THE ROSE
OF GOD

& The Eternal Security
Found in Christ

THE ROSE
OF GOD

& The Eternal Security
Found in Christ

Can a Christian, Once Saved, Lose Salvation?
A Complete, Biblical, In-depth Study
Confirming the Truth of Jesus' Covenant Love!

RICHARD O. WEBB

Genesis Cove ™
Biblical Books

The Rose of God & The Eternal Security Found in Christ
Can a Christian, Once Saved, Lose Salvation?
A Complete, Biblical, In-depth Study
Confirming the Truth of Jesus' Covenant Love!
© 2023-2026 by Richard O. Webb

Cover Concept: Richard O. & Lois M. Webb
Cover/Graphic Design: © 2023, 2024 by Richard O. Webb
"The Rose of God" Poem © 2023 by Richard O. Webb
"True Love" Poem © 1995, 2023 by Lois M. Webb
"Secure in Christ" Poem © 2023 by Richard O. Webb
End-Time Chart © 2024 by Richard O. Webb
BibleHearts™ Illustrations
© 1990, 2000, 2021 by Richard O. Webb

ISBN:
(Hardcover) 979-8-9887899-0-1, (Hardcover Color) 979-8-9887899-4-9,
(Paperback) 979-8-9887899-1-8, (Paperback Color) 979-8-9887899-3-2,
(eBook) 979-8-9887899-2-5

Library of Congress Control Number: 2023919307

All Scripture quotations in text are taken from the
King James Version of the Bible, unless noted from the
following versions that are also in the public domain:
WEB (World English Bible), NHEB (New Heart English Bible),
YLT (Young's Literal Translation)
Italics added by the author for emphasis

Published by Genesis Cove Biblical Books™
Clarkesville, Georgia
For permission requests visit GenesisCoveBiblicalBooks.com

This book was written by a praying human;
AI was not used in any of its creation.

This book is dedicated to my wife, Lois,
who came into my life many years ago, in 1996,
during a time when I was in great sorrow.

Your love and encouragement has been such
a wonderful blessing to me over the decades.
I am so grateful for the healing God has brought
into my life through your sweet and joyful spirit.

My love for you is indeed, eternal.

~

*"Having been reminded of the sincere faith
that is in you...Lois..."*

(2 Timothy 1:5, WEB)

Table of Contents

Preface

I wrote this book by accident. It started out as a much shorter Bible study that kept growing and fermenting in my heart over time. For over forty years, I have been praying and looking at a Christian's security in Christ and have become convinced, through the Holy Spirit and the Scripture, that our salvation is indeed *secure* in Christ Jesus.

Throughout these pages, you will find chapters that declare this eternal security as well as defend it. It has been my objective to present a thorough and sound biblical explanation of the everlasting covenant found in the salvation of Christ.

Beyond this, I have shared in God's Word what actually happens spiritually to a person when receiving Jesus as Savior. This is where the understanding of a believer's security in Christ is made most abundantly clear, bringing a realization and conviction that eternal life is *already* in the heart of one who has been truly born again of God's Spirit.

The revelation of God's secure love for you will indeed change every aspect of your life. For beyond presenting a mere doctrine, it is the knowledge of God's intimate relationship with you through His Son, Jesus Christ. For God has declared: "I have loved you with an everlasting love" (Jeremiah 31:3, *WEB*). And when you truly *know* you're secure in your relationship with God, you will draw near to His heart and—as the Apostle Paul said—"cry, Abba, Father" (Romans 8:15).

It is my prayer that you may know, having received such a "great salvation" (Hebrews 2:3), just how secure you are in the Rose offered to you by God, who is Christ Jesus Himself.

R.O.Webb

Author's Acknowledgment

My sincerest gratitude to the Name
of the Father, and the Son, and the Holy Spirit,
the "I AM"—Who has always been my Comforter.

It is only through the grace of my Lord Jesus Christ
that this book has been written.

*"But the anointing which ye have received of him
abideth in you, and ye need not that any man teach you:
but as the same anointing teacheth you of all things,
and is truth, and is no lie, and even as it hath taught you,
ye shall abide in him."*

(1 John 2:27)

*"Not to us, LORD, not to us, but to your name be the glory,
for your loving kindness and for your faithfulness."*

(Psalm 115:1, NHEB)

THE ROSE OF GOD

Christ, the Rose of God
Who bore the thorns of sin
Yet He Himself, being without
A single thorn within

Gave us life, made us new
Secure we are – in Him
For in His love, this thornless Rose
Has put away our sin

What Adam lost, this Rose has won
And more besides there be
For Christ, the thornless Rose of God
Has given...eternity

R.O.Webb

Chapter 1

A Narrow but Safe Introduction

Safe & Secure

When a person comes to Jesus Christ for new life and forgiveness of sins, how secure is his or her new position as a son or daughter of God? Is it possible for a true believer in Christ Jesus, having been born again (John 3:3), to ever become unborn? Within this book, I have highlighted many truths in the Word of God that have caused me to come to the conclusion that our position in Christ Jesus is an eternal position, where we are safe in the arms of a loving Father. I have also addressed Scripture that seems to cast doubt on this position, with the goal of adding clarity to the issue. It is to me a precious and priceless doctrine, one that in my opinion, adds to the life, love and godliness of the true believer in Jesus Christ.

To know such security in Christ is to experience the love of God that "casteth out fear" (1 John 4:18). For we can rest and rely on Jesus, who has borne "the chastisement of our peace" (Isaiah 53:5). Indeed, we may now draw *close* to God.

In a world with so much doubt and insecurity, how very important it is to know that your salvation is secure! Oh, how this truth reaches deep within the soul, giving it an anchor against all the waves of uncertainty around us. It is this love of God that the Bible declares we should know with certainty. As it is written:

> "And to *know* the love of Christ, which passeth knowledge, that ye might be filled with all the fulness of God" (Ephesians 3:19).

This is a love that will heal the brokenhearted, giving life to the heart that is thirsty for such a love which *does not fail.*

Perhaps the most important thing about knowing your security in Christ is that it means you are knowing Jesus Himself. You are understanding what His heart is for you and what He indeed went through in order to purchase you, His "pearl of great price" (Matthew 13:46). This assurance is foundational to the Christian's belief and is a truth that is brought forth abundantly throughout the Scriptures. For God did not intend for His redeemed children to live in fear of His wrath. And Jesus went to the cross to make sure we could have this fear removed and serve Him in an entirely new way. As it is written in Luke:

> "That he would grant unto us, that we being delivered out of the hand of our enemies might serve him *without fear,* In holiness and righteousness before him, all the days of our life" (Luke 1:74-75).

Ye Must Be Born Again

Before beginning this teaching, I want to clarify that the promises of our security in Christ are for those who have indeed turned to the Lord for the free gift of salvation. Jesus said, "Marvel not that I said unto thee, Ye must be born again" (John 3:7). And it is for those who have been born from above, through the Spirit of God and faith in Christ, that the hope of eternal life and salvation is sure.

Salvation is simply turning to Christ in faith for the forgiveness of sins. The Bible makes it clear that we have all sinned and the penalty for sin is death (Romans 5:12). Jesus bore our sin on the cross so that we may have eternal life and stand before God *completely forgiven*. And He bore our judgment so that we would be condemnation-free. To receive Christ, one only needs to pray a sincere prayer from the heart, saying, "Yes" to Him who knocks and asks to come into the door of each heart. As Jesus said:

> "Behold, I stand at the door, and knock: if any man hear my voice, and open the door, I will come in to him, and will sup with him, and he with me" (Revelation 3:20).

How do you know you have been born again? The answer to that question is actually very simple. For in salvation you are literally again born! You will experience this new life in Christ. Your heart will have a desire to follow Jesus. It's like getting a tattoo of the face of Jesus, not on your outer skin but on your heart. You will have a hunger to seek the Lord in your life and to grow in His Word. You will begin to associate with others who have also been born again—as your brothers and your sisters—for you share this new life in common. As it is written:

"We *know* that we have passed from death unto life, because we love the brethren. He that loveth not his brother abideth in death" (1 John 3:14).

And as it is also written:

"But whoso keepeth his word, in him verily is the love of God perfected: hereby *know* we that we are in him" (1 John 2:5).

For this new life in Christ will bear fruit in you. With some, it is very apparent right away and with others it becomes apparent over time, as they walk with the Lord. But this life, if indeed in you, will *continue* in you because it's the life of God in a heart that has accepted Christ—receiving His payment for sin on the cross.

And this new birth is like a seed, which after being germinated, grows and grows within you. It's spiritual life, given by God to the soul that simply receives Christ in faith.

Salvation, therefore, is free and easy for those who are sincere, *though it cost Christ everything.*

Salvation—Not Hard but Narrow

For salvation is not hard; it's just narrow.

As Jesus said:

"Enter ye in at the strait gate: for wide is the gate, and broad is the way, that leadeth to destruction, and many there be which go in thereat: Because strait is the gate, and narrow is the way, which leadeth unto life, and few there be that find it" (Matthew 7:13-14).

The meaning of this Scripture is that there is only one way to salvation, which is through an honest heart, calling on the Name of the Lord Jesus. As the Bible states:

"Let us draw near with a *true heart* in full assurance of faith" (Hebrews 10:22).

The path of salvation is a free gift, but it must be received in sincerity. God will come into your heart, change it and seat you with Him in heavenly places, if you simply turn to Him in repentance—seeing the need for salvation from your sin—and receive His eternal forgiveness in Christ.

Salvation can't be imitated, nor impersonated, nor pretended. It is in the realm of the heart and not of the mind only.

In 1980, I asked Jesus to come into my life as Savior. I was alone and prayed a simple prayer asking Him to forgive me of my sins and to come into my heart. I wrote it down in a notebook, so I could stand on the fact that I had given my life to Christ, turning to Him in faith. Now, many years later, He is still the all-encompassing thought in my life. Jesus saved me and has taken root, through the simple act of opening the door of my heart to Him.

For salvation is something that happens here, in this age —before the next one. It either happens in the heart of the believer or is missing in the heart of the unbeliever, or as we shall see—the *make-believer*. And make no mistake; salvation is free and easy—but narrow, since it involves the submission of the heart and will of an individual, which is necessary to receive Christ. Anything else is just thorns and thistles in the reality of the garden of God's salvation.

Believer, Unbeliever or Make-Believer?

The reason I'm mentioning this from the outset is because the Scripture clearly describes three types of individuals: the believer, the unbeliever and the one we will call the make-believer, as will be revealed in the following study.

We are already quite accustomed to thinking in terms of the believer or unbeliever, and these individuals need no clarification at all. But we must take notice of the fact that there are people who, for a season at least, may attend church, speak the Christian language and even have biblical knowledge—without ever having been *converted* to Christ within their hearts.

Jesus made this clear in the parable of the ten virgins, when He said:

> "Then shall the kingdom of heaven be likened unto ten virgins, which took their lamps, and went forth to meet the bridegroom. And five of them were wise, and five were foolish. They that were foolish took their lamps, and took no oil with them: But the wise took oil in their vessels with their lamps. While the bridegroom tarried, they all slumbered and slept. And at midnight there was a cry made, Behold, the bridegroom cometh; go ye out to meet him. Then all those virgins arose, and trimmed their lamps. And the foolish said unto the wise, Give us of your oil; for our lamps are gone out. But the wise answered, saying, Not so; lest there be not enough for us and you: but go ye rather to them that sell, and buy for yourselves. And while they went to buy, the bridegroom came; and they that were ready went in with him to the marriage: and the door was shut.

Afterward came also the other virgins, saying, Lord, Lord, open to us. But he answered and said, Verily I say unto you, I know you not" (Matthew 25:1-12).

In these verses, it is important to note that the ten virgins all looked similar outwardly. They all had their lamps burning and were together in their fellowship to meet the bridegroom. Yet, there was a big difference. Five of them had oil with them and five of them were without this oil. Oil represents the Holy Spirit in the Scriptures (1 Samuel 16:13; 2 Kings 9:3; Exodus 29:7), and it is He who gives the new birth and life in Christ. Even though these virgins all appeared the same, they differed significantly in that some had the oil and rebirth of the Holy Spirit within them, and some lacked it. Thus, some were revealed to be make-believers in contrast to the true believers. This is abundantly clear because when the time came to meet the bridegroom, He said to them, "I know you not." Indeed, they *never* had a relationship with the Bridegroom *at all.*

In Galatians 2:4, The Apostle Paul went so far as to name some individuals among the brethren and in the church as "false brethren unawares brought in, who came in privily to spy out our liberty which we have in Christ Jesus, that they might bring us into bondage."

Esau—Failing of the Grace of God

The Book of Hebrews speaks of those within the church who fall short of receiving salvation. And it actually contains a warning that those in the church should be:

"Looking diligently lest any man *fail of the grace of God*; lest any root of bitterness springing up trouble you, and thereby many be defiled; Lest there be any fornicator, or profane person, as Esau, who for one morsel of meat sold his birthright. For ye know how that afterward, when he would have inherited the blessing, he was rejected: for he found no place of repentance, though he sought it carefully with tears" (Hebrews 12:15-17).

This is quite an amazing statement, as it is confirming there may be those in the church who indeed *have not received Jesus and the grace of salvation* in their hearts at all! These verses declare that there may be those among us who "fail of the grace of God." To fail of the grace of God means to not receive the gift of salvation in the first place. And Hebrews describes this type of person as being like "Esau, who for one morsel of meat sold his birthright" (see Genesis 25:29-34). Just as Esau placed no value or faith on the birthright that could have been his, there are those within the church today who, within their hearts, reject the spiritual birthright of salvation.

This is mentioned earlier in Hebrews:

"Therefore we ought to pay greater attention to the things that were heard, lest perhaps we drift away. For if the word spoken through angels proved steadfast, and every transgression and disobedience received a just penalty, how will we escape if we neglect so great a *salvation*..." (Hebrews 2:1-3, *WEB*).

What is being neglected here is not one's good works but *salvation* itself. For if one who has heard the truth can truly "drift away," then, as we will see in this study, that individual was never saved and anchored *in Christ* in the first place. And these Scriptures serve as a warning to those who, like Esau, can declare:

"What good is the birthright to me?" (Genesis 25:32, *WEB*).

For there are those today—even within the church—who also say, "What good is the new birth to me?"

It is this class of people for whom the New Testament has many warnings and where confusion sometimes arises when presenting a discussion for the question: "Can a Christian lose salvation?"

We must first establish that one is indeed *a Christian*, in order to proceed with the blessed promises.

I recall being in a church service when a woman, who was present every Sunday and had attended the church for over *fifty years*, came forward to be saved. She stood up and declared in front of everyone that she had *never* received Christ in all those years. Oh, what a blessing that she did so on that day! But this illustrates that it's the heart and not the building, which matters to God. For God needs our permission to come into our hearts, no matter how long we have been around the things of Christianity. Christ will not force Himself upon us, nor can He be absorbed into us externally from our surroundings. He needs to be personally invited to enter each and every heart He knocks upon, by the free will He has given us.

I am not, in the following teaching, presenting a security for a *pretense* of Christianity. Please understand, the Bible clearly states that our security is *in Christ*, and it is only to those *in Him* that the blessed promises to the believer can be declared. These are in contrast to the warnings that are found written in the Scriptures for the unbeliever and make-believer.

A Sure Foundation

This study begins with Scripture that shows a believer's security in Christ. While much of this book deals with Scriptures that may *appear* to pose some doubt upon this position, it is not because the Scriptures pertaining to a believer's security in Christ are in any way lacking. For in writing this book, I felt that the verses of our security in Christ were so straightforward and so clear that there was no need to write in overabundance about them. Therefore, the latter proportion of this study contains much about explaining Scripture that is often misunderstood when skimming over the Word of God or when taking verses out of their intended context.

This is, in essence, a work of not only declaring our eternal security; it's also a work to fill in, with scriptural truth, any of the supposed "cracks in the floor" of this security. For the purpose in writing this book is to give a solid biblical foundation for the assurance of "the hope set before us" (Hebrews 6:18).

The New Covenant indeed provides security in Christ. And it is in this covenant that we have "fresh wine skins," without cracks, which *preserve* the wine of our new birth by grace. As Jesus said, in comparing the wine skins of the Old Covenant to the wine skins of the New Covenant:

> "Neither do people put new wine into old wine skins, or else the skins would burst, and the wine be spilled, and the skins ruined. No, they put new wine into fresh wine skins, *and both are preserved*" (Matthew 9:17, *WEB*).

It is my prayer that you may be found securely in the grace of God, and that being in Christ, you may rest in the comfort of the salvation which the Scriptures do abundantly promise you. God's gift of redemption in Christ is entirely free. Jesus paid for our sins on the cross so that we could be forgiven of them *all*. We need only turn to Him in childlike and sincere faith for the salvation of our souls, for "whosoever shall call upon the name of the Lord shall be saved" (Romans 10:13).

Having therefore received Christ, may we abide in the security of the salvation that Jesus purchased for us! For it's only through God's grace, as shown in the face of Christ, that we can rest on such a sure foundation in our salvation. And God has indeed given us *everlasting consolation*:

> "Now our Lord Jesus Christ himself, and God, even our Father, which hath loved us, and hath given us *everlasting consolation* and good hope through grace, Comfort your hearts, and stablish you in every good word and work" (2 Thessalonians 2:16-17).

It is through this "everlasting consolation" and "good hope through grace" that we can be established in "every good word and work." For such grace will always lead us closer to the Lord Jesus and thereby make us more fruitful in His Kingdom. So it is no wonder that Scripture declares:

> "These things I have written to you who believe in the name of the Son of God, *that you may know that you have everlasting life*" (1 John 5:13, *NHEB*).

Chapter 2

The Security of the New Nature

In Christ

When we are born of God's Spirit—through faith in Jesus—we are born again and our new nature takes on His attributes; for we are "*in Him*," as Scripture states:

> "According as he hath chosen us *in him* before the foundation of the world, that we should be holy and without blame before him in love" (Ephesians 1:4).

This term "in Him" or "in Christ" is repeated over and over in the New Testament. It seems so simple and is often overlooked, but this little "in" word has great significance for the Christian. Do you realize that when you were saved, you received a new heart that is literally *in* Christ Jesus? Your salvation is not just outward in the judicial appeasement of your sins on the cross of Christ; it is also internal, in that your canceled sin debt made way for Christ to come into your heart and change it, re-creating it *in Him*.

Indeed, you were in Adam when you were in your sin, but now as a new creation, you are *in Christ*. As the Scripture says: "For as *in Adam* all die, even so *in Christ* shall all be made alive" (1 Corinthians 15:22).

This is not figurative talk; it's the true spiritual reality for the believer who has received Christ as Savior. God now has your heart and can direct and guide you from within, for He Himself lives there. The Bible actually tells us that God has "raised us up together, and made us sit together in heavenly places *in Christ Jesus*" (Ephesians 2:6). In a real way, a Christian is already half resurrected. For although we still have the old sinful nature that we had before our salvation, our spirit is now truly "raised...up together...in Christ."

Spirit, Soul & Body

The Scriptures declare that man is spirit, soul and body. As it is written:

> "And the very God of peace sanctify you wholly; and I pray God your whole *spirit and soul and body* be preserved blameless unto the coming of our Lord Jesus Christ" (1 Thessalonians 5:23).

Our body is obviously our physical connection to this world and that which is most apparent to our natural senses.

Our soul is that place of the mind, will and emotions, which separates our life from that of a tree, for example. A tree has a body but not a soul.

The spirit of man is the place of our inner being and when reborn, connects us with God. It is the heart. As the Apostle

34

Paul said, "The grace of our Lord Jesus Christ be with your *spirit*" (Philemon 1:25).

For the spirit of man, being the heart, is the deepest part of a person. Peter described the spirit, the innermost being of the believer, as "the hidden man of the heart, in that which is not corruptible" (1 Peter 3:4).

Many people confuse the word "heart" for an emotional feeling. But the true heart of a person is far deeper than an emotional feeling of the soul. Indeed, it is the heart of hearts. It's the core of a being and is the very place of a Christian believer's rebirth and nature. It is no longer the heart of the old nature, about which was written in the Old Testament: "The heart is deceitful above all things, and desperately wicked: who can know it?" (Jeremiah 17:9). Rather, it is the new re-created heart or spirit in man, which Jesus was referring to when stating:

> "He that believeth on me, as the scripture hath said, out of his belly shall flow rivers of living water" (John 7:38).

The word "belly" in this verse is often translated as "innermost being," which is a very accurate description of a person's spirit, as it is the deepest "being" of the person. For Paul said:

> "For what man knoweth the things of a man, save the spirit of man which is in him? even so the things of God knoweth no man, but the Spirit of God. Now we have received, not the spirit of the world, but the spirit which is of God; that we might know the things that are freely given to us of God" (1 Corinthians 2:11-12).

Created in Righteousness

With the fall of man, the spirit died and man became sensual and fleshly in his nature. But in receiving Christ as Savior, our spirits were given life and we now have a connection with God that had been lost in Adam's sin. In fact, Christ has won back *more* than what Adam lost. For Adam's disobedience at the Tree of the Knowledge of Good and Evil gave us a sinful nature. Yet Christ's obedience at *the tree of the cross* declared us righteous before God *and* gave us a righteous nature. About this new nature Paul wrote:

> "Put on the new man, which *after God is created in righteousness and true holiness*" (Ephesians 4:24).

This new nature is our reborn spirit, which has literally been "created in righteousness and true holiness." Indeed, this is our new heart that was created according to the imprint of God, being "after God." And as John 3:6 says:

> "That which is born of the flesh *is flesh*; and that which is born of the Spirit *is spirit*."

So this new man, being born of God's Spirit—*is spirit,* for it is of God. Our sinful flesh may still be present with us as believers—and ever trying to exert itself—but our *spirits* have been re-created in righteousness and holiness because of our new birth in Christ. This is needed, as the Scripture states:

> "Follow peace with all men, and *holiness, without which no man shall see the Lord*" (Hebrews 12:14).

How can one possibly be holy in God's sight apart from the saving work of Christ and the new birth of the spirit? This is why God needed to re-create us in "righteousness" and in "true holiness." Indeed, this is God restoring His creation *to what He originally intended.*

Tested in Innocence

Now before their fall into sin, Adam and Eve were tested in innocence, revealing if they would become either righteous or sinful in the single act of obedience to God. This decision of whether they would listen to God or Satan—in the eating of the fruit of the tree—would impact their very nature. Through their sin and fall, the entire human race became sinful from birth (Genesis 2:16-17; 3:1-19).

But the Christian's rebirth is the opposite of this situation. Christ, the second Adam, has redeemed mankind through the cross. And in salvation, He re-creates the believer's spirit in *righteousness* itself. For in receiving Christ, we receive redemption from the fall of man. This is why Jesus emphasized to Nicodemus, "Ye *must* be born again" (John 3:7). Indeed, the issue of salvation is not about being outwardly good or bad but about receiving a new nature in righteousness, one that's in harmony with God, being born of God. This is made evident at the end of Jesus' Parable of the Banquet. For in the parable, the king—after inviting many to the banquet who refused to come—told his servants to go and gather whosoever will come:

> "Then saith he to his servants, The wedding is ready, but they which were bidden were not worthy. Go ye therefore into the highways, and as many as ye shall find, bid to the marriage. So those servants went out into the highways, and gathered together all as many as they found, *both bad and good*: and the wedding was furnished with guests. And when the king came

in to see the guests, he saw there a man which *had not on a wedding garment*: And he saith unto him, Friend, how camest thou in hither not having a wedding garment? And he was speechless. Then said the king to the servants, Bind him hand and foot, and take him away, and cast him into outer darkness; there shall be weeping and gnashing of teeth" (Matthew 22:8-13).

Jesus declares in this parable that it is the *garment*, which represents the *new birth*, that is required for salvation—not good works. For the good and bad were both gathered together to furnish the wedding with guests, all being clothed in wedding garments. But it was the one without a wedding garment who was singled out. That's because our outward self-righteousness or unrighteousness is not the issue in salvation. Rather, it is Christ's righteousness and the wedding garment of our new birth that matters—and by which we are saved. For upon salvation, Christ has both declared us righteous through the cross and created us in righteousness through His Spirit in the new birth.

The Second Adam

Now Adam *was never righteous before the fall*. If he had been, he *could not* have sinned, for his being would have been righteous and he would not have been able to sin. We sin quite easily in the flesh because its very nature is sinful. But if Adam had a righteous nature, it would have been as natural for him to be righteous as we are sinful, apart from Christ. However, Adam was innocent and was neither righteous nor sinful *before* the fall. And God did not want him to eat the fruit of the Tree of the Knowledge of Good and Evil, because in doing so, he would become corrupt not only in his disobedience but in his knowledge. As it is written:

"But of the tree of the knowledge of good and evil, thou shalt not eat of it: for in the day that thou eatest thereof thou shalt surely die" (Genesis 2:17).

Adam, however, in his test, did not choose God or righteousness. He chose Satan and sin, passing down this sinful nature to all of us. But Christ, the second Adam, has appeared and in obedience to the Father, has redeemed what Adam lost. For unlike the first Adam, Christ did obey—by which and through whom we are now *made righteous*. As it is written:

"He hath made him [Jesus] to be sin for us...that we might be *made the righteousness of God in him*" (2 Corinthians 5:21).

And again, it is written:

"For as in Adam all die, even so *in Christ* shall all be made alive" (1 Corinthians 15:22).

And consider Romans 5:19 as well:

"For as by one man's disobedience many were made sinners, so by the obedience of one shall many be *made righteous*."

For this is why the Bible states:

"Therefore if any man be *in Christ*, he is a new creature: old things are passed away; behold, all things are become new" (2 Corinthians 5:17).

We are a new creation in Christ Jesus and although our old nature, born of the fall of Adam, is sinful and does sin—

our new nature cannot sin, as it is born out of Christ's righteousness and is in Christ Himself. As the Scripture declares:

> "Whosoever is *born of God* doth not commit sin; for His *seed* remaineth in Him: and he *cannot* sin, because he is born of God" (1 John 3:9).

Born of God

Take note that this verse refers to the Christian's *new nature*, as it is speaking of "whosoever is born of God" and that God's "seed remaineth in Him." It is not just saying one won't *continually* sin—but may still sin at times—no; the actual wording of the Scripture in the Greek is more powerful. It says: *"he cannot sin" (literally: "he is not able to sin").*

Some Bible translations with paraphrases of the original text will translate this as "cannot *continually* sin," with the thought of emphasizing *continually* and giving the idea that the Scripture is merely referring to a continued practice of sinning. They do this because of the mood of the verb in the Greek and although this is still true, it is not the real meaning of this Scripture. For the word *continually* is not found in this Greek text at all, and reading it as such diminishes the strength and power of this verse. There is a Greek word for *continually* and surely it could have been added here. No; in fact, the mood of the verb, "cannot" is showing the continued fashion in which one who is born of God is unable to sin! Indeed, the verse may be understood to mean that one *continually cannot sin*, which is the same as saying, *"is not able to sin."*

So what am I implying—that a Christian never sins? No, not at all (unfortunately). What I am saying is that one needs to recognize how this verse is speaking of the reborn part of the believer—the spirit, the heart. This is the part of a believer that the Scripture declares, "cannot sin." Indeed, it is the spirit that is "in Christ." It is the reason that, as a born-again Christian, you dislike it when you fall into sin. Why? Because there is a part of you that doesn't agree and becomes grievous, because it didn't go along with the sin. That part is your spirit!

This verse should be understood exactly as it is written. Indeed, it is a radical statement, and people struggle with this Scripture because it doesn't seem to make sense *until* you see that it's referring to the spirit of man, that part which is "born of God." This is indeed what this verse is declaring when it says, "Whosoever is *born of God* doth not commit sin" and that "he cannot sin."

And this is why it says in Hebrews that the "the spirits of just men" are "made perfect" (Hebrews 12:23).

So how could this new nature become unrighteous and be separated from God, since it was "created in righteousness and true holiness" (Ephesians 4:24) and never agrees with sin?

Ponder this Scripture yet again:

"Whosoever is *born of God* doth not commit sin; for His *seed* remaineth in Him: and he *cannot* sin, because he is born of God" (1 John 3:9).

Chapter 3

The Security of Butterflies in Caterpillars

A New Heart

A Christian's new nature is like a butterfly emerging from the flesh of a caterpillar. It's this nature that has been born again and is now *in Christ*. Our challenge as believers in this life is to walk in the butterfly and yield to God's Spirit within us, as opposed to walking in the old self of the caterpillar.

Those who have been born from God have this new butterfly nature within their hearts, with a love and desire for Jesus. Indeed, they are no longer caterpillars! Now we may at times, to our dismay, still find ourselves walking in the old caterpillar ways—but we are still a new creation within the heart. As God promised in Ezekiel 36:26:

"A new heart also will I give you, and a new spirit will I put within you: and I will take away the stony heart out of your flesh..."

It is the work of God's *sanctification* in us that causes us to become Christ-like and walk more and more in the butterfly, rather than the caterpillar. But it's God's work of *salvation* that causes us to become the butterfly in the first place! Again, as it is written in 2 Corinthians 5:16-17:

"Wherefore henceforth know we no man after the flesh...Therefore if any man be in Christ, he is a new creature: old things are passed away; behold, all things are become new."

This is why, as a believer, it's so important to look at yourself as God sees you. He sees the new creation. He sees the butterfly!

We often judge ourselves from the orientation of our old flesh nature, when in fact we *are* the new nature. Indeed, the old nature is there, and it will remain with us until the day we go to be with the Lord. But we are, as believers, of the new nature itself. Look at how the Apostle Paul described this in Romans 8:9:

"But ye are *not* in the flesh, but *in the Spirit*, if so be that the Spirit of God dwell in you. Now if any man have not the Spirit of Christ, he is none of his."

So even though you still have the old nature of the flesh, you are no longer in it or of it. You may regrettably walk in its ways at times, but this verse declares that you are indeed "in the Spirit," if you are His and the Spirit of God dwells within you.

The Old Dirty Coat

To put it more simply, once I *was* the old dirty coat; it's who I was, and I was it. But in receiving Christ as Savior, He changed me on the inside. Now I find myself *wearing* the old dirty coat, but *I am no longer the old dirty coat itself.* I may be wearing this coat—but I am a new creation apart from it. This is what it means to become a new creature in Christ.

So as a Christian, this new nature is present even though the old nature is still there. But (and this is very important) —you are *not* two people! No, you're just one person and that person is the new one! Isn't it good to know that this is *who you really are?* For it's the spirit and *not* the flesh that determines who you are; and as a believer, your spirit has been made alive through the new birth by receiving Christ as Savior. This is why Paul said:

"Likewise reckon ye also yourselves to be dead indeed unto sin, but alive unto God through Jesus Christ our Lord" (Romans 6:11).

The word "reckon" applied here carries with it the meaning to "count, charge with, decide, conclude." Paul said this because, as a believer in Christ, your spirit is indeed alive unto God.

A Muddy Diamond

This is an amazing truth. It's like having a beautiful diamond covered in dirt. Our new nature is the diamond in Christ; our old nature is the dirt. No matter how much dirt is on the diamond, it's still a diamond. The dirt cannot destroy it. It is still holy in God's sight. This is why it's so important to see yourself as God does—*in Christ!* Suppose I took a very expensive diamond and put it in the ground for thirty years. If I then dug it out of the ground and offered it to you, would you reject it because it's muddy? Would you say it's no longer of value? No, because the dirt is separate from the diamond.

This is why Paul could make this stunning statement about himself, when describing his struggle with sin in his own energies. He said:

> "For that which I do I allow not: for what I would, that do I not; but what I hate, that do I. If then I do that which I would not, I consent unto the law that it is good. Now then *it is no more I that do it, but sin that dwelleth in me*" (Romans 7:15-17).

The Real You

What Paul is stating is that it's the sin in him and not the *real him* of the new nature that is the problem. Indeed Paul says, "It is no more I that do it." Who is the "I" here? It is the real person—reborn and created in righteousness—who doesn't agree with the sin of the flesh! This is the person speaking of doing "what I hate" and saying, "I consent unto the law that it is good."

Paul is revealing the law that's written in his heart under the New Covenant. Again, this is why true believers don't like to sin! It's actually a good indicator that you are indeed born again! The sin is not of your new nature.

But is Paul really saying it's not the real "him" doing it? That would sound so incredible and irresponsible except for the fact that he goes on to say it again:

"For I know that in me (that is, in my flesh,) dwelleth no good thing: for to will is present with me; but how to perform that which is good I find not. For the good that I would I do not: but the evil which I would not, that I do. Now if I do that I would not, *it is no more I that do it, but sin that dwelleth in me*" (Romans 7:18-20).

So Paul, once again, made the exact word-for-word statement about this struggle: "*It is no more I that do it, but sin that dwelleth in me.*" You see, Paul orientated himself according to his new nature and not his old nature, so he was able to speak this way. It was not irresponsible but the truth. Paul discerned his new nature from his old one. Again, this is such a wonderful truth for the child of God! It helps us to see and accept ourselves as God sees and accepts us in Christ. As it is written, "He hath made us accepted in the beloved" (Ephesians 1:6).

Notice how Paul spoke of the fact that nothing good dwells in him by saying: "For I know that in me (that is, in my flesh,) dwelleth no good thing." Paul is declaring that nothing good dwells in him, yet he needed to include the clarifying phrase, "that is, in my flesh." In other words, it's only his flesh he's referring to here, in which nothing good dwells. He's not speaking of his spirit, which has been born again in Christ.

Paul goes on to exclaim: "O wretched man that I am! who shall deliver *me* from the body of this death?" (Romans 7:24). This is Paul's way of saying, "Who will deliver me (the butterfly within, who wants to fly) from the caterpillar on the outside, fighting me with all its earth-bound legs?"

Paul then described the victory over all these struggles in the next chapter of the Bible, Romans 8, where he shared that only through the power of the Holy Spirit and not in one's own power, can a Christian have victory over the ways of the flesh and sin. For truly the butterfly takes flight in the wind of the power of God's Spirit.

And Paul encourages us that we are now alive in our spirit by his statement: "If Christ is in you, the body is dead because of sin, but the spirit is alive because of righteousness" (Romans 8:10, *WEB*). For although our caterpillar flesh is still sinful, our butterfly heart has been made new because of Christ's righteousness. As mentioned, Christ, unlike Adam, obeyed at *the tree of the cross*. In so doing, He redeemed what Adam lost, making us righteous in God's sight *and* in our spirits through the new birth.

The Everlasting Butterfly

And now this is the butterfly of the new creation that has eternal life, which has been "created in righteousness and true holiness" (Ephesians 4:24). *The caterpillar in all its potential waywardness is powerless to destroy this new butterfly's existence.*

Again, this is why Jesus said, "Ye must be born again" (John 3:7), for our eternity begins *before* we get to Heaven!

As the Apostle Peter also declared:

"Being born again, not of corruptible seed, but of incorruptible, by the word of God, which liveth and abideth for ever" (1 Peter 1:23).

Truly, this new nature, being born of the Spirit, is incorruptible as well as eternal.

Therefore, how could one ever become unborn? How can this new righteous nature ever become unrighteous? How can that which was born "of incorruptible" seed become corruptible? Does a butterfly become a caterpillar again? No, for Jesus said:

> "Verily, verily, I say unto you, he that heareth my word, and believeth on Him that sent me, *hath everlasting life*, and *shall not come into condemnation*; but *is passed from death unto life*" (John 5:24).

If a truly converted believer in Jesus Christ could be damned, how would "shall not come into condemnation" apply? Notice in this verse how Jesus revealed that *eternity has already begun* in the heart of a believer, as He stated that one "hath everlasting life" and has "passed from death unto life" already. The change has happened. So how can believers truly have everlasting life if they could lose it? (If they did lose it, did they ever really have *everlasting* life to begin with?) It is, after all, *ever-lasting*.

Remember that in Christ, we are already seated with Him in heavenly places. For the butterfly of your spirit is now alive in Christ. As it is written:

> "But God, being rich in mercy, for his great love with which he loved us, even when we were dead through our trespasses, made us alive together with Christ— by grace you have been saved—and raised us up with him, and made us to sit with him in the heavenly places in Christ Jesus" (Ephesians 2:4-6, *WEB*).

Chapter 4

The Security of Predestination

Free Will—Yet Chosen

The truth of predestination is found directly in the Scriptures. For Ephesians 1:4-5 declares predestination for the child of God when it states:

> "According as He hath chosen us in Him before the foundation of the world...*having predestinated us* unto the adoption of children by Jesus Christ to Himself."

Sometimes we have a hard time believing in predestination because we have difficulty understanding it. And since we don't understand it, we tend to negate it in our minds as unreal. But just because one may not understand predestination doesn't make it untrue. I may not understand how my computer functions in turning electricity into words, graphics and other elements—but I still accept the reality of it and turn the computer on. In the same way, predestination is a reality of God toward His children. And the Bible clearly states that the predestination of the child of God *is a fact.*

God's Foreknowledge

Predestination is not that God chooses some to go to Heaven and some to go to Hell, for the Lord is "not willing that any should perish, but that all should come to repentance" (2 Peter 3:9).

Rather, predestination is the working of God in accordance with His *foreknowledge.* God knows who will and will not receive Him ahead of time and makes sure that those who will receive Him actually do find Him. It is God's *foreknowledge* that sets His predestination into motion.

For the Apostle Paul, concerning the reason he was called out from the midst of his people, stated:

> "I say then, Hath God cast away his people? God forbid. For I also am an Israelite, of the seed of Abraham, of the tribe of Benjamin. God hath not cast away his people which he *foreknew*..." (Romans 11:1-2).

Here Paul states that God is saving a people He foreknew. Does that mean that in God's foreknowledge He saw our own righteousness and thus saved us? No, not at all. For the Prophet Isaiah said:

> "But we are all as an unclean thing, and all our righteousnesses are as filthy rags; and we all do fade as a leaf; and our iniquities, like the wind, have taken us away" (Isaiah 64:6).

So what did God see in His foreknowledge? He simply saw that we would *receive Him*. For in salvation, we receive what God has done for us in Christ. As it is written:

"But as many as *received* him, to them gave he power to become the sons of God, even to them that believe on his name" (John 1:12).

That's it. We received Him. We let God save us, sinners as we were, through the salvation of Christ. We can't boast in being saved, can we? If you were drowning and someone saved you, would you boast? Of course not.

And this foreknowledge of God happened *before* He set His predestination into effect to save us. For as Paul also wrote:

"For whom He did *foreknow*, He also did predestinate to be conformed to the image of His Son...Moreover whom He did predestinate, them He called; and whom He called, them He also justified; and whom He justified, them He also *glorified*" (Romans 8:29-30).

The Eternal God—who stands outside of time—has already foreknown, predestined, called, justified and *glorified* the true believer in Jesus Christ. Notice that these verses put our future glorification in Heaven in the past tense, as a *finished action* in the foreknowledge of God!

Since this glorification is already completed in the mind of the Lord when He calls us, how can a Christian believer in Christ subsequently become lost? In God's eyes, our glorification is as much a fact as our calling and our justification, all being seen beforehand in His foreknowledge.

Wheat & Sheep

This foreknowledge is what Jesus spoke of in the Parable of the Wheat and the Tares:

"Another parable put he forth unto them, saying, The kingdom of heaven is likened unto a man *which sowed good seed in his field*: But while men slept, his enemy came and *sowed tares among the wheat*, and went his way...He that soweth the good seed is the Son of man; The field is the world; the good seed are the children of the kingdom; but the tares are the children of the wicked one; The enemy that sowed them is the devil; the harvest is the end of the world; and the reapers are the angels. As therefore the tares are gathered and burned in the fire; so shall it be in the end of this world" (Matthew 13:24-25, 37-40).

Notice that the wheat is recognized apart from the tares in the foreknowledge of God. Indeed, the wheat is separate because the tares were sown "among" the wheat. This shows that the wheat never rose up from the seed of the tares, nor did the tares arise from the wheat! They may grow together and appear similar—but in full maturity they will be manifest according to what they are, the wheat being "the children of the kingdom" and the tares being "the children of the wicked one." For at the end of the day, one is *either* wheat or tare, sheep or goat, for Christ or opposed to Christ—in the foreknowledge of the Lord. This is why Jesus said:

"I am the good shepherd, and know my sheep, and am known of mine. As the Father knoweth me, even so know I the Father: and I lay down my life for the sheep...*My sheep hear my voice, and I know them, and they follow me*: And I give unto them eternal life; and they shall never perish" (John 10:14-15, 27-28).

Jesus also stated:

"Every one that is of the truth heareth my voice" (John 18:37).

The sheep are the ones who ultimately hear and follow the Good Shepherd. When one becomes saved, it is evidence of God's predestination in salvation and that he or she is of God's fold. *The reality that they would receive Christ was known in God's foreknowledge, just as the wheat was known, sown and separate from the tares.* This is what the Apostle Paul said concerning his own conversion:

"But when it pleased God, *who separated me from my mother's womb*, and called me by his grace, To reveal his Son in me, that I might preach him among the heathen; immediately I conferred not with flesh and blood..." (Galatians 1:15-16).

This is not to say that we are automatically saved and don't need to come to Christ for salvation. We absolutely do! But this salvation reveals what God *already* knew and planned to happen for those who would receive Him. We didn't know it—but God did. And it is through Jesus, the Good Shepherd, that God made the way for our sins to be forgiven. As He said:

"I lay down my life for the sheep" (John 10:15).

One will never know that he or she belongs to God's flock unless one lets Jesus into the heart by faith in the new birth of salvation. *This is the moment when one's free will and God's*

55

predestination embrace each other. This is why we preach the "whosoever" in the Gospel! As it is written:

> "For God so loved the world, that he gave his only begotten Son, that *whosoever* believeth in him should not perish, but have everlasting life" (John 3:16).

The "whosoever" of the Gospel is for all! And as mentioned, God is "not willing that any should perish, but that all should come to repentance" (2 Peter 3:9). But regarding those who *actually heed the call of Christ*, the Scripture reveals that they were known and chosen beforehand:

> "For many are called, but few are chosen" (Matthew 22:14).

Salvation from beginning to end is the work of God in bringing mankind back to Himself. It is entirely, unequivocally, and forever a work of God's grace toward those *who will receive Him.* And those who will receive Him are known, chosen and will be found by Him.

When in the garden of Gethsemane, Jesus prayed:

> "I have manifested thy name unto the men which thou *gavest* me out of the world: *thine they were*, and thou *gavest* them me" (John 17:6).

Here Jesus was saying that the disciples were already "thine," meaning the Father's, and that He manifested God's Name to these disciples.

Jesus also said:

"All that the Father *giveth me* shall come to me; and him that cometh to me I will *in no wise cast out*" (John 6:37).

These verses clearly show that God, the Father, is *giving* a people to Jesus. Notice that He said, "I will in no wise cast out" those who "cometh to me." How could we ever think a converted child of God, being of His sheep, could lose salvation? As Jesus said, yet again:

"And this is the Father's will which hath sent me, that of all which *He hath given me I should lose nothing*, but should raise it up again at the last day" (John 6:39).

The Back Door

Jesus declared in these verses that every believer whom God has seen in His foreknowledge *and has given to Him—* will indeed come to Him and that He "should lose nothing." What a blessed promise we have that Jesus will "lose nothing" of all those given to Him of the Father!

These are wonderful Scriptures that reveal the "back door" of God's hidden work in salvation. A people are being *given* to Jesus; this work is of God and it is through the power of the Holy Spirit.

We are accustomed to seeing the "front door" of salvation, which includes preaching, teaching, testimony and all the many other things that go into the sharing of the Gospel. And the Lord uses all these things—but it is the "back door" of the hidden work of the Spirit, by which human hearts are convicted and impacted for salvation.

Jesus showed us this "back door" again by saying:

"As thou hast given him power over all flesh, that he should give eternal life to as many as thou hast *given him*" (John 17:2).

For these verses in John's Gospel let us know some of what happens in the hidden work of the Spirit, toward the hearts of men. God is drawing a people to Himself. And these Scriptures reveal that it's not just about people coming to Jesus for salvation *but that these people were being given to Him*, having been empowered to come to Jesus.

In the Gospel of John, we find more Scripture regarding the Holy Spirit's working behind the scenes than in any of the other gospels. For John's Gospel is where the Holy Spirit was revealed as He who would come and convict, guide and comfort. Indeed, He is revealed by Jesus as the Comforter or "Paraclete" (John 14:26), which in the Greek means one who is a "helper, comforter, counsel for defense" and "called to one's aid."

Indeed, the Spirit of God *is* God Himself, being the third person in the Name "of the Father and of the Son and of the Holy Spirit" (Matthew 28:19, *WEB*). It is He who was promised by Jesus to come and live in the believer's heart (John 14:16).

So it is through this "back door" of the Spirit's working in the hearts of men that God's *foreknowledge* and *predestination* and man's *free will* come together in perfect harmony, in the orchestra of God's sovereign design.

This is why the Apostle Paul could emphatically declare:

"But we are bound to always give thanks to God for you, brothers loved by the Lord, because God chose you from the beginning for salvation through sanctification of the Spirit and belief in the truth, to which he called you through our Good News, for the obtaining of the glory of our Lord Jesus Christ" (2 Thessalonians 2:13-14, *WEB*).

The Helmet of Salvation

It is a sure comfort for the mind, this predestination of the Christian. It is deep thought, as it is an anchor into God's eternal purpose for our lives. Indeed, it protects our thoughts and minds from the wiles of the enemy, who would seek to turn away our hope of such an eternal security in Christ.

Many years ago, I was riding my motorcycle to work. As I turned off a main highway to go down a street, a car coming out of that same street ran a stop sign and hit my rear tire. The collision sent me airborne and I landed in the middle of the pavement. This road normally had lots of traffic at this time of the morning. But that day, there was literally no traffic—and it was a busy highway! Amazingly, by the grace of God, I was able to land on the highway without being run over.

However, when I landed, my head hit the pavement and I slid for a while. But I was wearing a good helmet. And it was on securely. So when I hit that asphalt, it felt as if I landed on a pillow. I still wonder if angels were involved in my landing, but I know for sure God was watching over me. And that helmet may have saved my life.

So why am I sharing this story? Well, the Apostle Paul says to "take the helmet of salvation" (Ephesians 6:17) as a protective piece of our Christian armor. It is noteworthy that Paul called this vital piece of equipment the helmet of "salvation" itself. For it covers your head and mind in battle.

How good it is for our minds to know and to be assured of our salvation in Christ!

When one is in doubt regarding the security of salvation, it's like wearing a helmet that is not fastened securely on the head. It's there, but it could fall off at any moment. This is something that actually happened once, while I was driving the same motorcycle with my wife riding on the back. She didn't have her helmet secured tightly and when we got up to speed, it flew off in the wind and bounced onto the highway. Thankfully, she was fine and we were able to pull over and safely retrieve her helmet from the road.

And once a helmet takes a hard hit like that, it must be replaced. But God's helmet of salvation never needs replacement! It just needs to be securely tied to the head, so the Devil can't blow it off with doubtful thoughts of insecurity about one's salvation in Christ. It is, after all, a helmet and a protective piece of equipment for the soul, which should be worn to protect the mind. This is why the Scripture says to "*take* the helmet of salvation."

Indeed, how comforting it is for the mind to understand, in securing the helmet, that God in His foreknowledge has eternally saved you. For God's predestination is one of the most powerful and convincing arguments for our eternal security! The fact is—God *had already* designed for you, as a born-again believer, to turn to Him and receive Him. How good it is to know that God not only has your back, but He has your head! For His salvation and the means by which you came to know the reality of Christ go far deeper than you or I could imagine:

> "O the depth of the riches both of the wisdom and knowledge of God! how unsearchable are his

judgments, and his ways past finding out! For who hath known the mind of the Lord? or who hath been his counseller? Or who hath first given to him, and it shall be recompensed unto him again? For of him, and through him, and to him, are all things: to whom be glory for ever. Amen" (Romans 11:33-36).

Bible ❤ Hearts™

"Who shall also confirm you unto the end,
blameless in the day of our Lord Jesus Christ.
God is faithful, by whom ye were called unto
the fellowship of his Son Jesus Christ our Lord."

1 Corinthians 1:8-9

by Richard O. Webb

Chapter 5

The Security of the Keeping Power of Christ

Presented Faultless

The Scriptures declare that God not only saves us—but that He keeps us as well! Jude summed it up quite wonderfully when he wrote:

> "Now unto Him that is able to *keep you from falling*, and to present you faultless before the presence of his glory with exceeding joy" (Jude 1:24).

And Jesus said of His own:

> "I give unto them eternal life; *and they shall never perish, neither shall any pluck them out of my hand.* My Father, which gave them me, is greater than all; and *no man is able to pluck them out of my Father's hand.* I and my Father are one" (John 10:28-30).

This statement of Jesus is even more powerful when you consider that the word "man" is not in the original language. In the Greek, it more accurately reads: "And *nothing (none, no one)* is able to pluck them out of my Father's hand." That is to say, no man, nor demon, nor anything else can pluck us out of Almighty God's hand!

Nor Things to Come

This truth is reiterated by the Apostle Paul in the book of Romans. For one of my favorite verses in Scripture states our security in Christ most clearly:

> "For I am persuaded, that neither death, nor life, nor angels, nor principalities, nor powers, nor things present, nor things to come, nor height, nor depth, nor any other creature, shall be able to separate us from the love of God, which is in Christ Jesus our Lord" (Romans 8:38-39).

The Word of God declares that nothing can separate believers from God's love. It states that even "life" itself can't separate us from the love of God! This includes *all* that could occur in life. If I were to lose my salvation, then wouldn't life have separated me from God's love? Demonic principalities cannot do it ("nor principalities"). So if a true believer could be tempted and drawn away into damnation—which is separation from God's love—how would this Scripture be true?

These verses also declare that not only the present but also the *future* can't separate me from God's love! Doesn't "nor things to come" include myself, revealing that I will never be apart from God's grace? Am I not in my future? How can this verse be true if I could separate myself from Him?

And consider the words: "nor any other creature, shall be able to separate us from the love of God." How could these words be true if I were able to separate *myself* from the Lord? Would not I be included in the phrase, "nor any other creature"?

He Is Able to Keep

The fact that the Apostle Paul was confident in God's keeping power is evident. For He also said:

> "For I know whom I have believed, and am persuaded that *he is able to keep* that which I have committed unto him against that day" (2 Timothy 1:12).

And Paul made the following statement as well:

> "Being confident of this very thing, that he which hath begun a good work in you will perform it until the day of Jesus Christ" (Philippians 1:6).

As these verses state, God did not save us to just leave us to ourselves until we (hopefully) make it home safely. That would only be half of salvation. For God's plan in Christ is not only to save us but to *keep us saved.* Doesn't that make sense? For look at the following Scriptures, which say:

> "But of him [God] are ye *in* Christ Jesus, who of God is made unto us wisdom, and righteousness, and sanctification, and redemption: That, according as it is written, He that glorieth, let him glory in the Lord" (1 Corinthians 1:30-31).

We see in these verses that it is God Himself who puts us *in* Christ. We did not choose Him, but He chose us (John 15:16). It was His doing.

And we can see this Christ, in whom we have been placed, is not only our wisdom, not only our righteousness, but He's our *sanctification and redemption* as well! For these verses declare that God is in this with us for all our days—even to full eternal redemption!

Indeed, He who started this work of grace for you is still at work *in* you! And Christ, being our very *sanctification*, will continue this miracle of grace in your life, transforming you into His image.

For we are God's. We are in His care. And His salvation has provided for us to be kept and to stand before Him faultless on that day when we see Him face to face.

Jude even said that we are "preserved" in Christ. For he started his epistle by stating:

> "Jude, the servant of Jesus Christ, and brother of James, to them that are sanctified by God the Father, and *preserved* in Jesus Christ, and called" (Jude 1:1).

We are not only sanctified by God the Father; we are also preserved in Christ Jesus. The translation of the word "preserve" in the Greek means: "to keep, to guard, to observe, to watch over." So God's salvation in Christ is never idle, because He keeps His eye on His treasured possession—you! For you are of great value to Him. As Peter said:

> "Forasmuch as ye know that ye were not redeemed with corruptible things, as silver and gold, from your vain conversation received by tradition from your fathers; But with *the precious blood of Christ*, as of a lamb without blemish and without spot" (1 Peter 1:18).

Your Price Tag

There is nothing that speaks of your worth to God more strongly than the fact that you were bought with Christ's blood. Do you think your place in this world is small? Do you say you have no special gift or talent to make you stand out and be "special"? Perhaps you ponder that you are insignificant and of little to no value upon this Earth. But have you seen the price tag that God has attached to you?

Jesus left Heaven and came to this Earth, being God in the flesh. He shed His precious blood to buy you and to keep you. You need not look at the way the world sets its value upon you. No, look to God and to Him alone. Truly, you are priceless to Him!

For Almighty God, who can do all things imaginable by His great power, suffered at the hands of cruel Roman soldiers to bring you back to Him. And although God has infinite power, He wanted to win you back through your own free will. Why? Because He desires a loving relationship with you. He didn't create you to be His robot. That would have been easy, yet loveless. He created you for friendship; and taking the risk of giving mankind free will, He made you with the capability of responding to Him with true love.

The risk of that free will would cost Christ the torment of the cross; and while upon it, He would also endure the extreme agony of separation from the face of God, the Father. But it was all worth it to Jesus. You are worth it to God! That's why He came—God on the cross—to restore you back to Himself. It's a love that began with His heart toward you. And upon receiving Christ, you became His prized purchased treasure. Do you not think He will therefore keep you? He paid *so* much for you!

And nothing you can do can add to His love. No amount of work or even self-hatred can add to what Jesus has done on the cross for you. It is only Christ, and Him crucified, Who has taken away all fear of God's holy wrath; for He was punished in our place. Self-hatred and condemnation may feel justified, natural, and even righteous, but only Jesus upon Mount Calvary has dealt the blow to our sin. Our feelings of unworthiness are not significant. *It's the beloved finished work of Christ that proves the love of God toward you and your value to God.* And it is only at the cross whereby the soul finds its truest acceptance, resting upon the very heart of God.

For Scripture says:

> "And you, that were sometime alienated and enemies in your mind by wicked works, yet now hath he reconciled In the body of his flesh through death, to present you *holy and unblameable and unreproveable in his sight*" (Colossians 1:21-22).

And you are His very jewel, as we read even in the Old Testament, in the Book of Malachi:

> "And they shall be mine, saith the LORD of hosts, in that day *when I make up my jewels...*" (Malachi 3:17).

Since you cost God so much—the shed blood of Christ—He will surely keep you for Himself! As the Apostle Peter declared:

> "You are a chosen race, a royal priesthood, a holy nation, *a people for God's own possession*" (1 Peter 2:9).

And this is why the Lord would have us draw near to His heart without fear. As it is written in the Song of Solomon:

> "O my dove, that art in the clefts of the rock, in the secret places of the stairs, let me see thy countenance, let me hear thy voice; for sweet is thy voice, and thy countenance is comely...My beloved is mine, and I am his" (Song of Solomon 2:14, 16).

For Jesus will surely keep those who are of His fold, as a Shepherd keeps His sheep. As it is promised in the Psalms:

> "The LORD shall preserve thee from all evil: he shall *preserve thy soul*. The LORD shall preserve thy going out and thy coming in from this time forth, and even for evermore" (Psalm 121:7-8).

And as the Apostle Paul stated:

> "And the Lord shall deliver me from every evil work, and will *preserve me unto his heavenly kingdom*: to whom be glory for ever and ever. Amen" (2 Timothy 4:18).

Chapter 6

The Security of the Sealing of the Holy Spirit

Until You Are Home

In biblical times, seals were used to keep and protect important contents. Often scrolls were sealed until they were delivered into the hands of the proper authorities by whom they would be opened. Jesus' tomb also had a seal, placed there by the Roman soldiers who had been ordered to guard it. As Matthew states:

> "So they went, and made the sepulchre sure, sealing the stone..." (Matthew 27:66).

The word "seal" in the Greek means to "authenticate, confirm, set a mark upon, keep secret." Its meaning involves *ownership* and the *protection* of that ownership. It comes from a word meaning: "to stamp for security or preservation."

Nowadays, we commonly think of a seal whenever we buy food or medicine in a package. There's usually some packaging designed to give assurance that the food or medicine hasn't been tampered with. It's intended to stay sealed until you get home and open the package for yourself.

In similar fashion, God has sealed you, the Christian, for Himself until He has *you* home. You are His possession upon receiving Christ as your Savior, and He has seen fit to seal you for Heaven and the Kingdom to come.

The Apostle Paul wrote:

> "And grieve not the Holy Spirit of God, whereby ye are *sealed* unto the day of redemption" (Ephesians 4:30).

This Scripture declares that we are sealed to "the day of redemption." This is the day of receiving our resurrected bodies in glory! This sealing, therefore, covers the entire duration of our pilgrimage here on Earth, within the tents of our sinful bodies of flesh.

For the Lord has a purpose in bringing you safely to His eternal Kingdom. And God's seal cannot be broken. As this verse clearly states, you are sealed to the day you come into glory and receive full redemption—and you are sealed by no less than the Holy Spirit of God Himself!

The Holy Spirit of Promise

Truly, this Holy Spirit is the guarantee of the security of our salvation. That He lives in our hearts is the proof that we belong to God *already*. For we are His possession and God— far from waiting until our day of death—has placed us *in*

Christ here and now, in His great love. As the Apostle Paul also wrote:

> "Now he which stablisheth us with you *in Christ*, and hath anointed us, is God; Who hath also *sealed* us, and given the earnest of the Spirit in our hearts" (2 Corinthians 1:21-22).

In addition, Paul wrote:

> "After that ye heard the word of truth, the gospel of your salvation: in whom also after that ye believed, ye were *sealed* with that Holy Spirit of promise, which is the *earnest* of our inheritance until the redemption of the *purchased possession*" (Ephesians 1:13-14).

The word "earnest" used here in the King James Version means "deposit." In the Greek, the meaning of the word involves part of a payment, given in advance, *to secure* an item that has not yet been received; it is a first installment and guarantee toward full ownership. For God has *already* put His deposit of the Holy Spirit in you. This is the proof and guarantee of your redemption and resurrection to come, having already entered into the Kingdom of God by the Spirit who now lives in you. And this deposit of the Spirit is the down payment for all God has for you, in redeeming you and securing your place in Heaven with Him.

Isn't it good to know that as a believer, you were sealed, not with plastic, not even with steel, but with the "Holy Spirit of promise"? Surely this is a seal that's safe, secure and worthy of our trust. After all, we are God's "purchased possession" and He is going to make sure we arrive safely home to Him.

73

Often we see Scriptures like this and think these promises are too simple, too reassuring, too uncomplicated to receive. But God has put His mark on you by giving you His Spirit, the blessed Comforter of God. And Jesus made the promise that:

> "I will pray the Father, and he shall give you another Comforter, *that he may abide with you for ever;* Even the Spirit of truth; whom the world cannot receive, because it seeth him not, neither knoweth him: but ye know him; for he dwelleth with you, and shall be in you. *I will not leave you comfortless*: I will come to you" (John 14:16-18).

With You Forever

Here we see a beautiful promise in connection with the Holy Spirit, which is: "He may abide with you *for ever.*" The word "abide" means to "remain." And this wonderful Comforter of God has been given with a promise—to remain with us always.

Now it should be mentioned that when Jesus said, "He *may* abide with you for ever," there is no doubt in connection with the word "may." For this verb in the Greek, being used in a "hina" clause as it is here, should be taken to be definitive in meaning and not just a mere possibility. (More will be discussed on this topic in *Chapter 14: Branches, Fruit & Fire.*) But a better understanding here would be: *He shall give you another Comforter, in order that He remain with you forever.* Clearly, there is no doubt in this verse that the Spirit that Jesus sends *will* remain in us forever. Indeed, He is being sent for this very purpose.

Jesus also promised in this passage: "I will *not* leave you comfortless." The word "comfortless" in the Greek means to be "bereaved, desolate, fatherless" or "an orphan." So how could it be possible to lose Christ, when He gives you such a promise? Has He not also said, "I will *never* leave thee, nor forsake thee" (Hebrews 13:5)? If words have any meaning, then "never" means "never," does it not?

Dear saint, do you not see that the Lord has placed Himself *always* with you?

Well, perhaps you think you might fail Him? But that's not the issue here. *Jesus' faithfulness to you* (by which He made such a great promise) is the issue. Does your unfaithfulness negate God's faithfulness? No! For it is written:

"If we are faithless, he remains faithful; for he can't deny himself" (2 Timothy 2:13, *WEB*).

Indeed, it is also written:

"He that is joined unto the Lord is one spirit" (1 Corinthians 6:17).

Since your spirit is one with His, how could He ever abandon you? Here the Word of God is not saying that we are "two," but "one," and therefore this truth removes even the *possibility* of the Christian being abandoned.

Oh, how difficult it is at times to simply receive "with meekness the engrafted word, which is able to save your souls" (James 1:21). Yet these are the reassuring words of a God who has promised to *never let us go*. Jesus said of His coming resurrection:

"At that day ye shall know that I am in my Father, and *ye in me, and I in you*" (John 14:20).

This is how close you are to God's heart!

God's Perfect Love

It is amazing, in a world that's full of so much coldness, that there truly is an answer for the human heart. It is the love and security of God that has come to remain within us, through the redemption in Christ. Many look high and low to fill their hearts, but the void can only be filled by Jesus, with His Spirit. And when He does fill it, we have the blessed promise that He has sealed us and will never leave us. This is a promise that will change every worry of your life into peace and every anxiety into hope. For without Christ in the heart, there is only fear in this world. But when Christ has indeed found His home within your heart, there abides an everlasting love that has conquered fear, as it is written:

> "There is no fear in love; but perfect love casteth out fear: because fear hath torment. He that feareth is not made perfect in love" (1 John 4:18).

Another word for "torment" in this verse is "punishment." And God's love has taken away your punishment through Jesus' atonement on the cross.

For God's love for you in Christ is like a circle, being unbroken, eternal and *perfect*.

And God has now taken ownership of you in Christ, for "ye are not your own...ye are bought with a price" (1 Corinthians 6:19-20). And this price is no less than the precious blood of Jesus Christ Himself.

Indeed, God saved you not only in the power of the resurrection but in the weakness and humiliation of the cross. Yet it was a cost He was willing to pay so He could have you as His own and put His Spirit within you! Why? Because He wanted to be *that* close to you.

For we read something very precious in the Book of Isaiah, where it is written:

"He shall see of the travail of his soul, and shall be satisfied" (Isaiah 53:11).

This verse can be interpreted in two ways, depending on who the "He" is in the sentence.

The first understanding is that God the Father will see the sacrifice of Jesus and be satisfied with the just payment for our sins. It means that He can therefore receive you freely, without wrath, as the debt has been satisfied and paid in full. Therefore, we can now come "boldly unto the throne of grace" (Hebrews 4:16) and find rest and peace in His presence. For in Christ, the just wrath of God has been *satisfied*.

The second truth in this verse is that Jesus Himself will see the travail of His own soul and be satisfied; for it would all be worth it to Him to go to the cross and save you. All the beating, the scourging, the thorns, the nails, the cross—as well as the abandonment and separation from God, the Father—was worth it to Him so that you would never know such abandonment! Jesus is truly *satisfied* with what His righteous soul has accomplished in bringing you back to the Father.

Either way, you can see the pure love of a God who has purchased you, put His Spirit inside you and sealed you. And His promise is to never leave you—no, not ever!

Chapter 7

The Security of Grace

The Law & the Strength of Sin

If it is possible for born-again believers to lose salvation, what must we do to secure it? What is the work? What is the "keeping effort" that we must maintain? What good thing must we continue to do in our own effort? What law must we keep?

In contrast to this thinking, the Scriptures declare that "we are not under the law, but under grace" (Romans 6:15) and "if by grace, *then is it no more of works*: otherwise grace is no more grace" (Romans 11:6).

What is grace? It is God's unmerited favor. It's God's love reaching down and saving you freely by *His* power. It is the opposite of salvation by good works *in your own power.*

But some may say, "If you teach the truth of grace, won't it promote sin?" On the contrary! It is in fact *the law* and not grace that promotes sin, as it is written:

"The sting of death is sin; and *the strength of sin is the law*" (1 Corinthians 15:56).

You see, the outward law will speak to our old nature which is dead in sin and rebellion. That's why the law actually causes sin to increase. Its commands are to the rebellion in us. This is why Paul the Apostle could write:

"For I was alive without the law once: but when the commandment came, sin revived, and I died" (Romans 7:9).

And Paul, in Romans 6:14, makes it clear that:

"Sin shall not have dominion over you: *for ye are not under the law, but under grace.*"

Notice how this verse states that it is the result of grace and not law, by which the dominion of sin is broken in our lives.

In Newness of Spirit

Indeed, the Spirit of God, in grace, will lead us into a loving relationship with our heavenly Father and produce fruit within us that the law could *never* produce. As it is written:

"But now we are delivered from the law, that being dead wherein we were held; *that we should serve in newness of Spirit*, and not in the oldness of the letter" (Romans 7:6, *NHEB*).

And again the Scriptures show the effect of grace:

"For the grace of God that bringeth salvation hath appeared to all men, teaching us that, denying ungodliness and worldly lusts, we should live soberly, righteously, and godly, in this present world" (Titus 2:11-12).

For grace, unlike any outward law, changes us on the inside and causes us to walk with the living Christ. Paul again made this clear when he wrote:

"...that I may win Christ, and be found in him, not having mine own righteousness, which is of the law, but that which is through the faith of Christ, the righteousness which is of God by faith. That I may know him..." (Philippians 3:8-10).

Notice that Paul did not rely on his own righteousness. Paul even went so far as to say that he had *no* trust in himself, declaring that he had "no confidence in the flesh" (Philippians 3:3). For Paul was no longer looking to himself, as he had done previously when living under the law. Instead, he was now looking to Christ and living under grace, with the end result being that he may "know him." And that which had previously been a lifestyle of simply looking to mere outward law became a living, loving relationship—the closeness of knowing Christ *Himself!*

For unlike law that is written on stone, the grace of God draws us close to His heart and enables us to walk in His ways. It no longer demands in fear; now God's grace *gives* in love. And the Father always wanted it so. That's why you can hear the yearning in these words of the Old Testament:

"Behold, the days come, saith the LORD, that I will make a new covenant with the house of Israel, and with the house of Judah: *Not according to the covenant that I made with their fathers* in the day that I took them by the hand to bring them out of the land of Egypt; which my covenant they brake, although I was an husband unto them, saith the LORD: But this shall be the covenant that I will make with the house of Israel; After those days, saith the LORD, *I will put my law in their inward parts, and write it in their hearts*; and will be their God, and they shall be my people" (Jeremiah 31:31-33).

Not Like the Old

Now God, in making a New Covenant, was sure to set it up to be fail-proof. For the Old Covenant failed, not due to God but because of man. Therefore, do you think God, in all His wisdom, would set up the New Covenant in similar fashion? Wouldn't you agree that He must have thought this through and made a covenant that would not fail because of man? Otherwise, would it not be just a repeat of the first covenant?

For indeed, the Lord designed this New Covenant to be accomplished by His grace and not by man's striving. Knowing man would fail, God designed it so He would not only atone for man's sin at the cross of Christ, but through this atonement—He could now gain access to the human heart by His Spirit. This is why He said: "I will put my law in their inward parts, and write it in their hearts." For God had in mind a better covenant. Once allowed in the heart, He could now re-create man with a new spirit, one that would follow Him through grace, not being under law. And as Ezekiel prophesied:

"Then will I sprinkle clean water upon you, and ye shall be clean: from all your filthiness, and from all your idols, will I cleanse you. A new heart also will I give you, and a new spirit will I put within you: and I will take away the stony heart out of your flesh, and I will give you an heart of flesh. And I will put my spirit within you, and cause you to walk in my statutes, and ye shall keep my judgments, and do them" (Ezekiel 36:25-27).

This prophecy speaks of the New Covenant. Notice that it is God who puts His Spirit within us and *causes* us to walk in His ways. This is grace. This is unmerited favor. As Paul the Apostle put it:

"For it is God which worketh in you both to will and to do of his good pleasure" (Philippians 2:13).

And all that this gift of grace requires is for one to freely receive it by accepting Christ as Savior. Truly, Jesus is the revelation of God's grace, proving that "God is love" (1 John 4:16). As it is written:

"For the law was given by Moses, but grace and truth came by Jesus Christ" (John 1:17).

As it is also written:

"But as many as *received him*, to them gave he *power* to become the sons of God, even to them that believe on his name" (John 1:12).

Servant or Son?

The Scripture above tells us that the grace of God in Christ's salvation gives *power*. This is not passive but active in saving, healing and restoring us back to all the Father made us to be, according to His original intent. And what did He make us to be? Not servants but sons and daughters of God.

God made you for Himself, for fellowship! And His purpose in Christ is:

> "To redeem them that were under the law, that we might receive the adoption of sons. And because ye are sons, God hath sent forth the Spirit of his Son into your hearts, crying, Abba, Father. Wherefore thou art no more a servant, but a son; and if a son, then an heir of God through Christ" (Galatians 4:5-7).

For as the father ran to his child in the Parable of the Prodigal Son—likewise, God runs to us in receiving Christ. The prodigal son's plan was to say:

> "Father, I have sinned against heaven, and before thee, And am no more worthy to be called thy son: *make me as one of thy hired servants*" (Luke 15:18-19).

But the son was never able to finish his last line: "Make me as one of thy hired servants." For the father would not hear it and interrupting him, said to his servants:

> "Bring forth the best robe, and put it on him; and put a ring on his hand, and shoes on his feet: And bring hither the fatted calf, and kill it; and let us eat, and be merry" (Luke 15:22-23).

Indeed, the father wanted a son, not a servant. Likewise, the heavenly Father is "merry" about the grace lavished upon us in His New Covenant! For the fattened calf, being Christ Jesus Himself, has indeed been slain; we may now be merry in our Father's arms, with the grace that makes us His sons and daughters. It is this beautiful grace that draws us close to God!

As it is written:

> "For the law made nothing perfect, but the bringing in of a better hope did; by the which we draw nigh unto God" (Hebrews 7:19).

A Better Hope

The law can neither keep us nor make us righteous in God's sight. The law will demand but never help. It cannot save but only condemns, leaving you without support and without hope. Those who rely on it thus rely upon themselves, not on Christ. For how can there ever be security or salvation by law? It cannot be found. And one should realize the hopelessness of the situation sooner rather than later and throw oneself upon God's answer—Jesus. As it is written:

> "For when we were yet without strength, in due time Christ died for the ungodly. For scarcely for a righteous man will one die: yet peradventure for a good man some would even dare to die. But God commendeth his love toward us, in that, while we were yet sinners, Christ died for us. Much more then, being now justified by his blood, *we shall be saved from wrath through him*" (Romans 5:6-9).

Notice something important in this passage: Because we have been justified by Christ's blood, "we shall be *saved from wrath* through him." So where is the possibility of God's wrath for the Christian, who is now *justified?* Where is the possibility of losing one's salvation? Indeed, "where sin abounded, grace abounded more exceedingly" (Romans 5:20, *WEB*). Gloriously, this is what God's grace does; it saves those who cannot save themselves!

For when Moses went up the mountain to receive the ten commandments, he came down only to break them to pieces. He then went back up the mount to receive the covenant a second time (Exodus 32:19; 34:1-2).

In similar fashion, we have broken the first covenant only to receive it again. But this New Covenant of grace, in God's wisdom, is indeed "a better hope," and will produce everlasting fruit in every heart that receives it. That's because divine grace does not depend on man but is the saving power of God. As it is written:

> "Not that we are sufficient of ourselves to think any thing as of ourselves; but our sufficiency is of God; Who also hath made us able ministers of the new testament; not of the letter, but of the spirit: for the letter killeth, but the spirit giveth life" (2 Corinthians 3:5-6).

And how far will God's New Covenant in Christ go to save you? The Bible declares that it is to the *uttermost*. For it is written:

> "Wherefore he is able also to save them to the *uttermost* that come unto God by him, seeing he ever liveth to make intercession for them" (Hebrews 7:25).

In the law, no security is found. But in grace there is an abundance of security—yes, eternal security.

Therefore, how can *you* lose what *God keeps?* It is, after all, a "better covenant, which was established upon better promises" (Hebrews 8:6).

Sloppy Agape?

Such wonderful love can sometimes be difficult to receive. And I have at times heard some fellow Christians use the word "grace" with disdain, calling it "sloppy agape" or something similar. The word "agape" is a Greek word and its meaning is an *unconditional sacrificial love*. It's the highest form of love in the Greek language. It is a love which is demonstrated with actions and does not rely upon the worthiness of its recipient. But some, by using this negative remark in describing the grace of God, imply that agape love is somehow overdone. The implication would be that grace is to blame for sin and that belief in its true meaning is being "soft" on sin.

For one may see a brother or sister in sin and therefore blame grace or the belief in such grace for that sin. But as mentioned, true grace will lead you closer to God and toward righteousness. This is because God's grace works in the heart and *is* His very love and sanctification in motion. Anyone in the Scripture who came close to the Lord's love and presence was certainly not being "sloppy" with such a true revelation. Just look at the words spoken by Job when the Lord was revealed to Him:

> "Wherefore I abhor myself, and repent in dust and ashes" (Job 42:6).

And consider Isaiah, who saw the glory of the Lord and exclaimed:

> "Then said I, Woe is me! for I am undone; because I am a man of unclean lips, and I dwell in the midst of a people of unclean lips: for mine eyes have seen the King, the LORD of hosts" (Isaiah 6:5).

Certainly, God's agape love is never sloppy, and we shouldn't use "cute" sayings to diminish its true meaning. People may be "sloppy" in walking with God but that is not the fault of grace. We must not negate the Word of God because of the way a situation appears in our eyes. God's love is never the problem. It was God's loving grace that motivated His Sacrifice at the cross. And this grace is truly unmerited, unearned, undeserved, unconditional favor— though Christ gave all to give it to us and to secure it for us before the Father.

Are there individuals who misuse this grace? Yes.

Indeed, there were also people in the Apostle Paul's day who twisted his words and took the meaning of grace as a license to promote sin. Paul even said that he was accused of this, declaring: "And not rather, (as we be slanderously reported, and as some affirm that we say,) Let us do evil, that good may come?..." (Romans 3:8).

However, the Apostle Peter said that Paul's writings were not the problem and stated that the problem was with the "unlearned and unstable," as Peter wrote:

> "As also in all his epistles, speaking in them of these things; in which are some things hard to be understood, which they that are unlearned and unstable wrest, as they do also the other scriptures, unto their own destruction" (2 Peter 3:16).

And Jude also mentioned ungodly people, who turned the grace of God into sensuality:

> "...ungodly people, turning the grace of our God into sensuality, and denying our only Master and Lord, Jesus Christ" (Jude 1:4, *NHEB*).

But in none of these Scriptures is there any mention of grace or the agape love of God as *being the problem.* Rather, it mentions "ungodly" people who deny not "their" Master and Lord but "our" Master and Lord Jesus Christ.

In contrast, the grace of God always brings healing to the heart of the one who receives it.

Are there issues that come up in the lives of Christians? Yes. Does the Lord sanctify His children? Yes. Is there discipline in the Lord? Yes. But is there condemnation? *No!* All these subjects will be covered in this study. For the New Covenant is His *unconditional love and grace* toward a people He has called and saved. This is not "sloppy agape," nor is it "messy grace," or any other degrading phrase that could be used to imply it is somehow erroneous. For God, and not we ourselves, knows the price paid at the cross for such a precious gift—as He Himself paid it.

Given such a marvelous grace provided to the born-again believer in Christ, how could salvation *ever* be lost? If salvation could be lost, then what law is one under, that must not be broken, to keep such a salvation? But the law always brings about God's wrath. As it is written:

"The law worketh wrath: for where no law is, there is no transgression" (Romans 4:15).

Yet, as believers in Jesus, we have a sure hope in our relationship with Him:

"For Christ is the end of the law for righteousness to every one that believeth" (Romans 10:4).

Chapter 8

The Security of No Condemnation

Controversy or Comfort?

In this chapter, we encounter a very precious verse in the Bible—Romans 8:1. Unfortunately, this verse has come with a bit of controversy. If we read from the King James Version it states:

> "There is therefore now no condemnation to them which are in Christ Jesus, who walk not after the flesh, but after the Spirit."

In reading the second part of this verse, namely: *"who walk not after the flesh, but after the Spirit,"* some have implied that there *is* condemnation if you, as a believer, should walk in the flesh and not the Spirit. Thus, they imply that the verse (and the "no condemnation") is conditional.

Interpreting this Scripture in this way diminishes what the Apostle Paul was stating in the chapters leading up to this verse in Romans and is in direct contrast to *all* of the Apostle Paul's writings.

Now I'm all for walking with God and in the Spirit; but was this really what Paul was saying in Romans, which is arguably one of the most liberating books of the Bible on the grace of God? Was Paul, who speaks of this grace in all his epistles, really making it conditional in this case? Is the walk of a Christian the *condition* for salvation or is it the *result* of salvation?

I remember a time when my wife, Lois, and I were singing a song that the Lord had given me, which is entitled, "No Condemnation." We were visiting a church and the Lord's Spirit was touching hearts and lifting heavy burdens. The song's chorus repeats: "There is now no condemnation, for those who are in Christ."

No sooner had we finished singing that song when the pastor of that particular church came up to the microphone and added that there is no condemnation *only* for Christians who walk not after the flesh, but after the Spirit. Adding this condition for grace hit like a lead weight (as I knew the truth of this Scripture), and I remember thinking that it was in direct contrast to what the Holy Spirit was doing in that meeting—healing, with His unconditional love.

Now some people explain the latter end of this verse by saying that it doesn't at all take away from the truth of having "no condemnation." They argue that Paul is speaking of how a true believer walks and is characterized, and the apostle is merely saying that we, having a new nature and being in Christ, do not walk after the flesh but after the Spirit.

So Paul is not making a condition for there being "no condemnation" for those in Christ, but he's describing the truth of those *in Christ as having a walk after the Spirit.*

While it is true that believers in Christ will bring forth the fruit of a life that follows after the Spirit, I don't think this interpretation adequately explains this particular verse. For by interpreting it as just stated, it's easy to come to the conclusion that there may still be condemnation for those who stumble in their walk with Christ.

When my wife and I sang our song in that church, it was directly quoted by the pastor to mean just that: condemnation for the Christian!

But there is another explanation pertaining to the second part of Romans 8:1, which gives us the best biblical answer for the meaning of the entire verse. Ironically, this answer involves words not found in Romans 8:1. For as it stands, the second half of Romans 8:1 is not biblical at all!

Who Walk Not after the Flesh but after the Spirit?

For indeed, the last ten words of Romans 8:1: "who walk not after the flesh, but after the Spirit," are *not in the oldest manuscripts of the Bible.* Furthermore, they are not quoted by *the earliest citations of the early church fathers.*

Most Bible translations are unanimous in omitting the last ten words of this verse, and you will often find a footnote stating that the oldest manuscripts do not support them.

So one might ask, can we trust the Bible? Absolutely! In fact, it's amazing to see that most variations within ancient text are *extremely* minor—not changing the idea of any doctrine in any way. If there is a discrepancy it is well documented, as with the verse being referenced here. The accuracy with which the Scriptures have been passed down to us over thousands of years is indeed wonderful. And the place where the inerrancy of the Bible is apparent is *in the original writings*, which were written through the Holy Spirit. As it is written:

> "Every Scripture is God-breathed and profitable for teaching, for reproof, for correction, and for instruction in righteousness, that each person who belongs to God may be complete, thoroughly equipped for every good work" (2 Timothy 3:16, *WEB*).

That's why it's important to use the most accurate manuscripts available when interpreting the Bible.

When it comes to manuscripts, it is the oldest ones that are deemed to be the most accurate. In this case, age is preferred even over quantity.

For example, suppose you wanted to accurately draw the earliest automobile and you were ready with twenty photographs of cars, taken around the 1930's.

There you are—ready to draw—when I enter the room with a few photographs of the automobile from 1886. Would you tell me that because you have more photos from the 1930's, they must be more historically accurate? No; you would have to concede that age is more accurate and that any true photograph dated prior to yours would need to be the basis from which you do your drawing.

All this is being expressed because the true reading of Romans 8:1 is:

"There is therefore now no condemnation to them which are in Christ Jesus."

This flows perfectly with the second verse, which says:

"For the law of the Spirit of life in Christ Jesus hath made me free from the law of sin and death" (Romans 8:2).

Paul the Apostle is clearly stating that by the principal of the new life of Christ in us, we have been set free from the old life and any condemnation! You are in Christ now, having been made a new creation. You are no longer under any threat of condemnation.

"No" Means "No"

It's good to remember that "no condemnation" in this verse applies to us not only when we are at our best but even when our walk is at its worst.

"No" means "No." And Christ has made the way for us, through His own bearing of our punitive judgment on the cross, to always stand before the Father without wrath.

This doesn't mean that God won't convict us of sin. He does this by His Spirit, changing us into the image of His Son. But Scripture declares He won't condemn us. The Lord may be corrective toward His children in love, but He's never punitive toward them in wrath.

For Jesus Himself bore that condemnation for us when He gave Himself for our sins. As it is written:

"The punishment that brought our peace was on him; and by his wounds we are healed" (Isaiah 53:5, *WEB*).

It is very important for one to understand what Jesus accomplished on the cross. Without this understanding, a Christian will always be striving in one way or another to attain God's favor. In contrast, if the believer truly understands this verse, he or she will rest in a secure and loving relationship with the heavenly Father, abiding in Him. And works will flow out of this relationship, through grace and love.

For Jesus Himself clearly stated that there is no condemnation for those who receive Him:

> "Verily, verily, I say unto you, he that heareth my word, and believeth on him that sent me, hath everlasting life, and *shall not come into condemnation*; but is passed from death unto life" (John 5:24).

And just in case there is any doubt regarding what the Apostle Paul meant when he wrote Romans 8:1, he clearly stated that there is no condemnation for those in Christ when writing these words, a little later in the same chapter:

> "What shall we then say to these things? If God be for us, who can be against us? He that spared not his own Son, but delivered him up for us all, how shall he not with him also freely give us all things? Who shall lay any thing to the charge of God's elect? It is God that justifieth. *Who is he that condemneth?* It is Christ that died, yea rather, that is risen again, who is even at the right hand of God, who also maketh intercession for us" (Romans 8:31-34).

Obviously, Paul believed that there was no longer *any* condemnation for those in Christ.

An Ancient "Copy & Paste"?

Interestingly, those words that are not actually part of Romans 8:1—"who walk not after the flesh, but after the Spirit"—were most likely copied there from Romans 8:4. There they correctly describe the fruit of our walk in the Spirit *after* salvation:

> "For what the law could not do, in that it was weak through the flesh, God sending his own Son in the likeness of sinful flesh, and for sin, condemned sin in the flesh: That the righteousness of the law might be fulfilled in us, *who walk not after the flesh, but after the Spirit*" (Romans 8:3-4).

In these verses, the words: "who walk not after the flesh, but after the Spirit" pertain to the life of a Christian *after* salvation, not as a condition *for* salvation.

Given the truth of the lack of any condemnation for those in Christ, how can a true believer *ever* be condemned?

If a believer, who is converted in Christ, was condemned —what would happen to his or her reborn spirit? Would it have to be *re-reborn*? How does that happen? Would Christ need to suffer and die all over again for another redemption?

In addition, how can the reborn human spirit—having been "created in righteousness and true holiness" (Ephesians 4:24)—ever die? The answer? It can't. It is now in Christ Jesus. Remember those last three words of our verse:

> "There is therefore now no condemnation to them which are *in Christ Jesus*" (Romans 8:1).

Chapter 9

The Security of Jesus' Eternal Sacrifice

Once & For All

We can usually grasp that Jesus' sacrifice on the cross covers all our past sins and even present sins—but what about our future sins? Does His sacrifice cover these as well?

The first thing you might ask yourself when looking at this question is how many of your sins were in the future when Jesus died for them 2,000 years ago? Were they not *all* in the future? In fact, when we receive Christ as our personal Savior, we enter into His finished work on the cross, which He accomplished long before we were even born. Scripture bears this out quite plainly, stating:

> "We are sanctified through the offering of the body of Jesus Christ *once for all*" (Hebrews 10:10).

And in Hebrews we also read:

"But this man [Jesus], after He had offered *one sacrifice for sins for ever*, sat down on the right hand of God" (Hebrews 10:12).

It is also written:

"For by *one offering* He hath perfected *for ever* them that are sanctified" (Hebrews 10:14).

Indeed, Jesus bore the entire weight of the sin of the world—past, present and future—upon Himself. As the Scriptures make clear and as has been mentioned in this study—Jesus is the second Adam who came to redeem all that was lost by the first Adam, in the fall of mankind. As the Apostle Paul stated:

"Wherefore, as by one man sin entered into the world, and death by sin; and so death passed upon all men, for that all have sinned" (Romans 5:12).

And Paul also said:

"For if by one man's offence death reigned by one; much more they which receive abundance of grace and of the gift of righteousness shall reign in life by one, Jesus Christ" (Romans 5:17).

This is why the Book of Hebrews can declare it was by one offering that Christ has put away our sin. This offering was fully accepted at the cross, where Christ bore the penalty for all of mankind's sin before God. And this sacrifice is *forever* in God's sight, as the Scripture states:

"How much more shall the blood of Christ, *who through the eternal Spirit* offered Himself without spot to God, purge your conscience from dead works to serve the living God?" (Hebrews 9:14).

For Jesus' sacrifice was accomplished through "the eternal Spirit," and when Jesus cried out: "It is finished" (John 19:30), He had completed the work of the atonement that paid our debt in full—*forever*.

But how did Jesus pay for our sins? To answer that question we need to ask, *what is the penalty for sin?* The Bible has an answer, as it says, "The soul that sinneth, it shall die" (Ezekiel 18:4). It also declares, "The wages of sin is death" (Romans 6:23). And what is death but separation? It is separation from this world and separation from God. Along with this death comes punishment, for God is righteous and just. As the Scripture states: "...these shall go away into everlasting punishment" (Matthew 25:46).

The Fish Tank

For God, being holy, cannot condone the presence of sin. This is because He is righteous and pure. We may not always understand the holiness of God, as we were born into a world contaminated by sin and therefore sin has been normal to us. So imagine if you were a fish, starting out life in a filthy fish tank. Having been born in that tank, you would never have known just how clean and clear the water could have been. You would have considered it normal for your environment to be dirty and full of sediment.

But God is like crystal-clear water—pure and without contaminants. That is what is really normal. Just because the fish in an unclean tank don't know the extent of their filthiness or how unclear their water is, this doesn't negate the fact that it's still a dirty tank. In fact, the fish in this cloudy water are so dirty they can't even see and perceive their own filth. For the dirtier they are, the less they see!

Now imagine if *you* were God, and you wanted to save *your* fish. In love, you had given them free will and you knew that their decisions had caused all this dirt to enter their tank. You had made the tank to be healthy and pure, but they caused it to be unclean. You also knew that your righteousness and holiness would not *and could not* accept them in this situation. Yet, the unconditional love you still had for them wanted to find a way to save them.

So you send your only son, being one with your very self, to become a fish and enter the filthy tank. He, being clean, would enter the tank and speak to the fish. This holy fish of yours would tell the dirty fish that if they listen to him, he would bring them back to purity and pristine water.

Some hear and receive what your chosen fish says about the reality of clean water. But some will not accept his words, saying, "We've lived here all our lives! We see nothing wrong with us or with this water!" In the end, those against you and against your fish, drag him up against the old dirty filter in the tank, causing him to be sucked into the current of the filter and die.

But now imagine that in your fish's death, he himself bore *all the punishment for the dirty fish in the tank before your eyes.* You, being God, are holy and just. It's not even possible for corruption to stand before you. Yet, in your love and due to your holy fish bearing the sin of the tank, you can now look upon this tank of fish through eyes of grace. That's because the sacrifice of your fish wasn't a death in vain; for you and your holy fish had a plan. And you knew that after the death of your fish, you would restore him, being one with yourself, to the place where he had been before entering the tank. And he, having borne the filth of the tank, would allow your just and righteous law to be fulfilled—for he paid its penalty in full. Because your very own fish bore the punishment for the entire dirty tank, it allows you to now look into the glass of the tank beyond the eyes of holiness *and with eyes of mercy.*

Now all the filth and corruption of the fish in the tank has been placed upon *your* holy fish. And in so doing, this fish removed—once and for all time—your just punishment for the entire tank.

Therefore, all you ask is that the fish of the tank accept what your holy fish has done for them—that they turn and receive the gift of your salvation. Because you will not force your salvation on them, you look for those who will say, "Yes" to your love. For thus it is fulfilled:

> "Mercy and truth are met together; righteousness and peace have kissed each other" (Psalm 85:10).

This is what Christ has done for those who receive Him—but He did more! For in His resurrection, He caused us to now be "justified" before God. As the Bible states:

> "Therefore being justified by faith, we have peace with God through our Lord Jesus Christ: By whom also we have access by faith into this grace wherein we stand, and rejoice in hope of the glory of God" (Romans 5:1-2).

The word "justified" in the Greek means "to make righteous." So God, through Christ, can truly see us as "holy and unblameable and unreproveable in his sight" (Colossians 1:22), because of Jesus!

And now, being holy in God's sight, He can send His Spirit to actually live in our hearts. He can guide and influence us and conform us to His ways of healing and peace.

As it is written:

"God hath sent forth the Spirit of his Son into your hearts, crying, Abba, Father" (Galatians 4:6).

The word "Abba" means "Papa" or "Daddy," and this is how dear you have become to the Father through Christ's sacrifice.

His desire was always to restore mankind's relationship with Himself—giving us the sure hope of one day being with Him in the cleanest tank of all.

For the very plan of redemption was set in motion because of the love that God has for you. It was a love He wanted in your heart.

As the Scripture declares:

"The love of God is shed abroad in our hearts by the Holy Ghost which is given unto us" (Romans 5:5).

Indeed, Jesus bore it all. The punishment for the evil of this world was placed on Him, at the cross, *once and for all time.*

The only punishment left for mankind is in refusing to receive what Christ has done. If one refuses to receive the forgiveness provided through Jesus, then his or her sins are still pending for judgment. *For there is no atonement for rejecting the atonement.* But for those who receive Christ, it means there is no punishment left. As Jesus said: "It is finished" (John 19:30), and those who say, "Yes" to Him and His salvation now have forgiveness and eternal life.

Before Him in Love

Surely God, in placing His wrath upon Jesus for the sins of the world, has caused us to be viewed "without blame before him in love" (Ephesians 1:4).

For this cross of Christ has taken away all that could keep you from drawing near to Him, and He to you. And through His cross all fear has been removed: fear of death, fear of abandonment, fear of rejection and the fear of what matters most to the human heart—the loss of His love. Anything that would separate us from God has been removed. As the Scripture encourages:

> "*Let us draw near* with a true heart in *full assurance of faith*, having our hearts sprinkled from an evil conscience, and our bodies washed with pure water" (Hebrews 10:22).

Do you see how God wants you to "draw near"? Do you see the "full assurance of faith" offered so you can draw near? Would God offer this full assurance to you if He didn't mean it? Would there be "full assurance of faith" if such a hope could be lost? Do you see the power in this blood of Christ shed for you? Do you see the security in the love that gave Himself for you? It is this love that removes *all* fear for the child of God! As has been stated, and as it is written:

> "There is no fear in love; but perfect love casteth out fear: because fear hath torment. He that feareth is not made perfect in love. We love him, because he first loved us" (1 John 4:18-19).

Chapter 10

Love Never Fails

Scripture Cannot Be Broken

The best way to describe our security in Christ would be to use the words found in 1 Corinthians 13. For the Apostle Paul, after describing the attributes of love, gave his final thought on the definition of love by simply saying that "love never fails" (1 Corinthians 13:8, *WEB*).

And in this statement of love's endless duration, we find the greatest truth about love. Love is something that endures *forever!* Such is the love of God toward His children. As He has indeed spoken:

> "I have loved thee with an everlasting love" (Jeremiah 31:3).

Therefore, for those who have accepted the redemption in Christ and have received His great salvation, how can a love that *never fails* ever be lost?

Jesus, when addressing the Pharisees about the Word of God, said:

> "The scripture cannot be broken" (John 10:35).

If this is true—and it is—then if God removed His love for His children, He would be *breaking* the Scripture. This is because the Word of God promises an unending, unfailing love for those who are His.

For to state that "love never fails" is not merely a pleasant saying; it is *the truth of God's Word.*

But regarding those who won't accept Christ, God will not force Himself upon them. This, too, is of His love. For to reject Christ is to also reject God. As Jesus said, "He that hateth me hateth my Father also" (John 15:23).

And Heaven is no less than a place filled with the love of God and love for God. For those who are His, this love has touched and changed their hearts.

Love—The Greatest Security

The Lord prophesied of His love and of the coming New Covenant when He spoke through Isaiah:

> "For this is like the waters of Noah to me; for as I have sworn that the waters of Noah shall no more go over the earth, so have I sworn that I will not be angry with you, nor rebuke you. For the mountains may depart, and the hills be removed; but my loving kindness shall not depart from you, neither shall my covenant of peace be removed," says the LORD who has mercy on you" (Isaiah 54:9-10, *NHEB*).

The words, "I will not be angry with you, nor rebuke you" are translated beautifully as, "Wrath is not upon thee, Nor rebuke against thee" in Young's Literal Translation of the Bible. For the Lord has *fulfilled His righteous wrath* through Christ.

Here it is stated again that God's love never fails, as His loving kindness "shall not depart from you." For His love is therefore—by definition—*eternal,* toward those who receive Him. And there is no circumstance by which His son or daughter can cause the removal of this love. For the mountains and hills may be removed but not God's love. Indeed, "loving kindness" in this verse is from the Hebrew word "hesed," which occurs over 240 times in the Old Testament. It is an unfailing, faithful, steadfast, loyal, merciful, kind, devotional, *covenant* love!

With promises like these in God's Word, how could we think for even a moment that we could ever lose salvation? Yes, God will cause us to grow and He disciplines us "for our profit" (Hebrews 12:10), but He will never condemn those who have turned to him in faith, receiving Christ as Savior. For He has made His promise, His covenant of peace, with those who put their trust in Christ.

If you have received Christ, you are in a most secure relationship with your Savior, as His love *never* fails. It's as simple as that, is it not? For "love is kind" (1 Corinthians 13:4). And it is written:

> "For I am persuaded, that neither death, nor life, nor angels, nor principalities, nor powers, nor things present, nor things to come, Nor height, nor depth, nor any other creature, shall be able to separate us

from the love of God, which is in Christ Jesus our Lord" (Romans 8:38-39).

The greatest security in all the world is God's love for you. Think of it: How many things in this world will *never fail*? Yet we often think of the Lord as being so ready and willing to let go of us! Do we not know for certain that He does truly love us and that our salvation is personal to Him? And do we not realize that if we were not with Him, He would indeed feel the loss?

This entire book is dedicated to the simple truth that you have security in this love. How could salvation ever be lost for the child of God, without His love failing?

But again—*love never fails!* Why not? Because God's love for you is perfect and unending, and it's more powerful than fear, as mentioned:

> "There is no fear in love; but perfect love casteth out fear" (1 John 4:18).

It is no wonder that God's love is perfect, because God *is* love. IT IS HIS VERY BEING. As it is written:

> "And we have known and believed the love that God hath to us. *God is love*; and he that dwelleth in love dwelleth in God, and God in him" (1 John 4:16).

And it is in His love that you can find rest, as He has said:

> "The LORD your God is in your midst, a mighty one who will save. He will rejoice over you with joy. *He will calm you in his love.* He will rejoice over you with singing" (Zephaniah 3:17, *NHEB*).

Why Hell?

But perhaps some will respond, "If God is so loving, why does He choose to send some to Hell?"

To answer this question, one must first understand that God doesn't "choose" to send people to Hell. He gives them what they have actually chosen upon Earth—separation from Him. And the Scripture, declaring that God is "not willing that any should perish, but that all should come to repentance" (2 Peter 3:9), shows His heart in not wishing any to be separated from Him.

However, God is also righteous and there is a penalty for rejecting the One who took our penalty upon Himself. Would you not be angry if you gave your life for the sin of the world, and that gracious act was rejected? Would it not be very personal to you? Why should we think it would not be very personal to God? For the true sin of the world is in rejecting Christ. For Jesus said that the Holy Spirit will convict the world of sin "because they believe not on me" (John 16:9). For love "doesn't rejoice in unrighteousness, but rejoices with the truth" (1 Corinthians 13:6, *WEB*).

Nevertheless, man chooses—by the free will that God has given him—*to separate himself from God*. This is happening here and now. In fact, if you were to reverse engineer Heaven and Hell, you would get the population of *planet Earth*.

But you may say, "What if one doesn't hear about Jesus?" Well, first and foremost, man is responsible to seek his Creator in earnest. As is is written:

"Because that which may be known of God is manifest in them; *for God hath shewed it unto them.* For the invisible things of him from the creation of the world are clearly seen, being understood by the things that are made, even his eternal power and Godhead; *so that they are without excuse*: Because that, when they knew God, they glorified him not as God, neither were thankful; but became vain in their imaginations, and their foolish heart was darkened" (Romans 1:19-21).

And those who reject God and His salvation through Christ remain in a state of corruption within their very *being*. What I mean by this is not just that their deeds are corrupt, but it's *who they are inside* that is corrupt—and that is the greater issue. So unless the spirit or "being" of a person receives the renewal and rebirth of the Holy Spirit, that one is still against Jesus, having not received the salvation that God offers in Christ. For Jesus said, "He that is not with me is against me" (Matthew 12:30).

People ultimately manifest *who they are* by their deeds. And Jesus said that "*men loved darkness* rather than light, because their deeds were evil" (John 3:19). In this verse we see that the evil deeds are manifesting the deeper reality that "men loved darkness." This is the reason for the evil deeds— the rejection of the light of Christ and the love of evil.

Notice these words in the Book of Revelation, when the angel that spoke with John declared the time of the end to be at hand:

> "And he saith unto me, Seal not the sayings of the prophecy of this book: for the time is at hand. He that is unjust, let him *be* unjust still: and he which is filthy, let him *be* filthy still: and he that is righteous, let him *be* righteous still: and he that is holy, let him *be* holy still" (Revelation 22:10-11).

We see in these verses that it is the *being* of a person (and not the doing) that is revealed, as it states, "He that *is unjust*, let him *be unjust* still." For the dead, in Hades, will *still be* the dead. They will not even cry out in repentance in such a state, as their very being is without Christ and without regeneration.

This can be seen in the events that Jesus spoke about in the story of the Rich Man and Lazarus:

> "Now there was a certain rich man, and he was clothed in purple and fine linen, living in luxury every day. A certain beggar, named Lazarus, was taken to his gate, full of sores, and desiring to be fed with the crumbs that fell from the rich man's table. Yes, even the dogs came and licked his sores. The beggar died, and he was carried away by the angels to Abraham's bosom. The rich man also died and was buried. In Hades, he lifted up his eyes, being in torment, and saw Abraham far off, and Lazarus at his bosom. He cried and said, 'Father Abraham, have mercy on me, and send Lazarus, that he may dip the tip of his finger in water and cool my tongue! For I am in anguish in this flame.' "But Abraham said, 'Son, remember that you, in your lifetime, received your good things, and Lazarus, in the same way, bad things. But here he is now comforted and you are in anguish. Besides all this, between us and you there is a great gulf fixed, that those who want to pass from here to you are not able, and that no one may cross over from there to us.' "He said, 'I ask you therefore, father, that you would send him to my father's house —for I have five brothers—that he may testify to them, so they won't also come into this place of

torment.' "But Abraham said to him, 'They have Moses and the prophets. Let them listen to them.' "He said, 'No, father Abraham, but if one goes to them from the dead, they will repent.' "He said to him, 'If they don't listen to Moses and the prophets, neither will they be persuaded if one rises from the dead'" (Luke 16:19-31, *WEB*).

Notice that the rich man, being in Hades, never cried out to Abraham *in repentance*. He did not say, "I was wrong and now I want God," nor did he ask, "Abraham, how can I be saved?" Not at all, as he is in his *eternal state*. That is why the Bible tells us to receive Christ today, saying:

"Behold, now is the accepted time; behold, now is the day of salvation" (2 Corinthians 6:2).

For although the rich man asked Abraham to send Lazarus to testify to his brothers, there was no mention of his *personal repentance* toward God. He feared for his brothers —yet possessed the same heart with which he denied God.

This story is not a parable, as some claim. It is a true account of what happened in the afterlife, following the passing away of these two individuals. For parables never include proper names as we see with "Lazarus" and "Abraham" in these Scriptures. So why does the story leave out the name of the rich man? David answered this in the Psalms, where he wrote:

"You have destroyed the wicked. You have blotted out their name forever and ever" (Psalm 9:5, *WEB*).

This rich man, with all the wealth he had upon Earth, gave no heed to faith or to God. In his lack, he fulfilled the words of Jesus, as He said:

"But whoever doesn't have, from him will be taken away even that which he has" (Matthew 13:12, *WEB*).

And God, in not allowing such a one to enter the Kingdom of Heaven, is not being unloving. *For the dead do not want Him. They had their entire lives on Earth to choose God and they did not do so. Therefore, there is no one in Hell who ultimately doesn't hate God. In the same way, there is no one in Heaven who doesn't love Jesus.*

Do you see? God will reach each and every one who is His, as Jesus said:

"All that the Father giveth me shall come to me; and him that cometh to me I will in no wise cast out" (John 6:37).

This is because God *wants* His children in Heaven! As Jesus also said:

"Father, I will that they also, whom thou hast given me, be with me where I am; that they may behold my glory, which thou hast given me: for thou lovedst me before the foundation of the world" (John 17:24).

Remorse or Repentance?

Sadly, those who reject Christ do not wish to be with Him. And God will not force them into Heaven, for that would not be loving. This is why we are not saved by remorse but in repentance—by turning in faith to Christ. Indeed, we see in Judas that he was remorseful but not repentant, as it is written:

"Then Judas, who betrayed him, when he saw that Jesus was condemned, felt remorse, and brought back the thirty pieces of silver to the chief priests and elders, saying, "I have sinned in that I betrayed innocent blood." But they said, "What is that to us? You see to it." He threw down the pieces of silver in the sanctuary and departed. Then he went away and hanged himself" (Matthew 27:3-5, *WEB*).

For remorse *is not* the same as repentance.

In remorse you may feel badly about the sorrow you have caused, but with repentance you go further, by actually turning to God in faith for forgiveness. You humble yourself and receive His free gift of salvation. Remorse may lead to repentance, but if it does not, it merely remains dead. As it is written:

> "For godly sorrow produces repentance leading to salvation, which brings no regret. *But the sorrow of the world produces death*" (2 Corinthians 7:10, *WEB*).

God is not looking for you to be punished in remorse but to gain salvation by faith—by turning to and accepting Christ in your heart.

You may assume if people feel badly about situations they wrongfully caused, it indicates they're turning to God. That's not necessarily true because guilt and self-condemnation are not the same as repentance. If that was the case, Judas would not have hung himself. For salvation is by faith, not by guilt. And those who do not turn to God are rejecting Him. Jesus even went so far as to say that those who reject Him—*hate* Him. He said, "They hated me without a cause" (John 15:25).

For God is not the One without love. His love is endless. It is man who is lacking love.

Where Was God?

One may consider all the problems in life and in this world and wonder, "Where was God when..?" But this is not Heaven and the world is in a fallen state. This is a world that crucified its Creator! God, in Christ, knows what it feels like to be on this Earth and to be broken by it. Due to the fall of *man*, sin and rebellion entered this world—touching even the Son of God, who humbled Himself to become the Son of Man and endured the road to the cross and His suffering upon it.

The "lack" of love you may feel is from a world that has rejected Christ as a whole. When is the last time you turned on the local news and the broadcast started with someone saying, "Welcome! Let us give praise and honor to the Name of the Lord!" You say, "That never happens!" Exactly—for that is how far this world has departed from God's original design. We were *always* meant to be in relationship with Him and to love Him.

How very sad that there was even a law given that said, "And thou shalt love the LORD thy God with all thine heart, and with all thy soul, and with all thy might" (Deuteronomy 6:5). It should not have had to be so! For we were made to love Him. Oh, how sad that such a love would need to be commanded by law! That is how far man had fallen from God's purpose in creation. But God had a plan that would be far better than an outward command of love. He sent His Son, Jesus, so we could truly love Him from our hearts, for the Bible states:

"We love him, because he first loved us" (1 John 4:19).

The Kingdom of Love

In the Kingdom of Heaven all goes according to God's will, which is—with love. This is why it it written:

"And God shall wipe away all tears from their eyes; and there shall be no more death, neither sorrow, nor crying, neither shall there be any more pain: for the former things are passed away" (Revelation 21:4).

And this is why, as in the true story of the Rich Man and Lazarus, the spiritually dead will need to be separated from the living, as it is written:

"For *without* are dogs, and sorcerers, and whoremongers, and murderers, and idolaters, and whosoever loveth and maketh a lie" (Revelation 22:15).

Indeed, God's love will reign supreme. It is for this purpose that you are saved. And it is to this end that God is still working, as Jesus said, "My Father worketh hitherto, and I work" (John 5:17). And it is His love—His endless love— that has not only called you into a relationship with Jesus but destined you for the full realization of His love in the Kingdom He has prepared for you.

This is a love that not only has you in the future—but here and now! Let all of us in the church humble ourselves before such a love that will *never fail!* For we are receiving this Kingdom now, securely in Christ. As it is written:

"So since *we are receiving a Kingdom that cannot be shaken,* let us give thanks..." (Hebrews 12:28, *NHEB*).

And as Jesus said:

"Fear not, little flock; for it is your Father's good pleasure to *give you* the kingdom" (Luke 12:32).

For God's love is personified in Christ. It is a love given to the point of death. And on the cross we see the love that bore our punishment and sin, our grief and our pain, our rejection and humiliation—all to bring us back to God.

Scripture says, "Love is strong as death" (Song of Solomon 8:6). Yet love is *even stronger* than death, as Scripture also says that "He is risen" (Matthew 28:6) and that Jesus "was raised again for our justification" (Romans 4:25)! For God does not desire punishment but salvation for those who turn to Him. As it is written:

> "So Christ was once offered to bear the sins of many; and unto them that look for him shall he appear the second time *without sin* unto salvation" (Hebrews 9:28).

For God is not carrying a big stick, ready to strike His own sheep and cast them from the fold. Indeed, "thy rod and thy staff they *comfort me*" (Psalm 23:4). The only "big stick" that God carried was the cross upon His back, as He walked toward Calvary for our sin.

And God is not willing to separate His true children from Himself—under any circumstance whatsoever. Jesus Himself experienced separation from God the Father *for us,* upon the cross. He did this so that we would *never* know such a separation from God. And now we, as believers, can stand before God "holy and without blame before him *in love*" (Ephesians 1:4).

Yes, we stand before Him in a love that "never fails."

True Love

The weight of this world with such suffering and tears
Can at times overwhelm and crush us with with fears.
It may seem life is hopeless and there is no way out,
But there's Someone Who cares, understanding the doubt.

I've know such deception, been betrayed with a kiss;
But Christ Jesus Himself has experienced this.
And His passionate cry, "Not my will but thine,"
Has transformed my life by God's love divine.

My Heavenly Father sent to Calvary's hill
The One whose shed blood is powerful still.
And on that cruel cross as He suffered and bled,
Jesus saw us today, feeling the tears that we've shed.

I'm awestruck and grateful that after He died,
He rose from the tomb and is here by my side.
I am now His, and He is now mine
And in Heaven's mansions, He'll share His new wine.

I'm changed forever — eternally free,
Clinging to promises Jesus gave me.
I'll go anywhere, that this whole world would know
That God cares for you, and His Son loves you so!

Mrs. Lois M. Webb

Chapter 11

True Conversion?

Clouds Without Water

Having written about our great and wonderful security in Christ, I'm now going to address the Scriptures that might *seem* to cast doubt upon this truth. It is necessary to understand these Scriptures as well—so that we can stand firm in our affirmations of this security in Christ.

This study began in contrasting the difference between the true believer and the make-believer. It is important to discuss the realities of the make-believers among us, in order to understand the many divine warnings spoken to them throughout the New Testament. Indeed, without such an understanding one may, as many do, confuse the warnings to false brethren as being warnings to the true church body. For as we will see, the New Testament has much to say regarding those who merely pretend and imitate Christianity.

We may all know people who have professed a belief in Christ and then proceeded to live like the Devil. They may have walked with Christ for a time, only to walk away into the ways of the world and *never* look back. Am I really saying that this is what it means to be *saved* by grace? Is it merely saying the right words at a given time, without any change of heart—and bearing no good fruit for the rest of one's life? Is that true salvation? Is this what Jesus meant when He said, "Ye must be born again" (John 3:7)?

Here is where a difficult question comes up: Was the person *really saved* to begin with?

True conversion will bring about fruit. It may not appear immediately, but eventually you will indeed know the tree by its fruit. Some believers are drawn away for a season, only to return to that true nature inside of them. Loss of fellowship with Christ will ultimately bring about misery for the believer. There is no joy for a Christian who walks in the flesh. It brings about sin, sadness, disharmony, loss of eternal rewards and ultimately, if need be, physical death (1 Corinthians 11:30). The Lord, in his mercy, will discipline His children in love to draw them back to His green pastures, but He *will not condemn them* (Romans 8:1). God is dealing with believers as sons and daughters and *not* as His enemies (Hebrews 12:5-11).

Others, however, *may never have been converted to begin with*. It is amazing to me how many admonitions are found in the epistles of the New Testament pertaining to false believers within the church. Regarding them, the Bible speaks of those who not only fail to receive Christ within their hearts but who also cause much deceit and harm within the church.

Jude wrote:

> "For there are certain men crept in unawares, who were before of old ordained to this condemnation, ungodly men, turning the grace of our God into lasciviousness, and denying the only Lord God, and our Lord Jesus Christ" (Jude 1:4).

Notice how Jude stated that these people were not denying *their* Lord God but "*the* only Lord God, and *our* Lord Jesus Christ." Jude specifically declared that Jesus was never *theirs*, but He is, in fact, *ours*. For these people did not have Christ as their Lord. Jude also went on to call them:

> "...clouds without water" (Jude 1:12).

He also stated:

> "These are they that separate themselves, sensual, *having not the Spirit*" (Jude 1:19).

Jude specifically referred to them as not having the Spirit and therefore as *not being born again.*

The Apostle Peter spoke of these individuals within the church in a similar way, by saying:

> "These are wells without water, clouds that are carried with a tempest; to whom the mist of darkness is reserved for ever" (2 Peter 2:17).

Denying the Lord That Bought Them?

Peter also called them "false teachers" (2 Peter 2:1), as well as "spots...and blemishes" (2 Peter 2:13) among the brethren, declaring that they:

"...bring in damnable heresies, even denying the Lord that bought them" (2 Peter 2:1).

The fact that they *denied the Lord that bought them* in no way implies these people ever *had* a personal relationship with Christ.

This verse is speaking of the blood of Christ that bought them and not the faith that saved them. For as you will see in this study, Jesus' blood was shed for the *entire world*, not just for those who accept Him. As it is written:

"And he is the propitiation for our sins: and not for ours only, *but also for the sins of the whole world*" (1 John 2:2).

(This is covered in greater detail in *Chapter 13: The Warning of Hebrews 10.*)

It is this Jesus whom the false believers deny and reject. Indeed, they are "wells without water" (2 Peter 2:17) because they do not have the water of the Holy Spirit within them. And as Jude mentioned, they:

"...were before of old ordained to this condemnation" (Jude 1:4).

The Apostle Peter repeated this same sentiment in saying that these individuals who deny the Lord are those:

"...whose sentence now from of old doesn't linger, and their destruction will not slumber" (2 Peter 2:3, *WEB*).

Surely if these people were ever saved, *their sentence from of old would have lingered, and their destruction would have slumbered,* would it not?

This verse is revealing that they have *remained* under such a sentence because they were *never* saved in the first place. And Peter went on to say...

Peter & A Clean Pig

"For if after they have escaped the pollutions of the world through the knowledge of the Lord and Saviour Jesus Christ, they are again entangled therein, and overcome, the latter end is worse with them than the beginning. For it had been better for them not to have known the way of righteousness, than, after they have known it, to turn from the holy commandment delivered unto them. But it is happened unto them according to the true proverb, The dog is turned to his own vomit again; and the sow [pig] that was washed to her wallowing in the mire" (2 Peter 2:20-22).

This is a strong admonition. But its context clearly shows that Peter is not speaking of those who have put a living *faith* in the Lord Jesus Christ but of those who have only "*known* the way of righteousness." He is not referring to those who have truly been saved but to those who have merely "escaped the pollutions of the world" through the "*knowledge* of the Lord and Saviour.*" One is not saved by knowledge alone; salvation requires faith and a changed heart. It is of note that Peter did not mention the word "faith" or "conversion" in these verses *at all.* A person may clean up his act outwardly, but that does not mean that he or she has received Christ. Just look at the many cults in the world that feign Christian principles.

Notice that Peter stated a dog returns again to its vomit. Why? Because it's still a dog and that's a natural thing for a DOG to do. And Peter said that a pig, after being washed, returns to its wallowing in the mire. Why? Because it never stopped being a PIG. In the same way, those who only have a head knowledge of salvation, without truly repenting within their hearts, will ultimately return to what they always were —natural, unregenerate individuals. Again, this is why Peter called these people "wells without water" (2 Peter 2:17).

Cursed Children?

The Apostle Peter also named these individuals "cursed children" (2 Peter 2:14). This word "children" is clearly a reference from the point of view of the church but not from God; for Peter fully revealed they were *never* the children of God in truth but only in falsehood. In addition to what Peter had to say about them, he wrote one of the most stunning statements in the entire New Testament. For when speaking *directly about these people*, he stated:

> "The Lord knoweth how to deliver the godly out of temptations, and *to reserve the unjust unto the day of judgment to be punished*" (2 Peter 2:9).

Peter declared in the second half of this verse that these false brethren were the *unjust* and were being *reserved* for the day of judgment! Surely, God is not fooled. He knows the ones who have turned to Him for salvation in true conversion and those who are acting deceitfully within the church. As the Scripture declares:

> "The Lord knoweth them that are his" (2 Timothy 2:19).

Do you see the separation here? Do you see how there is ultimately a distinction between the godly and the unjust? Is it not evident that one is delivered and the other is reserved? It's a deep thought, but it is one that the Scriptures do put forth. And the Lord is not deceived by the outward pretense of one pretending to be a Christian. He knows the heart and the heart is the issue. For out of it, man exercises the free will God has given him to accept or deny Jesus Christ. Indeed:

> "Man looketh on the outward appearance, but the LORD looketh on the heart" (1 Samuel 16:7).

And the Apostle Paul made this separation obvious, when he wrote:

> "To the pure, all things are pure, but to those who are defiled and *unbelieving*, nothing is pure; but both their mind and their conscience are defiled. *They profess that they know God, but by their deeds they deny him,* being abominable, disobedient, and unfit for any good work" (Titus 1:15-16, *WEB*).

Notice that Paul refers to individuals who are "unbelieving" and yet they "profess that they know God." The apostle declares in these verses that even though these people may speak of God, they nevertheless "deny him" and therefore—do not know Him.

There are many other Scriptures that bring out this point. Let's take the case of Judas, who was numbered among the "twelve" (John 6:70). He walked with Jesus and was sent out with the twelve disciples to cast out demons and to heal the sick. Yet, after washing the disciples' feet, Jesus said:

> "Ye are clean, but not all" (John 13:10).

He also stated:

> "I speak not of you all: I know whom I have chosen: but that the scripture may be fulfilled, He that eateth bread with me hath lifted up his heel against me" (John 13:18).

For Jesus had said:

> "Have not I chosen you twelve and one of you is a devil?" (John 6:70).

In these verses, Jesus is declaring that although Judas was chosen to walk with the disciples, he was never chosen in the spiritual sense; for the Lord said, "I speak not of you all: I know whom I have chosen." Jesus went so far as to call him a devil. Notice that Jesus didn't say Judas will *become* a devil, but that he *is* a devil.

So how could Judas have truly been in unity with the Lord's disciples? Would Jesus call a true disciple a devil? Although Judas was numbered with the twelve disciples and had "tasted...the powers of the world to come" (Hebrews 6:5), he was never actually one of the twelve disciples in his heart. This brings me to a key verse on the subject of eternal security and one that truly unlocks the meaning behind many verses of Scripture...

Of Us & Not of Us

> "They went out from us, but they were not of us; for if they had been of us, they would have continued with us: but they went out, that they might be made manifest that they were not all of us" (1 John 2:19).

The King James Version of the Bible includes the words "no doubt" in this verse. It reads: "For if they had been of us, they would *no doubt* have continued with us..." However, the words "no doubt"—which have been added to the King James Version—are not part of the original Greek. For clarity, I left them out in this study, as they are not needed, and I think the verse flows better without them.

Within this verse, we see an amazing revelation in Scripture: the "of us" and the "not of us." This also appears in other places in the epistles. Here, John declared that some followers had left the Christian fold. But he added that if they had really been "of us" and born-again Christians in the heart, they "would have continued with us." God's grace would have enabled them to continue. John stated that they left because they were never "of us" from the start.

I will be repeating the verse of 1 John 2:19 often in this study, in order to make the important point that Scripture clearly reveals those who do not remain in the faith as *not having salvation to begin with*. This verse is very significant in that it distinguishes those who "went out" and "were not of us" from those who were indeed saved and "continued with us."

What a precious promise to true believers that we, by His grace, *will* continue in Christ! In fact, John the Apostle also wrote:

> "Let that therefore abide in you, which ye have heard from the beginning. If that which ye have heard from the beginning shall remain in you, ye also shall continue in the Son, and in the Father" (1 John 2:24).

And if I may give my own paraphrase of that verse: *If the tree takes root, it will live!*

Chapter 12

The Warning of Hebrews 6

Falling Back into Judaism

The Epistle of Hebrews contains warnings that refer in particular to people who have shared in the heavenly powers to come, only to reject them later. It's important to keep in mind that this New Testament book was written to those who had turned from Judaism toward Christianity. As such, there are warnings written in the Book of Hebrews, addressing those individuals who—falling short of true salvation—were tempted to reject Christ and go back into Judaism, even though they had experienced the presence and the powers of the world to come.

Such a warning is found in the text of Hebrews 6:4-6, which states:

> "For it is impossible for those who were once enlightened, and have tasted of the heavenly gift, and were made partakers of the Holy Ghost, And

have tasted the good word of God, and the powers of the world to come, If they shall fall away, to renew them again unto repentance; seeing they crucify to themselves the Son of God afresh, and put him to an open shame."

Have Become Sharers

These Scriptures may *appear* to be saying that someone could be saved and then lost—but as we look into its context, we will see that the writer of Hebrews was not stating this.

These verses do speak of those who have been "enlightened," but as mentioned, salvation is not based on knowledge alone. Rather, salvation is through the step of putting one's faith in Christ. Even though some people have understanding, this does not mean they acted upon that understanding within their hearts.

This passage clearly refers to those who have shared in heavenly things and in fact, the words "were made partakers of the Holy Ghost" would more accurately be translated as "*have become sharers* of the Holy Ghost."

For in the Greek, the meaning of the verb translated as "were made" is primarily "to be, become, to come into being, come about, happen." For this reason, many versions of the Bible translate "were made" as "have become." And the word for "partaker" also has the meaning of "a participant, sharer, associate." Indeed, many translations interpret this word as "sharer."

Is it possible for those who "have become sharers of the Holy Ghost" to have done so without actually receiving salvation? Yes.

But before going into that, let's look at a couple of other places where this word—meaning "partaker/sharer"—appears in Scripture. It's only used a handful of times in the New Testament, most of which are found in the Book of Hebrews.

We read in Hebrews 3:1 that believers are "partakers" of a heavenly calling. For it says:

> "Wherefore, holy brethren, *partakers* of the *heavenly calling*, consider the Apostle and High Priest of our profession, Christ Jesus."

This verse is specifically speaking of a *calling* that is being shared and is clearly referring to *saved* believers. You cannot share in a *heavenly calling* without first having it. As Paul said:

> "Moreover whom he did predestinate, them he also *called*: and whom he called, them he also justified: and whom he justified, them he also glorified" (Romans 8:30).

There is no mere tasting of a heavenly calling. You either have it or you lack it. And the true church has this calling in common.

True Partakers of Christ

We also find this same word, "partakers," several verses later in Hebrews 3:14:

> "For we are made *partakers* of Christ, if we hold the beginning of our confidence stedfast unto the end."

Now this verse seems to be saying one thing, but it's actually saying something entirely different. Forgive me if I get a little complicated here, but we need to look deeply into this verse for a moment, as it reveals a very important truth.

This Scripture is significant because it is stating that we ARE MADE (*already*) partakers of Christ by reason of the fact that we hold our confidence unto the end. The verb tense in this verse is very important. Let's look at it again: "We *are made* partakers of Christ, if we hold the beginning...unto the end." Notice the holding of our confidence to the end *manifests* that we are, indeed, *partakers of Christ* in the first place—from the beginning. For it does not say we WILL BE MADE partakers of Christ if we endure, but we ARE MADE (present tense) partakers if we endure.

Therefore, for those who *do not endure*, it is thus manifest that they were never *truly* partakers of Christ. There is no other way to interpret this verse. For with salvation, God gives us endurance; and this endurance reveals that we are, truly, partakers of Christ. (More will be discussed on this verse later, in *Chapter 41: We Have Become Partakers of Christ!*)

So in light of this explanation, if one were *not* to endure, as in the case of those spoken of in the warning of Hebrews 6:4-6 who fell away, that person *could not have been a partaker of Christ to begin with!* Such a one may have partaken/shared in the Holy Spirit's presence—*without* fully accepting His ministry by receiving Christ. And as the warning of Hebrews 6 states—this one had merely "tasted" of these spiritual things but had not actually *eaten* of them.

It is through the Spirit that God's presence and power are made known to us. You need go no further than the Book of Acts to see this in Scripture. But just because one had encounters with the influence or power of the Spirit, does not *necessarily* mean there was a humble response, resulting in the partaking of Christ in salvation itself. Again, one may share in the presence of the Holy Spirit *without* fully receiving His ministry that leads to salvation in a relationship with Jesus. For the work and ministry of the Holy Spirit is to both draw us *to* and save us *in* Christ.

Sharing the Power & Presence of God

But are there any biblical examples of those who shared of the Holy Spirit without fully receiving Christ? Are there cases of some who were overshadowed by His presence, without accepting salvation itself?

Judas, again, is a perfect example of one who shared in the heavenly things of God, yet he was not a true believer. As mentioned previously, Jesus had said of Judas: "Have not I chosen you twelve and one of you *is* a devil?" (John 6:70) and yet we read in Matthew 10:1:

> "And when he had called unto him his twelve disciples, he gave them power against unclean spirits, to cast them out, and to heal all manner of sickness and all manner of disease."

Notice in this verse that Jesus called unto himself his "twelve" disciples. He didn't leave Judas, whom he knew and named a *devil*, out of this. So Judas certainly shared in these things but did not truly receive and own them in his heart.

In case there is any doubt regarding the word "twelve" being a group name for the disciples which perhaps didn't include Judas, the Gospel of Mark clearly states that Jesus specifically sent them all out in pairs. We read:

"And he called unto him the twelve, and began to send them forth by *two and two*; and gave them power over unclean spirits...And they cast out many devils, and anointed with oil many that were sick, and healed them" (Mark 6:7, 13).

So Judas was certainly sent out in a pair with another disciple. In fact, Peter stated that Judas "was numbered with us, and had obtained part of this ministry" (Acts 1:17).

We can see in these verses that the disciples were not only sent out together, *but they shared and partook in the power of the Holy Spirit.* Indeed, the Scripture says that Jesus "gave them power over unclean spirits." Judas was not excluded from this! He was involved and surrounded by the power and the works of the Kingdom to come, for the Word says: "They cast out many devils, and anointed with oil many that were sick, and healed them"—yet Judas himself was not a true believer.

These verses show that people can come under the influence of the power of God without fully receiving God in their hearts.

This can also be seen in the healing of the man at the pool of Bethesda. This man did not know Jesus nor follow Him. Yet Jesus healed him and the man, after being touched by the power of God in this way, didn't even know Jesus' name! After he was healed, the Pharisees caught up with this man and asked him who healed him. As it is written:

"The Jews therefore said unto him that was cured, It is the sabbath day: it is not lawful for thee to carry thy bed. He answered them, He that made me whole, the same said unto me, Take up thy bed, and walk.

Then asked they him, What man is that which said unto thee, Take up thy bed, and walk? And he that was healed wist not who it was: for Jesus had conveyed himself away, a multitude being in that place" (John 5:10-13).

This is quite amazing. The man was healed by Jesus through the power of the Spirit of God and didn't even know who it was who healed him! This demonstrates that God can work His power in the lives of people even before salvation.

A Personal True Story

This is something that I actually witnessed personally. Many years ago, I lived in a small apartment and there was an older man I would see occasionally, who was the manager of the apartment building.

One day I saw and greeted this man and he told me he wasn't feeling well. He said his back was causing him great pain. In fact, he was in such intense pain that he couldn't walk very well. As we were going up the stairs of the apartment building, I recall very distinctly the Lord gently putting on my heart to pray for him, then and there.

Now I had prayed for people in this way before, but I thought it odd because he wasn't a believer and did not confess Christ. And to be honest, after the Lord put that on my heart, I hesitated. This was partly because I wanted to be sure it was really the Lord, but the bigger reason was because I thought it strange to pray for an unbeliever in this way.

So I went up the stairs and into my apartment, and by this time I knew in my heart that it was actually the Lord. I remember lying down with my back on the floor, looking up at the ceiling, and saying, "Lord, I pray that You would give me another opportunity to pray for him."

The next thing I knew, maybe a few days later, I found myself right in this man's apartment. I can't remember the reason why, possibly to pay the rent, but there I was and I again felt the urging of the Holy Spirit to ask him if I could pray for his back. It was still causing him great pain. In fact, his daughter, who was a nurse, was coming by that very day to give him some strong pain reliever. He agreed to the prayer, so I put my hands on his shoulder to pray for him.

Now I'm going to be very honest here. I did not work up any faith. I didn't try to pray "hard." There was only *one thing* I wanted to do—just pray for his healing. That's it. For that was all the Lord required me to do. And I simply had a desire to fulfill what God had placed upon my heart.

So I prayed for this man gently, quietly asking Jesus to touch him and heal his back. As I prayed, he told me that he could feel heat on his back. He actually said it out loud, right after the prayer. He was shocked! He said he could see his back being healed, yet he didn't know how he could "see" that happening. He was not accustomed to *any* of the terminology we might use in church. Still, all his pain disappeared immediately, and he knew that Jesus had healed him. I didn't need to convince him of anything. He was telling *me* what had just happened to him.

It was beautiful to see the Lord move that way in this man's life. I had merely done what I felt led to do by the Holy Spirit. And to this day, I do not know if the man received the Lord. He did come to the church I was attending about a week later, where he shared with the congregation what had happened—not because I asked him to but because he wanted to share it. For his pain never came back and he knew God had given him a healing miracle. I honestly can't remember how much I spoke with him about the things of the Lord, but I know that I did share with him. I only recall the simplicity with which the Lord touched him.

I'm sharing this testimony to demonstrate that it was the Holy Spirit's presence and power which fell upon this man, even though at the time he did not profess Christ. How can we put limits on those whom God chooses to touch? It is His very Spirit at work in the world to touch the hearts of people and ultimately draw them to receive Christ.

God's Overlap

I call this God's "overlap," for His power has a way of spilling over. We can see this in the case of Saul, when after being anointed by Samuel, a band of prophets met Saul and he himself began to prophesy:

> "And when they came thither to the hill, behold, a company of prophets met him [Saul]; and the Spirit of God came upon him, and he prophesied among them. And it came to pass, when all that knew him beforetime saw that, behold, he prophesied among the prophets, then the people said one to another, What is this that is come unto the son of Kish? Is Saul also among the prophets?" (1 Samuel 10:10-11).

Amazingly, this same thing happened later in King Saul's life, during a time when he was trying to kill David! It not only happened to Saul but to his servants as well. As it is written:

"Saul sent messengers to seize David; and when they saw the company of the prophets prophesying, and Samuel standing as head over them, God's Spirit came on Saul's messengers, and they also prophesied. When Saul was told, he sent other messengers, and they also prophesied. Saul sent messengers again the third time, and they also prophesied. Then he also went...Then God's Spirit came on him also, and he went on, and prophesied, until he came to Naioth in Ramah. He also stripped off his clothes. He also prophesied before Samuel and lay down naked all that day and all that night. Therefore they say, 'Is Saul also among the prophets?'" (1 Samuel 19:20-24, *WEB*).

This is surely a story of God's "overlap" in the Old Testament. Saul and his men were trying to kill David when they all became sharers of God's Spirit and prophesied! How much more could this same overlap have been possible in the verses of Hebrews 6, with those who were "sharers of the Holy Ghost" and had "tasted...the powers of the world to come"?

No Overlap in Salvation

But even though we can see this "overlap" in the working of the Spirit of God, there is no such overlap when it comes to salvation itself. For although one may experience God's presence even without being saved, real salvation cannot be experienced without personally putting faith in Christ.

Remember the Parable of the Ten Virgins that was shared in the first chapter of this book? You may recall that the bridegroom was coming; and those five virgins who didn't have any oil remaining asked for some from the other five virgins who *did* have oil—to give them some. The response was:

> "Not so; lest there be not enough for us and you: but go ye rather to them that sell, and buy for yourselves" (Matthew 25:9).

For salvation, as in this parable, needs to be found and obtained individually. Those without the oil (the unsaved) could not share in the true salvation experience of the others, which was manifest by the oil they (the saved) still had with them.

As previously mentioned, in Christ we are "sealed unto the day of redemption" (Ephesians 4:30). No one can experience this personal sealing without being born again through faith in Christ. And you cannot be a sharer in this salvation *unless* you are truly His. This is revealed in Matthew 7:21-23, where Jesus said:

> "Not every one that saith unto me, Lord, Lord, shall enter into the kingdom of heaven; but he that doeth the will of my Father which is in heaven. Many will say to me in that day, Lord, Lord, have we not prophesied in thy name? and in thy name have cast out devils? and in thy name done many wonderful works? And then will I profess unto them, I never knew you: depart from me, ye that work iniquity."

We can obviously see in these verses that these people were not outside the church. They even called Jesus "Lord." But what makes these verses so chilling is Jesus' response to these individuals. He stated emphatically that He NEVER knew them; therefore He NEVER had a relationship with them. In saying this, Jesus revealed that they were not real Christians *at all*. If they were, perhaps He could have said: "I knew you once, but now I don't." But what Jesus declared was: "I *never* knew you."

It's not that these people were saved and then became lost—but that they were *never* saved, even though they were around the elements of Christianity. Unlike a real believer with Christ in the heart, they never had a relationship with Jesus. This is the difference between the believer and the make-believer.

Jesus demonstrated this again in the Parable of the Sower. In speaking of the seed sown on rocky ground, He stated:

> "And that sown on the rocky places, this is he who is hearing the word, and immediately with joy is receiving it, and *he hath not root in himself, but is temporary*, and persecution or tribulation having happened because of the word, immediately he is stumbled" (Matthew 13:20-21, *YLT*—also Matthew 4:16-17, Luke 8:13).

This is from Young's Literal Translation and shows the Greek word that is translated "temporary," which also means "for a season." This sounds exactly like our verses in Hebrews 6. For this verse demonstrates that people can be among the beliefs of Christianity, being influenced by the reality of the Lord for a season, yet without receiving Christ in their hearts; they *have no root*.

You see, this seed in its appearance was coming up like the other seeds in the ground. It was receiving the Word of God with joy. But the seed had "not root in himself." It had no depth of life in the soil. Indeed, its life was absent, without a root to be anchored in the hidden part of the ground. This is the issue that separated it from the true seeds. It came up in *appearance* as the good seed but there was a difference in the soil of the *heart*.

If one were to compare these temporary seeds to some within the church, it would appear outwardly that they had lost their salvation. However, the reality is that they were never truly converted, not being rooted in Christ.

The word "stumbled" in this verse means: "to become indignant, to offend" and is often translated as "to fall away," which is why this Scripture states they are "temporary." They were not saved to begin with, for they had not truly allowed Jesus to enter their hearts. If they had done so, they would have had the root of salvation within them.

Rooted in Christ

Born-again believers in Christ are anchored *in Him*. Christ has come to live personally inside the individual Christian's heart. As the Apostle Paul stated in Colossians 2:6-7:

> "As ye have therefore received Christ Jesus the Lord,
> so walk ye in him: Rooted and built up in him..."

True believers have the reality of Christ within them and are not just sharing an experience of heavenly things—as Paul states again in Ephesians 3:16-18:

> "That he would grant you, according to the riches of his glory, to be strengthened with might by his Spirit in the inner man; That Christ may dwell in your hearts by faith; that ye, *being rooted and grounded in love*, May be able to comprehend with all saints what is the breadth, and length, and depth, and height;

And to know the love of Christ, which passeth knowledge, that ye might be filled with all the fulness of God."

Tasting or Eating?

Now the warning within Hebrews 6 has much to say about *tasting*. Indeed, it declares that they "tasted of the heavenly gift" and they "tasted the good word of God, and the powers of the world to come." The choice of the word "tasted" is very revealing here, in that it doesn't say they *ate* "the heavenly gift" or *ate* "the good word of God, and the powers of the world to come"—only "tasted."

It's like going to a food vendor and getting a small cup of ice cream to sample. You're not sure if you like that flavor and haven't yet made up your mind if you want to purchase it. You sample it, you taste it, but haven't committed to it in any way; in fact, you didn't even pay for it. Such is the case with these people who taste *but do not eat* or appropriate Christ within them for salvation.

See what David said in the Psalms:

"O taste and see that the LORD is good: blessed is the man that trusteth in him" (Psalm 34:8).

We can see in this verse that the tasting precedes the trusting. For it is after the tasting that David said, "Blessed is the man that trusteth in him." This is such an apparently simple verse, but it shows that you could taste of the Lord without putting your trust in Him. Why else would the Scripture encourage us, after tasting and seeing that the Lord is good, to then trust? For as with our sample of ice cream, one may taste and then buy the flavor, while another may taste and reject it. But both have tasted.

Can this tasting be what causes people to turn to the Lord? Sure. That is what David is encouraging. It is also the reason Peter instructed the newly born-again Christians, after tasting and then receiving Christ, to grow by the milk of God's Word:

> "As newborn babes, desire the sincere milk of the word, that ye may grow thereby: If so be ye have tasted that the Lord is gracious" (2 Peter 2:2).

But there are others who—after tasting—*fall short of receiving Christ*, as stated here in Hebrews 6. These individuals indeed tasted the real thing but did not become "newborn" as in the verse just stated in 2 Peter. They didn't simply listen to the Gospel message and reject it; they tasted the Spirit, power and glory of the Kingdom to come *and rejected it.* They didn't merely hear about it; they experienced it. That's why this warning in Hebrews 6 is so emphatic and goes so far as to say: "For it is impossible for those *who were once enlightened, and have tasted...If they shall fall away,* to renew them again unto repentance; seeing *they crucify to themselves* the Son of God afresh, and put him to an open shame" (Hebrews 6:4-6).

The reason this Scripture is so strong is because in this situation, one had indeed *experienced* the Kingdom. So how can you bring someone back to the point of repentance when they had already been at that point and refused, having seen the power and experienced the glory to come? Since they truly tasted the sample and did not want it, how can you bring them back to even taste it again? It's not that God would not save them, but "they crucify *to themselves* the Son of God afresh."

Nevertheless, Christians are called to share and shine our light in a world full of darkness. God knows the state of each individual—*more than we ever could*—and He gives us grace to share His light so that those who hear might believe.

For those who say, "Yes" to Christ, they will therefore *eat*, and He will indeed enter their hearts in salvation. As Jesus said:

> "I am the living bread which came down from heaven: if any man eat of this bread, he shall live for ever: and the bread that I will give is my flesh, which I will give for the life of the world" (John 6:51).

Notice that Jesus didn't say, "If any man *taste* of this bread, he shall live forever." No, for *tasting is not enough* for salvation. Jesus said we must *eat* of this bread.

This is why Jesus declared so emphatically, "Ye must be born again" (John 3:7). It's because salvation, like eating, is something that happens *within you*. As the Apostle Paul stated:

> "Test your own selves, whether you are in the faith. Test your own selves. Or do you not know as to your own selves, that *Jesus Christ is in you..?*" (2 Corinthians 13:5, *NHEB*).

This is also what is meant behind Jesus' words to the Pharisees in Luke 17:20-21:

> "And when he was demanded of the Pharisees, when the kingdom of God should come, he answered them and said, The kingdom of God cometh not with

observation: Neither shall they say, Lo here! or, lo there! for, behold, *the kingdom of God is within you.*"

For our salvation is not about an outward observation with the eyes but is an inward conversion of the heart, through the Spirit of God, by faith in Jesus Christ.

It is no less than:

"Christ *in you*, the hope of glory" (Colossians 1:27).

Thorns & Briers

This difference in the hearts of individuals who merely taste—but do not eat—is further demonstrated as we continue with the warnings of Hebrews 6, as it is written:

> "For the earth which drinketh in the rain that cometh oft upon it, and bringeth forth herbs meet for them by whom it is dressed, receiveth blessing from God: But that which beareth thorns and briers is rejected, and is nigh unto cursing; whose end is to be burned" (Hebrews 6:7-8).

Bringing forth "thorns and briers" can hardly be applied to a Christian who has truly been born from above. Paul makes this clear when he says: "But the fruit of the Spirit is love, joy, peace, patience, kindness, goodness, faith, gentleness, and self-control..." (Galatians 5:22-23, *WEB*)

Jesus Himself spoke of these fruits as an *indicator* as to whether one was truly a believer or not, when He taught:

> "Ye shall know them by their fruits. Do men gather grapes of thorns, or figs of thistles? Even so every good tree bringeth forth good fruit; but a corrupt tree bringeth forth evil fruit. A good tree cannot

bring forth evil fruit, neither can a corrupt tree bring forth good fruit. Every tree that bringeth not forth good fruit is hewn down, and cast into the fire. Wherefore by their fruits ye shall know them" (Matthew 7:16-20).

Notice that Jesus actually said: "A good tree *cannot* bring forth evil fruit." So how could a true Christian with a regenerate spirit produce only "thorns and briers," which is considered "nigh unto cursing; whose end is to be burned"? Truly such a one would not have even brought forth the first fruit of salvation itself!

Things That Accompany Salvation

And continuing with the warning, Hebrews 6:9 reveals something important that confirms this very truth. It's just a little verse, but it has great significance. We read:

"But, beloved, we are persuaded better things of you, and things that accompany salvation."

Here we see that the entire warning of Hebrews 6, *did not apply to those with salvation* in the first place! For it was a warning for those who were not truly saved but were only *sharing* in these things. Why else would the Scripture then say: "We are persuaded of better things of you...things that *accompany salvation*"?

This verse could have easily been written without that ending. It could have simply stated that "we are persuaded better things of you." We could then consider it a sentiment of encouragement, yet we wouldn't have a reason for the encouragement itself. But in stating the reason, being that these better things are "things that accompany salvation," we not only have a reason for the hope but a cause to rejoice in it as well!

For by including that last line, it is again confirmed that salvation (or the lack of it) is the true issue here. The Scripture doesn't say *we are persuaded of better things that accompany your faithfulness.* No; it goes further and deeper, to the very foundation itself, in declaring—"we are persuaded better things" that "*accompany salvation.*" For salvation is the heart of the matter, and one either has it or lacks it. And salvation brings with it the entire package, as Paul stated:

> "But of him [God] are ye in Christ Jesus, who of God is made unto us wisdom, and righteousness, and sanctification, and redemption: That, according as it is written, He that glorieth, let him glory in the Lord" (1 Corinthians 1:30-31).

The meaning therefore, is that the warning of Hebrews 6 was *not* for those with true salvation. There is just no other way to explain this little but powerful verse that states "better things" that "accompany salvation."

For as mentioned earlier, the Apostle John gave us the complimentary verse and key into understanding these Scriptures of Hebrews 6 as well, when he stated:

> *"They went out from us, but they were not of us; for if they had been of us, they would have continued with us: but they went out, that they might be made manifest that they were not all of us" (1 John 2:19).*

Chapter 13

The Warning of Hebrews 10

The Willful Sin of Rejecting Christ

The Book of Hebrews has another warning, similar to the one addressed in Hebrews 6, which some have used to say that a Christian can lose salvation. It is found in Hebrews 10:26-31:

> "For if we sin willfully after that we have received the knowledge of the truth, there remaineth no more sacrifice for sins, But a certain fearful looking for of judgment and fiery indignation, which shall devour the adversaries. He that despised Moses' law died without mercy under two or three witnesses: Of how much sorer punishment, suppose ye, shall he be thought worthy, who hath trodden under foot the Son of God, and hath counted the blood of the covenant, wherewith he was sanctified, an unholy thing, and hath done despite unto the Spirit of grace? For we know him that hath said, Vengeance belongeth unto me, I will recompense, saith the

Lord. And again, The Lord shall judge his people. It is a fearful thing to fall into the hands of the living God."

The willful sin in the beginning of this verse is not any ordinary sin. Who, then, would be saved? Are not our sins willful in the moment (in the flesh, anyway)? Let us be honest here. As it is written in 1 John 1:8:

"If we say that we have no sin, we deceive ourselves, and the truth is not in us."

In fact, the Apostle John declares that for the true believer in Jesus:

"The blood of Jesus Christ...cleanseth us from *all* sin" (1 John 1:7).

If this be so (and it is), it is evident that these verses in Hebrews could *never* be speaking of a saved Christian. For then how could *all* sins be forgiven if a willful sin is not?

To clarify this, let's read the Scripture leading up to Hebrews 10:26-31. It is:

"Not *forsaking* the assembling of ourselves together, as the manner of some is; but exhorting one another: and so much the more, as ye see the day approaching" (Hebrews 10:25).

Those are the words that are followed by:

"For if we sin willfully after that we have received the knowledge of the truth, there remaineth no more sacrifice for sins..." (Hebrews 10:26).

Note that the context is speaking of a "forsaking" of the assembly. This is not the same thing as missing a church service or taking some time apart to seek the Lord, as did Paul when he was in Arabia (Galatians 1:15-17). No; for the word "forsaking" here in the Greek means "to desert."

This is actually a case of forsaking or deserting Christianity itself. The context clearly demonstrates it. For the warning about this "willful sin" is given in such a way that after committing it:

"...there remaineth no more sacrifice for sins."

Obviously, this is speaking of *those who are rejecting the first and only sacrifice of Christ!* Again, the context shows the meaning of these verses.

For this is the willful sin of rejecting Jesus after receiving *only* "the knowledge of truth." Let's look at it again:

"For if we sin willfully after that we have received the knowledge of the truth, there remaineth no more sacrifice for sins..."

This Book of Hebrews was written to Jewish believers to encourage them in Christ and to warn those among them who were still doubtful and of an undecided heart, convincing them of the truth that the Messiah had come and had shed His blood for forgiveness, in fulfillment of Old Testament prophecies.

This Scripture is not referring to one who has received the Lord and salvation itself, but it applies to those refusing Christ after receiving *only the knowledge of truth—before salvation.* Again, this is the "willful sin" referenced here.

Therefore, these verses in Hebrews 10 pertain to those *without* a like faith—those having only a mere knowledge of the truth that *could* save them.

If one willfully rejects Christ and His atoning sacrifice, another atonement will not be available. For Jesus is the only promised Messiah. That is why this warning says that "there remaineth no more sacrifice for sins" for those who reject this truth. This is not speaking of those who, by faith, have the new life of Christ within them. It is referring to those who reject Jesus and the salvation purchased for them by His blood.

Adversaries

This is evident because of the fact that the verses in Hebrews 10 compare such a person who rejects this truth to one who *despised* the Covenant, as it says:

> "He that despised Moses' law died without mercy under two or three witnesses: Of how much sorer punishment, suppose ye, shall he be thought worthy, who hath trodden under foot the Son of God..." (Hebrews 10:28-29).

These verses are making the direct comparison that as one despised *the Old Covenant* under Moses, he or she is despising *the New Covenant* under Jesus. This section of Scripture goes further in referring to these individuals, who have sinned willfully by rejecting Christ's plan of salvation, as "adversaries." For it states that what remains for them is:

> "...a certain fearful looking for of judgment and fiery indignation, which shall devour the *adversaries*" (Hebrews 10:27).

Can this be said of one who has been born again of Christ's Spirit? Never! Is this about someone who is regenerate, with a new spiritual nature? No! For the Apostle Paul said Christians have:

"...received the Spirit of adoption, whereby we cry, Abba, Father" (Romans 8:15).

And is this "Spirit of adoption" permanent? Absolutely! For:

"...the gifts and the calling of God are irrevocable" (Romans 11:29, *WEB*).

How could this warning for God's enemies ever apply to those whom Jesus called "My sheep"—declaring "they shall never perish"?

As it is written:

"My sheep hear my voice, and I know them, and they follow me: And I give unto them eternal life; and they shall never perish, neither shall any man pluck them out of my hand. My Father, which gave them me, is greater than all; and no man is able to pluck them out of my Father's hand. I and my Father are one" (John 10:27-30).

Jesus also promised:

"Verily, verily, I say unto you, He that heareth my word, and believeth on him that sent me, hath everlasting life, and shall not come into condemnation; but is passed from death unto life" (John 5:24).

Surely, as God's sons and daughters, we cannot be classified as His "adversaries."

Insulting the Spirit of Grace

There is a significant phrase at the end of these verses in Hebrews 10, where the Bible describes this type of individual as having:

> "...done despite unto the Spirit of grace" (Hebrews 10:29).

The word "despite" is more accurately translated in the Greek as "insult," which is in accordance with the majority of Bible translations. This is very revealing as to the type of person to whom this Scripture applies.

Indeed, you would insult someone by not receiving a gift offered to you, would you not? And who gives the gift of salvation? The Holy Spirit is He who makes the truth and reality of Christ's salvation personal to the individual.

This is why the verse is more accurately translated that such a one has "insulted the Spirit of grace."

For the context of this Scripture is not speaking about those who are already *in the grace* of the Lord Jesus Christ; it is aimed at those who are outside the Kingdom—those in particular who are "on the fence" in their hearts, considering going back into Judaism and rejecting Christianity.

In addition, the next verse goes on to say:

> "For we know him that hath said, Vengeance belongeth unto me, I will recompense, saith the Lord. And again, The Lord shall judge his people. It is a fearful thing to fall into the hands of the living God" (Hebrews 10:30-31).

This reference to the Old Testament verse that says, "The Lord shall judge his people" (Deuteronomy 32:36) is a Scripture with which a Hebrew would be familiar. The word "judge" means "to decide"—and surely God would decide between those who received the sacrifice of His Son and those who rejected Him, having:

"...trodden under foot the Son of God..." (Hebrews 10:29).

The Blood of the Covenant Wherewith He Was Sanctified

Now one might assume these warnings found in Hebrews 10 are pertaining to true believers, because of the wording found in Hebrews 10:29, which mentions:

"...the blood of the covenant, wherewith he was sanctified..."

The assumption that this *must* be about believers arises because it says, "wherewith he was sanctified."

But first we must realize that this Scripture mentions the *blood* of the covenant specifically and *not* the New Covenant itself. This is the blood that was shed for the *purchase* of the New Covenant, and the blood is the prerequisite for receiving the New Covenant. Indeed, it's the blood that made atonement for the ratifying of the covenant itself, making it available to all who believe.

We must remember when reading, "the blood of the covenant, wherewith he was sanctified" (Hebrews 10:29) that the blood of Jesus was shed for the *entire world*, not just for believers. As mentioned, John the Apostle wrote concerning the effect and scope of Christ's blood:

"And he is the atoning sacrifice for our sins, and not for ours only, but also for the *whole world*" (1 John 2:2, *WEB*).

This verse clearly tells us that Jesus' blood has already been shed for the sins of the entire world, even for those who reject Him. So all those sins are *already* paid for? Yes! Surely, this Scripture reveals an amazing truth.

For indeed, as John says, Christ is the atoning sacrifice "*for the whole world.*" His blood has already been shed for the sins of all. What love, what grace, that the world has been sanctified, set apart by the *blood* of Jesus for forgiveness *already*!

Why, then, is not the whole world saved, receiving the New Covenant and therefore bound for Heaven? The answer is because His blood has sanctified everyone for forgiveness; but forgiveness is only appropriated by our faith, through the work of the Holy Spirit. When one receives Jesus as personal Savior, he or she *then* enters into the New Covenant through the "sanctification of the Spirit" and obtains the salvation that was *already* purchased by Christ's blood. Peter states this in 1 Peter 1:2, where we read:

"Elect according to the foreknowledge of God the Father, *through sanctification of the Spirit, unto obedience and sprinkling of the blood of Jesus Christ:* Grace unto you, and peace, be multiplied."

The blood of Christ has already been shed for the entire world, but it is through the power and sanctification of the Holy Spirit that one receives this atonement by faith. Yes, this sanctification is "*unto* obedience and sprinkling of the blood of Jesus Christ." And this is what makes a believer different from an unbeliever. Unbelievers have not received the gift of forgiveness that was *already* paid by the blood of Christ for them.

So being sanctified by the blood indeed refers to the entire world, whereas being sanctified by the Spirit refers to the individual. Jesus shared this within a parable referring to His Kingdom, saying that His blood would buy the whole world in order to save the treasure of those who believe, hidden within the world. He said:

> "Again, the kingdom of heaven is like unto treasure hid in a field; the which when a man hath found, he hideth, and for joy thereof goeth and selleth all that he hath, and buyeth that field" (Matthew 13:44).

The field represents the entire world, bought by the blood of Jesus, for which He bore all sins. The man who sold all that he had refers to Jesus, who gave *all* by shedding His blood, sacrificing His life to atone for the sins of the world. And the treasure represents the called-out believers who, by faith through the power and sanctification of the Holy Spirit, *receive* this gift of forgiveness, made possible by the blood of Christ.

Therefore, when Hebrews 10:29 speaks of the "the blood of the covenant, wherewith he was sanctified," it cannot be assumed that this warning is to the treasure of true believers bought within a portion of the field, who have truly accepted Christ in their hearts for salvation.

No; the entire field itself was bought through Christ's blood. And this is a warning to those who reject the blood that was shed as a provision for their salvation.

This Scripture in Hebrews would have been clearly understood by the Jews, to whom this book of the Bible was addressed. They would acknowledge the importance of shed blood for one's forgiveness. Given the Old Testament law concerning the blood of sheep and bulls and other animals, which were types and shadows of Christ's blood to come, the Hebrews would have known all too well that the blood should not be ignored or considered "unholy" (Hebrews 10:29).

Those who reject the blood of the covenant provided for them by Jesus for salvation have no future hope of atonement. Another Savior will not come and die for their sins, nor for the sin of rejecting Christ's sacrifice.

The writer of Hebrews 10 is undoubtedly giving a warning to those who have come away from Judaism and toward Christianity, urging them not to turn back to the law and to Judaism. And in a larger sense, this warning is for anyone who rejects the gift of Christ's blood for forgiveness.

Of Them That Believe

As we continue in Hebrews 10, we find further clarification as to whom these warnings were addressed in the first place. Notice the end of the admonition, where we find these few, yet powerful words:

> "But we are not of them who draw back unto perdition; but *of them that believe* to the saving of the soul" (Hebrews 10:39).

So those who draw back to perdition, to whom all these warnings were addressed, are obviously not *of those* who believe!

And thus the warning of Hebrews 10 concludes with words that are similar in meaning to the those found at the end of the warning of Hebrews 6 (which was covered in the last chapter):

> "But, beloved, we are persuaded better things of you, and things that accompany salvation." (Hebrews 6:9).

Therefore, how could this warning of Hebrews 10 be addressed to born-again Christian believers, having like faith in Christ, about losing their salvation? For truly, by grace, we are:

> "...of them that believe."

Bible ♥ Hearts™

"I am the vine, ye are the branches: He that abideth in me, and I in him, the same bringeth forth much fruit: for without me ye can do nothing."

John 15:5

by Richard O. Webb   HEARTOFTHELORD.ORG

Chapter 14

Branches, Fruit & Fire

Three Types of Branches

Jesus said in John 15:1-6:

> "I am the true vine, and my Father is the husbandman. Every branch in me that beareth not fruit he taketh away: and every branch that beareth fruit, he purgeth it, that it may bring forth more fruit. Now ye are clean through the word which I have spoken unto you. Abide in me, and I in you. As the branch cannot bear fruit of itself, except it abide in the vine; no more can ye, except ye abide in me. I am the vine, ye are the branches: He that abideth in me, and I in him, the same bringeth forth much fruit: for without me ye can do nothing. If a man abide not in me, he is cast forth as a branch, and is withered; and men gather them, and cast them into the fire, and they are burned."

This allegory in John 15 speaks of three different types of branches and how they relate to the vine.

A Branch in Christ Taken Away

The first one is the branch that is said to be "in me" but produces so little fruit that it is barely recognized as fruit. We read about this branch in verse 2:

> "Every branch *in me* that beareth not fruit *he taketh away.*"

This branch—described as "in me" or *in Christ*—was taken away by the husbandman, for we read that "he taketh away." It is interesting to note that in the Greek, the word which is translated as "taketh away," also means "to raise, lift up, take up, remove." Indeed, the word has the meaning "to bear" or "to carry off" as well.

This is a reference about those who were truly saved but had not shown much of Christ's life within them. They had the fruit of salvation, since Jesus could say that they are "in me"—but they didn't bear any significant fruit *after being saved.*

Now in Matthew 7:16, Jesus said, "Ye shall know them by their fruits" in reference to those who were His, as opposed to those who were not in His fold. But in this particular allegory, these individuals had apparently borne fruit unto salvation—yet they had allowed the flesh to rule in their lives to such an extent that it was said they "beareth not fruit" after the experience of salvation. In other words, they allowed the flesh to smother the life of the Spirit within them. Indeed, they had the fruit of salvation—but in their lives and in their walk they reflected the life of the flesh over the life of the Spirit to such an extreme that Jesus could say, "Every branch in me that beareth not fruit he taketh away."

So these believers were taken up and away by the husbandman himself. *They did not fall to the ground* but *"he taketh away."* Notice that the husbandman's hand had a *direct role* in their removal, as he personally took them away. They did not just drop off the vine but were *taken up.*

This verse is referring to a particular believer, *in such a hardened state*, being taken home early in physical death. This does not imply that *all* believers who go home "early" are in such a state, but it refers specifically to those that "beareth not fruit." Paul spoke of this when saying: "For this cause many are weak and sickly among you, and many sleep" (1 Corinthians 11:30). But this *is not condemnation;* it is *correction*. Such a one would have loss of rewards *but not loss of salvation, nor would he or she fall under God's wrath.* It is vitally important to understand this distinction.

For if the Christian believer does not recognize the difference between the Lord's discipline in love and the punishment of the wicked in eternal damnation, one will *never* understand the security of the salvation in Christ. There are many verses that show this distinction and the Apostle Paul made this very clear when he, in speaking of a particularly sinful believer, said in 1 Corinthians 5:5:

> "To deliver such an one unto Satan for the destruction of the flesh, *that the spirit may be saved* in the day of the Lord Jesus."

Paul states in this Scripture that even though the flesh or body was given over to destruction (or death), the spirit would, in fact, still "be saved in the day of the Lord Jesus."

Spirit May Be Saved & The "Hina" Clause

It is important to note that the word "may" used in this Scripture spoken by Paul cannot be interpreted to mean only the *possibility* of being saved, as some have put forth when interpreting this verse. (They argue that it implies one *may* be saved, with the idea also being that one *may not* be saved.)

For although the verb in the Greek is in the subjective mood (which indicates possibility), when used in what is known as a "hina" clause (as it is in this case), it should be viewed as *something that will in fact happen* and not as the mere possibility of something happening. This thought is *usually* understood when translated into English—but not always.

"Hina" is the Greek word for "that, so that, in order that" and when used with a verb in the subjective mood, the verb then becomes the equivalent of the indicative mood—or of that which *will indeed happen.*

Such a Greek construction is seen in Mark 3:14, which translates: "He appointed twelve, *that they might be with him, and that he might send them out to preach.*" The meaning is not that they might, maybe, hopefully—be with Jesus and get sent out to preach. No; the construction is much more definitive and means that they will, in fact, be with Him and be sent out. Again, this is usually understood, but I mention it here to show that the wording of 1 Corinthians 5:5 is not stating a mere possibility of the spirit being saved, but the actual fact of it *being* saved.

We see this same usage of the Greek found in John 13:18, which states: "I speak not of you all: I know whom I have chosen: but that the scripture *may be fulfilled*, He that eateth bread with me hath lifted up his heel against me."

It is undoubtedly clear that when Jesus spoke this, He meant that the Scripture would, in fact, be fulfilled. There is no question about the Word coming to pass. For again, the use of "may" in this verse pertains to that which will *indeed* happen. This thought would be clearly understood in the Greek, but again, it might be missed in the English translation.

Let's look at one more verse. In 1 John 3:8 we read: "For this purpose the Son of God was manifested, *that he might destroy* the works of the devil." Do we really think there is any question whether or not Jesus *would* destroy the works of the Devil? This is the very reason for His appearance in the flesh. The more accurate translation is that "the Son of God was manifested *in order that He may* destroy the works of the devil."

For the word "that" in these "hina" clauses is better translated from the Greek as "in order that" or "so that." This wording gives a much clearer understanding of the meaning as it was originally intended to be understood.

So in getting back to our verse spoken by Paul in 1 Corinthians 5:5, it would more accurately be translated and understood as:

> "To deliver such an one unto Satan for the destruction of the flesh, *so that* the spirit may be saved in the day of the Lord Jesus."

The "spirit being saved" is not in question here at all. Based on the preceding words, "so that," the word "may" in this construction of the Greek is actually stating what *will* certainly happen—which is the spirit being saved in the day of the Lord Jesus.

Now it should also be noted that in this particular discipline, Satan had no effect on the destruction of the *spirit* but only of the body of *flesh*. Here Paul was clearly speaking of the *flesh* in terms of the *physical body* (see examples of this usage in Mark 13:20, John 1:14, etc.). For the *flesh nature itself* will not be destroyed until Christians are with the Lord. And although this verse, as with our Scripture of the branch that "he taketh away," may appear to be of extreme discipline —it is *not* of condemnation. As mentioned previously, Christ has borne a believer's punishment (Isaiah 53:5). Still, God loves us too much to waste our time here on Earth, if it is spent only in corruption and in the ways of the flesh—or in hurting others. He saved us for much better things!

There will be more on this subject in the next chapter of this book: *Chapter 15: Damnation or Discipline?* But certainly our verse in John 15, pertaining to the branch that the husbandman/Father takes up, is *not* stating that a believer, one who is truly saved, can subsequently be lost. No; for we will now read about another branch, which is said to be quite different from this one, as described in verse 6 of John 15...

A Branch Not in Christ

"If a man *abide not in me*, he is *cast forth* as a branch, and is withered; and men gather them, and cast them into the fire, and *they are burned*."

Notice here that Jesus is not referring to one "in me," as we noted about the branch "in me that beareth not fruit." In contrast, Jesus specifically said, "If a man *abide not in me*..."

There is no connection to Christ here, which is very significant. Also note that—unlike the previous branch that "he taketh up"—this branch is "cast forth" and "men gather them, and cast them into the fire, and *they are burned.*" In this case, the husbandman's hand is not involved in taking them up or away, but rather they are cast forth of themselves, ultimately to be thrown in the fire.

It is important to realize that Jesus spoke these words to the disciples immediately after Judas had left to betray Him. And this verse is a perfect example of those who, being among the church, are nevertheless not part of the true church.

These words are also very similar to what Jesus said in Matthew 5:13, when speaking to the Jewish people prior to His rejection and crucifixion:

> "Ye are the salt of the earth: but if the salt have lost his savour, wherewith shall it be salted? it is thenceforth good for nothing, but to be cast out, and to be trodden under foot of men."

For those who would turn away from Jesus are those who ultimately *do not want Him* and therefore do not have Him living within them. And these words speak precisely of what befell the Jewish nation which, as a whole, turned from Christ and rejected Him (Luke 19:43-44).

Remember our verse in 1 John 2:19, the one speaking of those who did not abide in Christ? It says:

> "They went out from us, *but they were not of us.*"

Yes, they went out from us—cast forth as a branch. So this verse is revealing that they were *not Christ's to begin with,* for it declares emphatically—*"they were not of us."* Thus, this branch was never truly *in Christ* and is *cast forth* of itself, to eventually be *burned*. This is the way of all unbelievers and make-believers who would ultimately reject Christ. They cast themselves from their Creator, who is the only true Shepherd of their souls. Holding on to their rebellion, they go their own way, denying the need for Jesus and His salvation.

But in contrast, consider Paul's words in 1 Corinthians 1:8, referring to the Lord's keeping of His true believers:

"Who shall also confirm you *unto the end*, that ye may be blameless in the day of our Lord Jesus Christ."

Since God indeed will confirm you (the Christian) "unto the end," how can this verse, which talks about being cast forth and thrown in the fire, apply to a born-again believer? This is why interpreting Scripture with Scripture—through the help of the Holy Spirit—is so important. For God's Word is one harmonious truth.

A Branch Bearing Fruit

Lastly, the third type of branch mentioned in this Scripture is referring to a believer who is walking with the Lord. It speaks of one who is growing by grace, through the Spirit of God. As Jesus said:

"He that abideth in me, and I in him, the same bringeth forth much fruit: for without me ye can do nothing" (John 15:5).

Truly a branch's life is in the vine, as it is the vine that gives sap and life to the branch.

Jesus' allegory of the branches is similar to His parable of the sower found in Matthew 13:18-23, which was mentioned earlier in this study. That parable also shows the different reactions to God's working in the hearts of people. There are some rejecting the Gospel and having the seed taken from them, some reacting with joy to the Gospel but having no root in themselves and lacking conversion itself, some who are saved yet growing with thorns and not to maturity, and some who are saved and producing fruit that is thirty, sixty and one hundred-fold. The Bible addresses all people and in these verses about branches, as in the Parable of the Sower, it reveals the conditions of people's hearts.

When I was younger in the Lord, I used to think that the Bible was speaking *only* to Christians. I probably thought this because Christians were, for the most part, the only ones interested in what the Bible had to say! Yet I have come to understand that the Word of God is written for all types of people—to believers, unbelievers, make-believers and false believers. His Word addresses everyone so that the truth of God's Word may be a witness to all. And the Bible clearly states that although those who reject Christ will go their own ways and be cast out, those who are indeed rooted in Christ will remain in Him. Remember again those sweet words of Jesus:

> "All that the Father giveth me shall come to me; and him that cometh to me I will in no wise cast out" (John 6:37).

Did you catch that? Jesus said He *"will in no wise cast out"* those who come to Him! So how could those branches that are being cast out to the ground to be burned *ever* refer to a true believer? No way!

Chapter 15

Damnation or Discipline?

Eating & Drinking Damnation?

The Apostle Paul, when instructing the Corinthian church in regard to the institution of the Lord's Supper, stated:

> "For he that eateth and drinketh unworthily, eateth and drinketh damnation to himself, not discerning the Lord's body" (1 Corinthians 11:29).

Was Paul saying that believers in Christ may, in fact, lose their salvation? Let's look into this verse and some others similar to it, that we may understand them in light of the eternal security promised for the child of God, which is found in Scripture.

The context of this verse, referring to the Lord's Supper, can be found within 1 Corinthians 11:26-34. The King James Version is as follows:

> "For as often as ye eat this bread, and drink this cup, ye do shew the Lord's death till he come. Wherefore

whosoever shall eat this bread, and drink this cup of the Lord, unworthily, shall be guilty of the body and blood of the Lord. But let a man examine himself, and so let him eat of that bread, and drink of that cup. For he that eateth and drinketh unworthily, eateth and drinketh *damnation* to himself, not discerning the Lord's body. For this cause many are weak and sickly among you, and many sleep. For if we would judge ourselves, we should not be judged. But when we are judged, we are chastened of the Lord, that we should not be condemned with the world. Wherefore, my brethren, when ye come together to eat, tarry one for another. And if any man hunger, let him eat at home; that ye come not together unto *condemnation*. And the rest will I set in order when I come."

First of all, one must understand the proper translation of the word "damnation" used in this portion of Scripture. I like the King James Version of the Bible very much, but in this case it's just not accurate. The Greek word used here that is translated as "damnation" primarily means "judgment." This involves a verdict or decision, as in one made by a judge, often (but not always) with a negative outcome. The decision as to what that judgment might be is determined according to the use of this word in context.

Virtually every other translation of the Bible, including the updated New King James Version, uses the word "judgment" in this Scripture instead of "damnation," as damnation would be going a step further by determining the outcome of the specific judgment itself. The text should actually read:

"For he that eateth and drinketh unworthily, eateth and drinketh *judgment* to himself, not discerning the Lord's body" (1 Corinthians 11:29).

We also should note that the word "condemnation" used in the last verse of our text uses the exact same Greek word and should also be translated as "judgment":

"Wherefore, my brethren, when ye come together to eat, tarry one for another. And if any man hunger, let him eat at home; that ye come not together unto *judgment*" (1 Corinthians 11:33-34).

This specific word is found in many other verses of the King James Version and is translated, unfortunately, as damnation or condemnation, instead of judgment.

See Romans 13:2: "Whosoever therefore resisteth the power, resisteth the ordinance of God: and they that resist shall receive to themselves *damnation,*" 1 Timothy 5:12: "Having *damnation*, because they have cast off their first faith," James 3:1: "My brethren, be not many masters [teachers] knowing that we shall receive the greater *condemnation,*" and in 1 Timothy 3:6: "Not a novice, lest being lifted up with pride he fall into the *condemnation* of the devil."

The words I have placed in italics are all this exact same Greek word and should all be translated as "judgment." Certainly, the Devil himself will receive a judgment which *leads to* condemnation, so the usage of "condemnation" in that last verse from 1 Timothy would seem to be accurate. But the similarity between the Devil and a believer with pride goes no further than a judgment—as the believer receives "no condemnation" (Romans 8:1). This is why the word "judgment" is the better and more accurate terminology here.

Also consider Romans 5:16, where the exact same Greek word, being used as "judgment," is differentiated from a different Greek word, specifically used for "condemnation":

"For the *judgment* was by one to *condemnation*, but the free gift is of many offences unto justification."

In this case, the judgment led to condemnation; but again, the judgment or decision is a separate act from the condemnation itself.

Jesus gave an example of this meaning when He used this word in John 9:39:

"For *judgment* I am come into this world, that they which see not might see; and that they which see might be made blind."

This same word was used in the Septuagint (the Greek translation of the Old Testament), as we read in Exodus 18:22, which states:

"And let them *judge* the people at all seasons: and it shall be, that every great matter they shall bring unto thee, but every small matter they shall *judge*: so shall it be easier for thyself, and they shall bear the burden with thee."

You can understand by this verse how the word "judge" can be quite different from condemnation.

In the King James Version, James 5:12 reads: "But above all things, my brethren, swear not, neither by heaven, neither by the earth, neither by any other oath: but let your yea be yea; and your nay, nay; lest ye fall into *condemnation*."

However, in the Greek—this word is also correctly translated as "judgment," which is reflected in all major literal translations of the Bible.

James 5:9 also says: "Grudge not one against another, brethren, lest ye be *condemned*..." but again, the oldest and most reliable biblical manuscripts—as well as the large majority of Bible translations—accurately translate this word in the Greek as "judged."

There are verses where the Bible *does* include the specific word meaning *condemnation*, as translated from the Greek. Examples are found in 2 Peter 2:6, which states: "And turning the cities of Sodom and Gomorrha into ashes *condemned* them with an overthrow..." and in Matthew 12:41: "The men of Nineveh shall rise...and shall *condemn* it..." These are among many other examples found in the New Testament. However, it's not the same Greek word as those being discussed here, which primarily mean "judgment."

Drunk at the Lord's Supper

Therefore, it is significant to note that the Scriptures within 1 Corinthians 11 concerning the Lord's Supper refer to judgment—not to condemnation or damnation. *This is not God striking them down in condemnation but humbling them from the strength and pride of their flesh.* It is correction but not condemnation. This judgment was toward believers who were using this holy occasion as a carnal party and selfishly fighting one another over the food and drink involved in it. They were literally getting drunk at the Lord's Supper, as stated in 1 Corinthians 11:20-21:

> "When ye come together therefore into one place, this is not to eat the Lord's supper. For in eating

every one taketh before other his own supper: and one is hungry, and another is *drunken*."

This is rather difficult to imagine, but it's exactly what Paul described as taking place during this special time, which is intended for Christians to reflect on the body and blood of Christ and His sacrifice for us on the cross.

Surely the Lord did not want such a practice of behavior to spread throughout the church. That's why He dealt with it in this manner. Nevertheless, this is not speaking of damnation or of losing salvation, as we read in verse 30:

"For this cause many are weak and sickly among you, and many sleep."

The term "sleep," which is used for death, was the Apostle Paul's favorite term for those who had passed away *in Christ*. He did not use this term when speaking of the *physical death* of those facing an eternity without Christ. But Paul used the term "sleep" when referring to the death of believers (see: Acts 13:36; 1 Corinthians 15:6, 15:18, 15:20, 15:51; 1 Thessalonians 4:13-15; 5:10).

The lack of damnation for believers is brought out very clearly in verses 31-32:

"For if we would judge ourselves, we should not be judged. But when we are judged, we are chastened of the Lord, *that we should not be condemned with the world*."

Did you see that? We are chastened "that we should *not* be condemned with the world." And in Christ, we are no longer *of* the world! This word "chastened" means "disciplined." Again, we are not speaking of condemnation or of losing your salvation because: "There is therefore now no condemnation to them which are in Christ Jesus" (Romans 8:1). No; we are speaking of discipline here.

And as mentioned in the previous chapter, when Paul states: "Many are weak and sickly among you, and many sleep," it does not mean that *everyone* who is weak or sickly —and sleeps in what may appear to be a premature death— is therefore judged by God. Although infirmity might be a result of God's dealing with a person, it is not *always* the case and a doctrine of such cannot be inferred within this verse or in other Scriptures. For Paul himself said:

> "Brethren, I beseech you, be as I am; for I am as ye are: ye have not injured me at all. Ye know how through *infirmity of the flesh* I preached the gospel unto you at the first. And my temptation which was in my flesh ye despised not, nor rejected; but received me as an angel of God, even as Christ Jesus" (Galatians 4:12-14).

In contrast to Paul's situation, the verses from 1 Corinthians 11 addressed a specific group of believers who had behaved according to their flesh and had thereby caused quite a disruption in the church.

An Unnecessary Discipline

Indeed, these verses in Corinthians were dealing with unruly individuals who were mishandling the Lord's supper and setting a bad precedent. Notice how the Word says that "if we would judge ourselves, we should not be judged." This indicates that the situation involved issues of the heart. In other words, this discipline didn't have to take place. When we judge or discern ourselves, we are looking within our hearts, allowing the Lord in His grace to help us, heal us and conform us to His will. These followers were not looking inwardly, nor at the value of their relationships with Jesus. They were instead treating the Lord's Supper with recklessness and causing harm to the church.

There is always some measure of discipline that we experience as Christians, since we are without understanding in many ways. As we read in the Book of Hebrews:

> "God deals with you as with children, for what son is there whom his father doesn't discipline?" (Hebrews 12:7, *WEB*).

God disciplines us for our spiritual health. In fact, God's discipline shows His calling and favor upon you; just look in Genesis 37-47, and see what the Lord put Joseph through!

However, the discipline mentioned in 1 Corinthians 11, the writer declared, *didn't have to happen.* Paul was explaining in verse 31 that if these believers had acknowledged the carnal issues within them, they:

> "...should not be judged."

More Examples...

Other examples of this type of discipline are found in Scripture. We see it in Colossians 3:22-25, which states:

> "Servants, obey in all things your masters according to the flesh; not with eyeservice, as menpleasers; but in singleness of heart, fearing God: And whatsoever ye do, do it heartily, as to the Lord, and not unto men; Knowing that of the Lord ye shall receive the reward of the inheritance: for ye serve the Lord

Christ. *But he that doeth wrong shall receive for the wrong which he hath done: and there is no respect of persons."*

The context of these verses has to do with servants and their masters; and the verse: "He that doeth wrong shall receive for the wrong which he hath done" actually appears to apply to the masters themselves. I say this because the Apostle Paul specifically stated that "there is no respect of persons" with the Lord and this would make more sense if said to benefit the servant, in his lower position. Paul, therefore, would have been comforting the servant by saying that God has no regard for a person's position and that the masters who treated their servants wrongfully would receive for the wrong they had done. This is indeed confirmed in Ephesians 6:9, which states: "And, ye masters, do the same things unto them, forbearing threatening: knowing that your Master also is in heaven; *neither is there respect of persons with him."*

The point made is that the Lord would deal with such injustice. With believers, it may be a judgment but never condemnation; and if referring to unbelievers, then the judgment could ultimately result in condemnation itself, if they do not turn to the Lord.

A similar verse is found in Hebrews 13:4, which states:

"Marriage is honourable in all, and the bed undefiled: *but whoremongers and adulterers God will judge."*

In this passage, the writer of Hebrews may be speaking in general terms regarding the ways of unbelievers. But even if not, there is still a difference between the judgment of a believer and that of an unbeliever.

The Apostle Peter made this truth clear when he stated:

"For the time is come that judgment must begin at the house of God: and if it first begin at us, *what shall the end be of them that obey not the gospel of God?* And if the righteous scarcely be saved, where shall the ungodly and the sinner appear?" (1 Peter 4:17-18).

These verses show that there is clearly a distinction between the judgment of the righteous and the judgment of the wicked "that obey not the gospel of God." For Peter declares that the righteous will indeed be *saved*, but he then adds, *"Where shall the ungodly and the sinner appear?"*

Though both groups may be judged, one is corrective and the other is punitive. One judgment is remedial and unto life, while the other is a sentence unto death. We must be certain to differentiate between the two when reading Scripture. Indeed, as believers in Christ, we should always read God's Word *through the eyeglasses of the cross*. For any punitive judgment—the one that leads to condemnation—has *already* been borne by Christ on our behalf.

This mercy is even foreshadowed in the Old Testament under law. For when David sinned greatly, it was the sacrifice at the threshing floor of Ornan (which would become the future temple site) that stopped the outpouring of God's wrath (1 Chronicles 21:1-27). This is a type and picture of Jesus—the everlasting Sacrifice—stopping *all* the wrath of a holy God toward believers, "once for all" (Hebrews 10:10).

This is why Jesus said:

> "Most certainly I tell you, he who hears my word and believes him who sent me has eternal life, and *doesn't come into judgment*, but has passed out of death into life" (John 5:24, *WEB*).

For this judgment of which Jesus spoke is referring to condemnation, and believers have no part in this type of judgment.

Therefore, if a believer is judged in Scripture, it is for correction and sanctification but *not condemnation*. Yet again, as the Apostle Paul said, this type of judgment does not have to happen. For he stated: "If we would judge ourselves, we should not be judged" (1 Corinthians 11:31).

This only occurs when Christians harden themselves by not keeping their hearts open to the Lord. The issue is not about living perfectly but about living *openly* with Jesus.

If we harbor sin, without going to the Lord for help, He may need to get our attention another way. For the Savior is our *only* help from sin! The problem is never really the sin itself but the hiding from Christ, denying His will and avoiding His grace. Jesus is *always* present and willing to forgive, strengthen, heal and restore us in our walk and sanctification with Him. As the Scripture declares:

> "Let us therefore come boldly unto the throne of grace, that we may obtain mercy, and find grace to help in time of need" (Hebrews 4:16).

Shipwrecked

We find additional examples of this kind of discipline elsewhere in the Bible, such as when Paul wrote to Timothy:

"Holding faith, and a good conscience; which some having put away concerning faith have made shipwreck: Of whom is Hymenaeus and Alexander; *whom I have delivered unto Satan, that they may learn not to blaspheme*" (1 Timothy 1:19).

We can see that such discipline is *not normal* and need not take place if one is "holding faith, and a good conscience." Can you imagine being delivered to Satan, in order to learn not to blaspheme? Is not Satan the ultimate blasphemer?

(This situation is not the same as the blasphemy of the Holy Spirit. See *Chapter 31: Blasphemy Against the Holy Spirit?*)

What the Apostle Paul was saying is that these men were delivered to be humbled in the flesh so that they would become truly humble in attitude. Did you notice they were not given over to condemnation? Indeed, condemnation will not reform anyone. As extreme as this discipline was, there was the purpose "that they may learn not to blaspheme." This hope would denote having salvation (1 Corinthians 5:12). And by writing this, Paul again demonstrated that this type of discipline *could have been avoided*. That Paul considered such a one as Hymenaeus saved is alluded to in 2 Timothy 2:16-21, where he apparently speaks of the same individual (with this uncommon name) by saying:

"But shun profane and vain babblings: for they will increase unto more ungodliness. And their word will eat as doth a canker: of whom is *Hymenaeus* and Philetus; Who concerning the truth have erred, saying that the resurrection is past already; and overthrow the faith of some. Nevertheless the foundation of God standeth sure, having this seal,

The Lord knoweth them that are his. And, Let every one that nameth the name of Christ depart from iniquity. *But in a great house there are not only vessels of gold and of silver, but also of wood and of earth; and some to honour, and some to dishonour.* If a man therefore purge himself from these, he shall be a vessel unto honour, sanctified, and meet for the master's use, and prepared unto every good work."

Castaway?

For Paul was sensitive about his own life and walk, as he said:

"I therefore so run, not as uncertainly; so fight I, not as one that beateth the air: But I keep under my body, and bring it into subjection: lest that by any means, when I have preached to others, I myself should be a castaway" (1 Corinthians 9:27).

By sharing this, Paul showed that he was responsive in his walk with the Lord.

The usage of the word "castaway" here in the King James Version is not the best translation from the Greek, as the word primarily means "not passing the test" or "disqualified." It is not translated as *castaway* anywhere else in the Bible, nor do the majority of Bible translations use that word. The New King James Version accurately updated it as "disqualified."

For Paul was not referring to being a castaway in salvation, as the context of this verse shows he was speaking of being *disqualified* in regard to *eternal rewards*. As he said in the verses leading up to this:

"Know ye not that they which run in a race run all, *but one receiveth the prize*? So run, that ye may obtain. And every man that striveth for the mastery is temperate in all things. Now they do it to obtain a corruptible crown; but we an incorruptible" (1 Corinthians 9:25-26).

Paul wrote that "one receiveth the prize." Therefore, he could not have been speaking about salvation. If that was the case, Paul would have been saying that he was running to be the *only one* who would be saved—which is contrary to all of this apostle's teachings, let alone the entire Bible as well. Clearly, Paul was referring to heavenly rewards.

An In-Tune or Out-of-Tune Instrument?

In these verses, Paul revealed that the Christian's walk has great eternal value. A life surrendered to the Lord, though unrecognized by the world, is recognized by God. And a life surrendered to Jesus will know the grace, empowerment and guidance of the Holy Spirit to help in his or her daily walk with Christ.

For our salvation is like a beautiful stringed instrument, with our spiritual walk being the strings. When we are in tune with the Lord, we give off the sweet melody of Jesus. But when we are out of tune with Him, though we still have the instrument of salvation, its sound has now become inharmonious with its true self.

This is why, as believers, we need to remain humble before the Lord, recognizing that apart from Him we "can do nothing" (John 15:5). This humility provides the safest harbor for abiding with Jesus. We need to acknowledge that

He is our "righteousness, and sanctification, and redemption" (1 Corinthians 1:30). Indeed, we do not even have sanctification of ourselves, apart from yielding to His Spirit of grace in order to overcome our natural flesh. It is in this place, keeping our hearts open and in tune with Jesus in every way, where we find peace—because "Christ...is our life" (Colossians 3:4). As it is written in Micah 6:8 so beautifully:

> "He hath shewed thee, O man, what is good; and what doth the LORD require of thee, but to do justly, and to love mercy, and to walk humbly with thy God?"

The Example of the Fathers

Indeed, humility brings harmony, but the pride of the flesh always brings discord. This is why the Apostle Paul gave the example of the fathers, who were "all baptized into Moses" (1 Corinthians 10:2, *WEB*) and drank from Christ, the Rock (1 Corinthians 10:4), yet nevertheless fell into error.

For when speaking of them, he said:

> "Now these things were our examples, to the intent we should not lust after evil things as they also lusted. Don't be idolaters, as some of them were. As it is written, "The people sat down to eat and drink, and rose up to play." Let's not commit sexual immorality, as some of them committed, and in one day twenty-three thousand fell. Let's not test Christ, as some of them tested, and perished by the serpents. Don't grumble, as some of them also grumbled, and perished by the destroyer. Now all these things happened to them by way of example,

and they were written for our admonition, on whom the ends of the ages have come. Therefore let him who thinks he stands be careful that he doesn't fall" (1 Corinthians 10:6-12, *WEB*).

Verses such as these are not pertaining to a fall from salvation for one who truly knows the Lord. For Paul himself abundantly affirmed the true believer's security in Christ. Also, as Christians, we are not baptized *into Moses* and the Old Covenant of law and wrath—but *into Christ Himself* and the New Covenant of grace. This covenant is based on "better promises" (Hebrews 8:6), for we are now "in Christ" (2 Corinthians 5:17). Concerning the fathers of Israel to whom Paul referred, many did not even have a relationship with the living God, for as Paul also said: "They are not all Israel, which are of Israel" (Romans 9:6).

Nevertheless, pertaining to believers, Paul spoke these words as a warning of discipline that can take place when believers harden themselves from the ways of the Lord and remain in a rebellious state. Paul therefore says that these are "examples" of the error of following our own ways over God's ways. It's important to realize that the Bible addresses not only our salvation but our *sanctification* as well. And Paul is advising humility over pride by saying: "Therefore let him who thinks he stands be careful that he doesn't fall."

And as it is written:

"When pride cometh, then cometh shame: but with the lowly is wisdom" (Proverbs 11:2).

So as mentioned previously, when a true believer is in an unrepentant posture and unresponsive to the Lord, God may discipline such a brother or sister, if necessary. But this is not the same thing as saying one who is a true Christian has lost his or her salvation, or that God has taken His love away from such a person.

For if you had an expensive instrument (one you bought with your blood!) and it was severely out of tune, would you throw it in the trash? Or as a parent, would you completely and utterly disown your child? You may discipline him or her severely if need be, but such a one would still be *your child— born of you—right?* How much more can this be said of the One who is called: "Everlasting Father" (Isaiah 9:6, *WEB).*

Pardon or Merely Probation?

Now if the Lord were to utterly reject us after our receiving Him as Savior, would not salvation itself be in question? Are we truly *pardoned* by Christ's sacrifice for us on the cross or are we merely *on probation?* Are we saved from the prison of eternal damnation, only to have the fear of returning to that same prison always hanging over us? Surely our redemption, by the precious blood of Christ, is more than a temporary period of probation.

For although God may discipline, we are still in Christ and under His New Covenant—if we are indeed His. He may save His own *through* fire, if necessary, but not *to* fire. For as the Apostle Paul wrote:

> "If any man's work shall be burned, he shall suffer loss: but he himself *shall be saved*; yet so as by fire" (1 Corinthians 3:15).

And as mentioned previously, Paul, who wrote the portion of Scripture concerning the Lord's Supper, also wrote about a rather hardened believer who was severely out of tune, as we read in 1 Corinthians 5:5:

> "To deliver such an one unto Satan for the destruction of the flesh, that the spirit may be *saved* in the day of the Lord Jesus."

Notice the difference between the flesh and the spirit of the Christian referenced in this verse. The spirit person of the believer is the real person. That person will be "saved in the day of the Lord Jesus." God may discipline in this way, *if need be,* but again, this is not *punitive* for the child of God; it is *corrective.*

This verse of 1 Corinthians 5:5—as well as our verse in 1 Corinthians 11:30 regarding those who "sleep"—is very similar to the verse mentioned previously in *Chapter 14: Branches, Fruit & Fire,* when Jesus said, "Every branch in me that beareth not fruit he taketh away" (John 15:2).

Remember how this branch was "taken away" or "taken up" but nevertheless, it did not fall to the ground like the other branches that "are burned" (John 15:6)?

A Sin Unto Death?

The Apostle John echoed this as well, when he stated:

> "If any man see his brother sin a sin which is not unto death, he shall ask, and he shall give him life for them that sin not unto death. *There is a sin unto death*: I do not say that he shall pray for it" (1 John 5:16).

In this verse, John is showing that there are situations which require the taking home of a brother or sister who may be in such a state that it would be better to leave this Earth early than to continue in waywardness.

This interpretation of John's statement of "a sin unto death" goes hand in hand with the verses being covered here. For if one who is truly a believer in Christ, yet through rebellion and an unrepentant attitude continues in a hardened state—the Lord may take such a one home in the "sleep" (1 Corinthians 11:30) of *physical* death.

Indeed, we have been bought with a price. We belong to God. So if all opportunities have been spent in order to have His child turn to his true self in Christ, the Scripture would be fulfilled:

> "Every branch in me that beareth not fruit he taketh away" (John 15:2).

However, as mentioned in *Chapter 14: Branches, Fruit & Fire*, this is not spiritual death but physical death for the believer. Again, the issue is not so much the sin but *the hardening of oneself to the Lord, who is the Shepherd of our souls.* That is why Paul said: "If we would judge ourselves, we should not be judged" (1 Corinthians 11:32). God is always there to restore; but if we do not turn to Him, He will chasten us back to Him, if need be. Yet it is always in love—for we are now His, bought with His blood. As it is written:

> "*For ye are bought with a price*: therefore glorify God in your body, and in your spirit, which are God's" (1 Corinthians 6:20).

Now this "sin unto death" in 1 John 5:16 could also apply to those who (as mentioned in *Chapter 12: The Warning of Hebrews* 6) are among Christianity for a season, ultimately to turn away and deny the Christ they *never actually received.*

Their turning away, if after tasting of the Kingdom to come, would truly be "a sin unto death"—for they "crucify to themselves the Son of God afresh, and put him to an open shame" (Hebrews 6:6).

As noted, this is not just a case of an unbeliever's rebellion toward Christ, which we see all around us and for which we preach the Gospel. No; it applies to those who had greater revelation into the *true reality of Christ* and then turned away from receiving Him. This is why Scripture says so strongly: "For it is impossible...If they shall fall away, to renew them again unto repentance; seeing they crucify *to themselves* the Son of God afresh, and put him to an open shame" (Hebrews 6:4-6). For they did not want this Savior who was clearly revealed to them. And as has been already covered, they were rejecting Jesus *after receiving revelation knowledge of His Spirit and experiencing the power of the Kingdom to come.*

This is similar to the "blasphemy against the Holy Spirit" (Matthew 12:31, Mark 3:28-30, Luke 12:10), as will be covered in *Chapter 31: Blasphemy Against the Holy Spirit?* This is essentially the same sin, as there is a purposeful and willful denial of God's revealed Spirit—who gives repentance and salvation through Christ—which is ultimately the lot of *all* who reject God.

If John was speaking in this way in 1 John 5:16 of the "sin unto death," then the "death" would be interpreted as *spiritual* death.

But in either explanation—the physical death of the believer or the spiritual death of the unbeliever—*there is no such reality found in Scripture for the spiritual death of a Christian who has indeed received Jesus!*

This is because he or she has been born again of the Spirit of God and "created in righteousness and true holiness" (Ephesians 4:24). Indeed, such a one has already "passed from death unto life" (John 5:24) and is now a new creation "in Christ" (2 Corinthians 5:17).

Discipline & Grace

But perhaps someone might question: "Why this talk of discipline and a "sin unto death," anyway? I thought we, as believers, are "not under the law, but under grace" (Romans 6:14).

Yes, we as believers are *fully* under the New Covenant of Grace. But this freedom doesn't mean that we are not being sanctified to become more Christ-like. As Paul said:

> "For whom he did foreknow, he also did predestinate to be *conformed to the image of his Son...*" (Romans 8:29).

This is why the Lord has not only put us under His grace, but He also gives us His Spirit to sanctify us! For He does not want us jumping off cliffs in our freedom! This is what Paul meant when he exhorted:

> "For, brethren, ye have been called unto liberty; only use not liberty for an occasion to the flesh, but by love serve one another. For all the law is fulfilled in one word, even in this; Thou shalt love thy neighbour as thyself. But if ye bite and devour one another, take heed that ye be not consumed one of another" (Galatians 5:13-14).

For grace does not lead us to lawlessness and death but rather, it leads to obedience and life. And it is this very saving grace that causes us to become more like Christ. As it is written:

> "For the grace of God that bringeth salvation hath appeared to all men, Teaching us that, denying ungodliness and worldly lusts, we should live soberly, righteously, and godly, in this present world; Looking for that blessed hope, and the glorious appearing of the great God and our Saviour Jesus Christ; Who gave himself for us, that he might redeem us from all iniquity, and purify unto himself a peculiar people, zealous of good works" (Titus 2:11-14).

The Law of Christ?

Living in Christ means that we can now follow, not an external set of rules but the living, loving Jesus—who through the Holy Spirit, dwells in us and causes us to walk in His ways. This is why it is written:

> "For the law of the Spirit of life in Christ Jesus hath *made me free* from the law of sin and death" (Romans 8:2).

Notice that these two "laws" are stated as being within you. You have the law of the Spirit and the law of sin. And by speaking this way, the Apostle Paul was describing these two laws as opposing principles, similar to the "law" of magnetism, when two magnets repel each other.

And through the "law of the Spirit of life in Christ Jesus" we have victory over the "law of sin and death."

For the law of the Spirit of life is not like the external law of Moses. Rather, it is the power and principle of Christ's righteousness within you. Indeed, it is Christ working in you "to will and to do of his good pleasure" (Philippians 2:13).

And we also read in Galatians:

"Bear ye one another's burdens, and so *fulfil the law of Christ*" (Galatians 6:2).

For in walking with Christ, His will is fulfilled through you by His power. This is the law or principle of Christ at work within you! It is not our "righteousness" that counts—but His righteousness. We cannot carry Him, but He carries us. This is why we don't bear *the root of the Spirit* but *the fruit of the Spirit*, which includes:

"...love, joy, peace, longsuffering, gentleness, goodness, faith..." (Galatians 5:22).

And this is why Jesus stated:

"He that hath *my commandments*, and keepeth them, he it is that loveth me" (John 14:21).

Notice that the Lord said, "my commandments," which is not the term He used when speaking of the external law of Moses. For when speaking of that law, He said, "It is also written in *your* law" (John 8:17) or "Is it not written in *your* law" (John 10:34). This differs from the way Jesus spoke of *His* commandments, which are empowered by the Holy Spirit within us. Notice how this difference is referenced in the beginning of the Book of Acts, where we read:

"The former treatise have I made, O Theophilus, of all that Jesus began both to do and teach, Until the day in which he was taken up, after that he *through the Holy Ghost had given commandments* unto the apostles whom he had chosen" (Acts 1:2).

We see in this Scripture that Christ's commandments are given "through the Holy Ghost," which means they are given with God's power to fulfill them! For this is not like the Old Covenant of external law, but it's the New Covenant of internal grace! This is what it means to "walk in the Spirit." As it is written:

> "If we live in the Spirit, let us also walk in the Spirit" (Galatians 5:25).

And this is why Paul the Apostle could also say:

> "Walk in the Spirit, and ye shall not fulfil the lust of the flesh" (Galatians 5:16).

Indeed, God has made each of us who are in Christ a new creation in harmony with Himself. And we now have God's power indwelling us, enabling us through His Spirit to walk with Him. And the law is now written in our hearts and not on tablets of stone, as Paul said:

> "...not that we are sufficient of ourselves to account anything as from ourselves; but our sufficiency is from God, who also made us sufficient as servants of a new covenant, not of the letter but of the Spirit. For the letter kills, but the Spirit gives life" (2 Corinthians 3:5-6, *WEB*).

For God has given us power through His Spirit to overcome the sin which so readily desires to exert itself upon us through the flesh. This too, is grace. And our walk in Christ is by the sanctification of the Spirit, never by the condemnation of law.

Christ Has Borne the Punitive Penalty

We must always keep in mind that *Christ has borne the punitive penalty* for those who have received Him as Savior. *God will not undo nor forget what Jesus accomplished for us upon the cross!* No, not ever! This divine accomplishment is clearly stated in the Book of Isaiah:

> "But he was pierced for our transgressions. He was crushed for our iniquities. *The punishment that brought our peace was on him*; and by his wounds we are healed" (Isaiah 53:5, *WEB*).

Obviously, God's discipline for the believer is *not the same* as His wrath for the unbeliever. This is not a matter of being small on sin. It's a matter of being big on Christ. For God knows the cost of the blood of His Son, and through that blood alone can we stand before God!

One who rejects Christ's sacrifice on the cross for remission of sin has no hope to escape the just wrath of God's holiness. In contrast, with those who receive Christ, there is an Advocate and Friend—One entering into the very holiness of God's presence and removing *all* of God's wrath by His own blood. As is written:

> "*For God hath not appointed us to wrath*, but to obtain salvation by our Lord Jesus Christ" (1 Thessalonians 5:9).

And as it is also written:

> "Much more then, being now justified by his blood, *we shall be saved from wrath through him*" (Romans 5:9).

by Richard O. Webb

Chapter 16

Faith—What if I Don't Have Enough?

Saving Faith

When we ask Christ to enter our hearts in salvation, He puts within us His Spirit and we are born again, as the Apostle Peter wrote:

> "Being born again, not of corruptible seed, but of incorruptible, by the word of God, which liveth and abideth for ever" (1 Peter 1:23).

This very Holy Spirit is He who prompted our faith in Christ *in the first place*. Indeed, whether we realized it or not, it was His working in our hearts that drew us to Christ. For Jesus said:

> "No man can come unto me, except it were *given unto him* of my Father" (John 6:65).

And about that which was "given" to us, the Apostle Paul also said a wonderful thing. He declared that:

"God hath dealt to every man the measure of faith" (Romans 12:3).

And it is with this measure of faith that one enters into the finished work of Christ on the cross, being "sealed unto the day of redemption" (Ephesians 4:30).

So sweet is this Spirit of God, who even gives faith itself! As it is written:

"But the fruit of the Spirit is love, joy, peace, longsuffering, gentleness, goodness, *faith*..." (Galatians 5:22).

Some translations use the word "faithfulness" in this verse instead of "faith," but a more prominent usage of this word in the original Greek, as translated in the King James Version, is actually "faith." If you have truly given your heart to Jesus, then you are indeed born of His Spirit. A fruit of this Spirit is the faith you now possess in your heart.

Faith of the Son of God

And we find this wonderful faith elsewhere in Scripture, where Paul the Apostle also made this amazing statement:

"I am crucified with Christ: nevertheless I live; yet not I, but Christ liveth in me: and the life which I now live in the flesh I live by *the faith of the Son of God*, who loved me, and gave himself for me" (Galatians 2:20).

Notice that Paul stated he was living by "the faith *of* the Son of God." Many translate this as "faith *in* the Son of God" and that does make sense, but the actual Greek is rendered as "*faith of* the Son of God"—as seen here in the King James Version.

Young's Literal Translation of the Bible translates this verse from the Greek as: "...in the faith I live of the Son of God" and this shows the exact same meaning.

But does it seem to make no sense, this "*faith of* the Son of God"? Actually, it's demonstrating Christ's life in the believer. Paul is literally saying that he is living by the faith *of another.* And it's no wonder, since he also said that he is crucified with Christ and that Christ is *living* in him. This is Paul describing the Christian's walk in the Spirit. As mentioned, Paul wrote in Philippians 2:13:

> "For it is God which worketh in you both to will and to do of his good pleasure."

This inner working of God includes the faith and anchor you have in Christ. For surely, as a believer, your life is *in* Him. As Paul also declared:

> "For ye are dead, and your life is hid with Christ in God. When Christ, *who is our life*, shall appear, then shall ye also appear with him in glory" (Colossians 3:3-4).

Hearing of Faith

There is yet another beautiful expression of this faith found in the Scripture. Galatians 3:2 reads:

> "This only would I learn of you, Received ye the Spirit by the works of the law, or by *the hearing of faith*?"

And this question is repeated in Galatians 3:5:

> "He therefore that ministereth to you the Spirit, and worketh miracles among you, doeth he it by the works of the law, or by *the hearing of faith?*"

This is quite a phrase: "the hearing of faith." And that's how it's actually written in the original Greek. Paul states that miracles were done by this "hearing of faith." It sounds odd, but it is wonderfully accurate. For it doesn't say miracles where done *by* faith—but by *the hearing of faith.* This is how faith originates—through the hearing and receiving of God's Spirit and His Word. And it shows that true faith is found in our connection to Christ. It is inspired by His Spirit and comes from a relationship with Jesus.

Often when the Lord has spoken to my heart, I knew it was Jesus because He produced a faith in me that I didn't have before He spoke. His touch creates a faith with substance, one that mere presumption cannot reproduce.

In 1996, when I first met my wife, Lois, I knew nine days after I met her that she would become my wife. I remember exactly where I was when the Lord revealed this to me. The result of His spoken word left me with a love and a faith that was sure in my heart. As it is written:

> "The grace of our Lord was exceeding abundant with faith and love which is in Christ Jesus" (1 Timothy 1:14).

And this faith that Jesus imparted to me remained steady. My heart *knew* what He had impressed upon it and six months later, to my joy, Lois and I were married. That was many years ago (1997), and the impact of that "hearing of faith" changed my life!

The Lord has moved in my life this way many times. And each and every time, because of the faith that was deposited in my heart, I knew it was Jesus speaking and not my own thoughts. The faith remained. I knew.

It is the same when we read the Word of God. His Spirit makes truth known to us. Faith arises in our hearts and these ancient words on the pages of the Bible become specific and relevant to our own daily lives. For God is real! And as the Apostle Peter wrote:

> "We have not followed cunningly devised fables, when we made known unto you the power and coming of our Lord Jesus Christ, but were eyewitnesses of his majesty" (2 Peter 1:16).

Deep Calling Unto Deep

Jesus rebuked the Pharisees of His day by saying:

> "You do not have His word abiding in you" (John 5:38).

And with this statement, He revealed that God's Word should indeed abide and remain in us. With the believer, this faith is deep. Indeed, as David said,

> "Deep calleth unto deep" (Psalm 42:7).

For God's Word abides as a conviction deep inside the heart. It is a faith that has strengthened the saints and has kept martyrs faithful to the truth that "Jesus Christ is Lord" (Philippians 2:11). This is the kind of faith that comes directly from God, and rather than our keeping it—*it keeps us.* It is the faith that overcomes and is found in the heart of every true believer, for:

"Whatsoever is born of God overcometh the world: and this is the victory that overcometh the world, even our faith" (1 John 5:4).

As a Christian, have you not known His faith in you? Have you not experienced that "underneath are the everlasting arms" (Deuteronomy 33:27)? Have you not understood the words of Jesus when He said, "Without me ye can do nothing" (John 15:5)? And have you not yet seen that at the end of yourself—He is there?

Remember this Scripture? Jesus said that "no man can come unto me, except it were *given unto him* of my Father" (John 6:65). So this salvation of yours—this faith of yours— was indeed *given* to you. It is not a matter of *how much* faith or *if you have enough* faith; no, what really matters is whether or not *you indeed have it.* This is the reason why, when the disciples asked Jesus to increase their faith, He basically replied by saying anything is possible if you have faith in the first place:

> "And the apostles said unto the Lord, Increase our faith. And the Lord said, If ye had faith as a grain of mustard seed, ye might say unto this sycamine tree, Be thou plucked up by the root, and be thou planted in the sea; and it should obey you" (Luke 17:5-6).

For if you are saved, you have been enabled to see with the eyes of faith. Yes, you responded to the call. But the work of faith itself is a gift of God. As it says in Ephesians 2:8-10:

> "For by grace are ye saved through faith; and that not of yourselves: it is the gift of God: Not of works, lest any man should boast. For we are his workmanship, created in Christ Jesus..."

His Workmanship

You see, this whole package is of God—the grace and the faith—the entire workmanship. For this verse makes it apparent that we are not our own workmanship. We are not co-partners or co-captains in this work of salvation. It is too great a salvation for us to touch! No, we are "*his workmanship.*" We only received what was given to us. The Apostle Paul put it so simply when he wrote: "What hast thou that thou didst not receive? now if thou didst receive it, why dost thou glory, as if thou hadst not received it?" (1 Corinthians 4:7).

One can hardly boast in what is received! If I bought you a fancy sports car and handed you the keys, would you boast about your part in receiving it from me? Rather, you would boast in the fact that I gave it to you. Yet God does indeed honor those who yield to Him and receive Him. But the work of salvation, from beginning to end, is *His.* For who else could re-create you and put you "in Christ Jesus"? As it is written:

> "But of him [God] are ye in Christ Jesus, who of God is made unto us wisdom, and righteousness, and sanctification, and redemption: That, according as it is written, He that glorieth, let him glory in the Lord" (1 Corinthians 1:30-31).

It's a wonderful and precious thing, this salvation that has been given to us in Christ Jesus! For God is reaching down to the lowly and weak to make them rich. In the Book of James we read:

> "Hath not God chosen the poor of this world [to be] rich in faith, and heirs of the kingdom which he hath promised to them that love him?" (James 2:5).

Truly God has *chosen* the poor to be rich in faith. Indeed, He has quickened hearts to receive Him.

The Substance of Faith

To the one who is born again, having received Christ as Savior, the faith within is not simply mental assent; it is a substance and reality deep within the heart. The Scripture tells us:

> "Now faith is the *substance* of things hoped for, the *evidence* of things not seen" (Hebrews 11:1).

This is not something that is worked up emotionally; rather, it's a spiritual reality and anchor for the soul, a faith given by the Spirit of God. The Lord causes this faith to grow in us as we yield in walking with Him, but its beginnings are made available by the spiritual sight given to us through God's grace.

Why did Noah have faith to build the ark? It was because God had spoken to him (Hebrews 11:7). And why did Abraham go forth without knowing where he was going? We find the answer in Hebrews 11:8. It was because God had called him. God's grace always tags us first, giving the vision and inspiring the faith. And as mentioned, this kind of faith reaches deep within the heart, in the place where we *know*. As Paul the Apostle wrote:

> "Now we have received, not the spirit of the world, but the spirit which is of God; *that we might know* the things that are freely given to us of God" (1 Corinthians 2:12).

If you have a true faith unto salvation, it will remain. Yes, this "measure of faith" (Romans 12:3) that was *placed in you* was sparked by the Spirit of God Himself and is alive. As it is written:

> "In whom we have boldness and access with confidence by *the faith of him*" (Ephesians 3:12).

And as Jesus said:

> "The words that I speak to you *are Spirit, and are life*" (John 6:63, *WEB*).

Indeed, His words are living within us, as John also made known:

> "If that which ye have heard from the beginning shall remain in you, ye also shall continue in the Son, and in the Father" (1 John 2:24).

Let us also remember the Scripture which tells us that we can be *confident* of this work of Christ in us, as Paul wrote:

> "Being confident of this very thing, that he which hath begun a good work in you will perform it until the day of Jesus Christ" (Philippians 1:6).

Therefore, it is no wonder that the Word of God tells us to be:

> "Looking unto Jesus the author and finisher of our *faith*" (Hebrews 12:2).

Chapter 17

Free Will—What if I Leave Christ?

Some That Believe Not

Some might say, "I have free will. What if I walk away from Jesus?"

So the thought is that after salvation, one may separate himself or herself from Christ. And at first this sounds logical, as it would seem that if you wanted to get out of your salvation, God wouldn't force you to stay. But if one really felt this way from the heart, how could he or she have salvation in the first place? Indeed, part of the provision of salvation is a new heart itself!

Now Hebrews 11:15 refers to a people who may think of leaving, as it states:

"And truly, if they had been mindful of that country from whence they came out, they might have had opportunity to have returned."

But do these words actually pertain to those who have been reborn of God's Spirit, or are they about those who observe godly things from a distance? Let's see what Jesus said about those who followed Him, only to turn away when they could no longer bear His words. We read about this in John, chapter 6...

"But there are some of you that believe not. For Jesus knew from the beginning who they were *that believed not*, and who should betray him. And he said, Therefore said I unto you, that no man can come unto me, except it were given unto him of my Father. *From that time many of his disciples went back, and walked no more with him*" (John 6:64-66).

It is evident within these verses referring to some "disciples" who "went back"—that these individuals had not given their hearts to the Lord; they were merely entertaining and observing things from a distance. For Jesus had stated resoundingly that "there are some of you that believe not." These are the "disciples" who walked away. So when this is the situation, yes—you are "free" to go. But truly, this would demonstrate that you were not "there" from the start.

That is why Jesus said: "No man can come unto me, except it were given unto him of my Father." Notice that these are the people who remained—those to whom it was *given*. This is because salvation is a spiritual experience that involves rebirth. Upon receiving Christ, God changes your heart and joins you to His Spirit. And that's why it is written:

"But he that is joined unto the Lord is one spirit" (1 Corinthians 6:17).

It is indeed the work of God, by grace, that resurrects and joins your spirit to His Spirit. How then could a person remove one's heart, that part which is the real person, to walk away from Christ? Think of it naturally. Is it possible to become *unborn?*

Power to Become

As John 1:12-13 says:

"But as many as received him, to them gave he *power to become the sons of God,* even to them that believe on his name: Which were born, not of blood, nor of the will of the flesh, nor of the will of man, but of God."

We need to fully understand what happens to us when we allow the Lord into our hearts and receive His gift of salvation. This salvation is not only an *external* justification from the law and its demands; it's also an *internal* changing of our wills and our desires toward God's will and His desires. This is why John said that to "as many as received him, to them gave he *power to become the sons of God.*" And as has been mentioned in this study:

"It is God which worketh in you both to will and to do of his good pleasure" (Philippians 2:13).

This is why we have "so great a salvation" (Hebrews 2:3, *WEB*). For in His wisdom, God knew He would not only forgive us by the cross—but change our hearts through His Spirit to be like His heart. Otherwise, we would just up and leave Him, returning to our rebellion.

It's like a manufacturing company needing to do a recall of a product from stores. They address the issue by recalling the item in question, so it can be repaired. But this only solves *half* the problem. They also need to fix the problem within the factory itself. Otherwise, they would just be repeating the same faulty manufacturing process by which the product was recalled in the first place!

So you see? God not only saves you from your sin in the plan of salvation, but He also fixes the "factory" of sin which was you! He did this through the power of the Holy Spirit when you were born again in Christ. Again, as it is written:

> "Therefore if any man be in Christ, he is a *new creature*: old things are passed away; behold, all things are become new" (2 Corinthians 5:17).

This is important. For unlike the Old Covenant which speaks to the *outward* righteousness of a man while under law, the New Covenant speaks of the *inner* righteousness of the new creation *in Christ*. This righteousness in Christ is eternal, having been created by the Holy Spirit in the new heart of one who is born again. For the new creation is:

> "...created in righteousness" (Ephesians 4:24).

This is unlike the righteousness of the Old Covenant which speaks of the outward behavior under law:

> "If a righteous man turns from his righteousness and practices iniquity...will he live?...Because of the unfaithfulness and sin he has committed, he will die" (Ezekiel 18:24).

In contrast, the righteousness of the New Covenant speaks of the righteousness of the reborn spirit, being *in Christ*:

"Whosoever is *born of God* doth not commit sin; *for his seed remaineth in him: and he cannot sin, because he is born of God*" (1 John 3:9).

For in this New Covenant, God Himself has made us forever righteous in Christ! And He Himself promises to keep us. This is clearly demonstrated in Jeremiah 32:40, where we read the promise of the coming New Covenant...

They Shall Not Depart

"And I will make an everlasting covenant with them, that I will not turn away from them, to do them good; but I will put my fear in their hearts, that *they shall not depart from me*."

In this verse, God was specifically referring to the future New Covenant that came to pass through Jesus' atonement on the cross. This is the same covenant that we, as believers, enter upon receiving Christ as Savior. Notice the words "...they shall not depart from me." For the Lord knows how to save His people from themselves! God's Word in Ezekiel 36:26-27 speaks of this covenant as well, stating:

"A new heart also will I give you, and a new spirit will I put within you: and I will take away the stony heart out of your flesh, and I will give you an heart of flesh. *And I will put my spirit within you, and cause you to walk in my statutes, and ye shall keep my judgments, and do them*."

For prior to Christ, your "freedom" and desires were in Adam, which weren't really free at all. It was just a "freedom" for the old nature to exert itself. But due to salvation, your freedom and desires are now "in Christ" because of your new nature. "For as in Adam all die, even so in Christ shall all be made alive" (1 Corinthians 15:22).

This total salvation plan of God is like eating a meal. It enters your system, changes you on the inside and adds proteins to your body (hopefully!). Your free will was exercised in receiving the meal itself. But now that you have eaten it, you are changed. Indeed, you can't even return the meal once fully eaten and digested! In similar fashion, you have "eaten" of Christ. And this meal has changed you forever! In speaking of His sacrifice on the cross, Jesus said:

> "I am the living bread which came down from heaven: if any man eat of this bread, he shall live for ever: and the bread that I will give is my flesh, which I will give for the life of the world" (John 6:51).

This is why when we read of individuals in the Old Testament, like Saul (1 Samuel 15:26-28) or Solomon (1 Kings 11), who turned from the ways of the Lord—we must remember that in the *New Covenant*, God has made remedy for this situation by giving us a new spirit and placing us IN CHRIST! (1 Corinthians 1:30). This is why Jesus "is the mediator of a better covenant, which was established upon better promises" (Hebrews 8:6).

Free Will in Accepting Christ

For whether you realized it or not, when you used your free will in accepting Christ, He made some eternal changes to your spirit! It's a good thing, too, because who could remain saved in his or her own power? Have you not yet seen the vileness and depravity of your old nature? Ah, such blessed news is the Gospel—an amazing plan devised by God, through the cross and His Spirit, to utterly save those who call on Jesus in childlike, true faith! It is indeed a salvation with complete assurance. For one can rest in Jesus, drawing "near with a true heart in full assurance of faith" (Hebrews 10:22). Therefore, the question is not about whether or not you would leave the Lord. The question is always: have you actually *received* Him? This is not about mental assent. As it is written in James 2:19:

> "Thou believest that there is one God; thou doest well: the devils also believe, and tremble."

Conversion actually involves a changed heart, after putting trust in Jesus for salvation. As Jesus declared:

> "Verily, verily, I say unto thee, Except a man be born again, he cannot see the kingdom of God" (John 3:3).

And Jesus also said:

> "Verily I say unto you, Except ye be *converted*, and *become* as little children, ye shall not enter into the kingdom of heaven" (Matthew 18:3).

Notice the word "converted" in this verse, which literally means to be "turned" or "changed." Also notice that in salvation, you indeed "become" something new. If you are truly born from above, your heart, your will and your freedom are now joined with the Lord. Your liberty would never take you away, because the heart that He has given you now cries out, "Abba, Father." As it is written:

> "For ye have not received the spirit of bondage again to fear; but ye have received the Spirit of adoption, whereby we cry, Abba, Father" (Romans 8:15).

"Thy mercy, O LORD, is in the heavens;
and thy faithfulness reacheth unto the clouds."

Psalm 36:5

by Richard O. Webb

HEARTOFTHELORD.ORG

Chapter 18

The Sermon on the Mount

Under the Law

It is important to keep in mind that when Jesus was teaching the Sermon on the Mount, He was speaking to Jews who were under the law. Jesus Himself was born under the law, as it is written:

> "But when the fulness of the time was come, God sent forth his Son, made of a woman, made under the law, To redeem them that were under the law, that we might receive the adoption of sons" (Galatians 4:4-5).

Although this sermon takes place in the Book of Matthew, chapters 5-7, the New Covenant had not yet begun, as Jesus had not yet gone to the cross. For it was Jesus' blood that ratified the New Covenant and made it possible to receive forgiveness and a new nature. This is why we find that the veil of the temple was not torn at the beginning of the Book of Matthew; rather, it was torn at the end, in Matthew 27:51, indicating that the entrance by grace into God's presence had only then begun.

Therefore, when Jesus was teaching this sermon, He was speaking as one under the law to those who were under the law. It's important to know that before there can be an outpouring of God's grace, we first need to realize the *need* for such grace. This is why God gave His holy law in the Old Testament. So we find here, in the beginning of Jesus' Sermon on the Mount, that far from removing the law and its demands, Jesus actually intensifies its demands. This is how Jesus began His ministry.

The Magnification of the Law

Indeed, the Book of Isaiah prophesies of Jesus:

"He will magnify the law" (Isaiah 42:21).

And this is exactly what Jesus did with His words on the mount. For He repeatedly stated, "Ye have heard that it was said by them of old time...But I say unto you." And when He did this, He magnified the law and enlarged it to include the very thoughts of the heart. In doing so, Jesus brought out the fact that sin was not just external in deed but rooted in the very nature of mankind. Consider His words:

"Ye have heard that it was said by them of old time, Thou shalt not kill; and whosoever shall kill shall be in danger of the judgment: But I say unto you, That whosoever is angry with his brother without a cause shall be in danger of the judgment: and whosoever shall say to his brother, Raca [empty-head], shall be in danger of the council: but whosoever shall say,

Thou fool, shall be in danger of hell fire. Therefore if thou bring thy gift to the altar, and there rememberest that thy brother hath ought against thee; Leave there thy gift before the altar, and go thy way; first be reconciled to thy brother, and then come and offer thy gift. Agree with thine adversary quickly, whiles thou art in the way with him; lest at any time the adversary deliver thee to the judge, and the judge deliver thee to the officer, and thou be cast into prison. Verily I say unto thee, Thou shalt by no means come out thence, till thou hast paid the uttermost farthing" (Matthew 5:21-26, also Luke 12:57-59).

Jesus was revealing the sin problem of mankind, showing that it's far worse than we had known. Indeed, by comparing fallen sinful humanity to the holiness of God, He was revealing that the issue of our brokenness before God goes much deeper—to our very nature—exposing us to the wrath of a pure and holy God.

The Lord continued in the same manner, saying:

"You have heard that it was said, 'Do not commit adultery.' But I tell you that anyone who looks at a woman to lust after her has already committed adultery with her in his heart" (Matthew 5:27-28, *NHEB*).

Again, Jesus was teaching that it is not just outward actions that reveal the sin of man but the inward condition. And He went so far as to say:

"And if thy right eye offend thee, pluck it out, and cast it from thee: for it is profitable for thee that one of thy members should perish, and not that thy whole body should be cast into hell. And if thy right hand offend thee, cut it off, and cast it from thee: for it is profitable for thee that one of thy members should perish, and not that thy whole body should be cast into hell" (Matthew 5:29-30).

Jesus was declaring that the demands of the law were much higher than even the self-righteous Pharisees could have imagined. He boldly stated:

"For I say unto you, That except your righteousness shall exceed the righteousness of the scribes and Pharisees, ye shall in no case enter into the kingdom of heaven" (Matthew 5:20).

Why did Jesus speak this way? There are many incidents in the gospels were Jesus showed abundant mercy to sinners. One need go no further than the Parable of the Prodigal Son to see this mercy. Indeed, it was the Pharisees to whom Jesus spoke the harshest words, not to those found in their sin. But Jesus spoke the righteous judgments of the Sermon on the Mount in order to bring the self-righteous to an awareness of their need for salvation.

For the sermon He taught was full of the true fire and brimstone of God; but its purpose was to bring out the realization of the complete and utter depravity of man's own righteousness before a holy God.

As the Apostle Paul explained:

"Wherefore the law was our schoolmaster to bring us unto Christ, that we might be justified by faith. But after that faith is come, we are no longer under a schoolmaster" (Galatians 3:24-25).

The Ministry of Condemnation

So the law brings us to Christ by humbling us. Its purpose is to show us the filth of our sin, like looking at a mirror, but it offers no cleansing or salvation in itself. As it is written:

> "Because by the works of the law, no flesh will be justified in his sight; for through the law comes *the knowledge of sin*" (Romans 3:20, *WEB*).

And as Paul also wrote:

> "The letter *killeth*" (2 Corinthians 3:6).

That is what the law does: it kills you (and rightfully so!) and just leaves you there—slain. And Paul actually went so far as to call the Old Covenant a ministry of death and condemnation! For he said the following in comparing the Old Covenant of law and the New Covenant of the Spirit:

> "But if the *ministration of death*, written and engraven in stones, was glorious, so that the children of Israel could not stedfastly behold the face of Moses for the glory of his countenance; which glory was to be done away: How shall not the ministration of the spirit be rather glorious? For if the *ministration of condemnation* be glory, much more doth the ministration of righteousness exceed in glory" (2 Corinthians 3:7-9).

What amazing Scriptures, telling us that the Old Covenant was indeed a ministry of death and condemnation! And Jesus, in His Sermon on the Mount, was speaking under this ministry, as He clearly brought out the point that the problem with mankind is not the sin but the *sinner*. It is thus revealed that *we are found in a corrupted state of sin in our very nature, which cannot attain to God's righteousness.* As the Prophet Isaiah pointed out:

> "But we are all as an unclean thing, and all our righteousnesses are as filthy rags; and we all do fade as a leaf; and our iniquities, like the wind, have taken us away" (Isaiah 64:6).

Indeed, Jesus' sermon kills us. It slays the very heart of the self-righteous, who think they can stand before God's holiness on their own merit. Jesus, when speaking to sinful mankind on the mount, went to such an extent as to say:

> "Be ye therefore perfect, even as your Father which is in heaven is perfect" (Matthew 5:48).

Alas, every form of religion falls to the dust with such words. For how can you be perfect without Christ? But the good news of the Gospel gives abundant hope to those who have cried out for God's mercy. As it is written:

> "For if by the trespass of the one, death reigned through the one; so much more will those who receive the abundance of grace and of the gift of righteousness reign in life through the one, Jesus Christ" (Romans 5:17, *WEB*).

Saints, do you see it? Do you grasp what this Jesus has done in taking the guilt and punishment for all our sins on the cross? He has cleared the way for all to be forgiven because no one could be forgiven by the law! For it is written:

> "And by him all that believe are justified from *all things*, from which ye could *not* be justified by the law of Moses" (Acts 13:39).

Made Alive in Christ

This is why Jesus is Savior. He Himself is our redemption, releasing us from being under the law. And in this New Covenant, instead of fear we have faith before God. Instead of death and condemnation, we have life and justification. For "He is our peace" (Ephesians 2:14), and He has blotted out the handwriting of the law that was against us. As it is written:

> "And you, being dead in your sins and the uncircumcision of your flesh, hath he quickened together with him, *having forgiven you all trespasses; Blotting out the handwriting of ordinances that was against us, which was contrary to us, and took it out of the way, nailing it to his cross*; And having spoiled principalities and powers, he made a shew of them openly, triumphing over them in it" (Colossians 2:13-15).

So to a Christian, *being justified in Christ*, the warning in the Sermon on the Mount in regard to wrath and the fire of Hell—does not apply. For a believer has been born again and *made righteous* because of Christ. The law has completed its work in leading us to Christ and to an everlasting salvation. Indeed, we have received a new nature with the law now written in our hearts. And that was God's plan all along. As Jesus said:

> "Think not that I am come to destroy the law, or the prophets: I am not come to destroy, but to fulfil. For verily I say unto you, Till heaven and earth pass, one jot or one tittle shall in no wise pass from the law, till all be fulfilled" (Matthew 5:17-18).

Fulfillment of the Law

Jesus went to the cross to fulfill the righteousness of the law on our behalf. Then He went a step further and gave us a new nature, as Paul the Apostle said:

> "And that ye put on the new man, which after God is created in righteousness and true holiness" (Ephesians 4:24).

Yes, the law is now written in our hearts and it is empowered not by our righteousness but by the Spirit of the living God, who through the new birth, now lives inside of us.

For the believer trusting in Christ, the law has been fulfilled by Christ's substitution for our sins on the cross. Indeed, Christ was raised for our justification. As Scripture says of Jesus, He is the One:

> "Who was delivered for our offenses, and was raised again for our justification" (Romans 4:25).

As previously mentioned in this study, the word justified means "to make righteous." This means that the act of God raising Christ from the dead *proves* our sins were paid in full! The Lord need not suffer for them any longer! Our sins were so fully paid that God the Father could raise Jesus from the dead—as there was no more need for further punishment to be applied to Christ. It was done—so done, in fact, that the Father could now declare us *righteous!*

However, the law still applies to those who reject Christ, and its holy demands still hover over them. As Jesus said, He didn't come to destroy the law—but to fulfill it; and He did this by providing the atonement for it. And those who refuse to receive Christ's work on the cross still face the reality of God's just and holy law. As it is written:

"Knowing this, that the law is not made for a righteous man, but for the lawless..." (1 Timothy 1:9).

So for some, the ministry of condemnation still stands, until the lost soul cries out to Christ in utter despair and hopelessness. And it's in that place of hopelessness where room is made in the heart of fallen mankind to look up to the face of Jesus—and to desire His salvation; for Christ is the only hope for all.

It is to this end that Jesus spoke the judgments in the Sermon on the Mount. But those who have knelt at the feet of Jesus abide now in His New Covenant, which frees us from any condemnation of the law.

"For the law was given by Moses, but grace and truth came by Jesus Christ" (John 1:17).

Chapter 19

Talents & the Unprofitable Servant

Servant or "Servant"

In the Gospel of Matthew we find the Parable of the Talents, which speaks of a servant being "cast...into outer darkness." Is this speaking of a saved believer losing salvation? Surely not, for as we study this parable (and similar ones like it), we will discover its true meaning. Jesus said:

> "For the kingdom of heaven is as a man travelling into a far country, who called his own servants, and delivered unto them his goods. And unto one he gave five talents, to another two, and to another one; to every man according to his several ability; and straightway took his journey. Then he that had received the five talents went and traded with the same, and made them other five talents. And

229

likewise he that had received two, he also gained other two. But he that had received one went and digged in the earth, and hid his lord's money.

"After a long time the lord of those servants cometh, and reckoneth with them. And so he that had received five talents came and brought other five talents, saying, Lord, thou deliveredst unto me five talents: behold, I have gained beside them five talents more. His lord said unto him, Well done, thou good and faithful servant: thou hast been faithful over a few things, I will make thee ruler over many things: enter thou into the joy of thy lord.

"He also that had received two talents came and said, Lord, thou deliveredst unto me two talents: behold, I have gained two other talents beside them. His lord said unto him, Well done, good and faithful servant; thou hast been faithful over a few things, I will make thee ruler over many things: enter thou into the joy of thy lord.

"Then he which had received the one talent came and said, Lord, I knew thee that thou art an hard man, reaping where thou hast not sown, and gathering where thou hast not strawed: And I was afraid, and went and hid thy talent in the earth: lo, there thou hast that is thine.

"His lord answered and said unto him, Thou wicked and slothful servant, thou knewest that I reap where I sowed not, and gather where I have not strawed: Thou oughtest therefore to have put my money to the exchangers, and then at my coming I should have received mine own with usury. Take therefore the talent from him, and give it unto him which hath ten talents.

"For unto every one that hath shall be given, and he shall have abundance: but from him that hath not shall be taken away even that which he hath. And cast ye the unprofitable servant into outer darkness: there shall be weeping and gnashing of teeth" (Matthew 25:14-30).

This Parable of the Talents is similar in many aspects to the Parable of the Ten Minas (or Coins) of Luke 19:11-27. The Parable of the Ten Minas was demonstrating what a servant's ability would be when receiving a single mina or coin, whereas this parable speaks of receiving one or more talents—given according to one's known ability.

For in this parable there are three servants, with each one being given a different amount of talents. A talent is a measure of weight regarding the money used at that time. It has nothing to do with actual talents in the sense of one being "talented." In this case, the reference is to a form of money by which one could gain increase from the exercise of it.

He who received the five talents was able to trade up to five more talents. He was not able to go beyond this—but could use the five to make five more. For this the lord of that servant gave the commendation:

"Well done, [thou] good and faithful servant: thou hast been faithful over a few things, I will make thee ruler over many things: enter thou into the joy of thy lord" (Matthew 25:21).

In a similar fashion, the second servant, who had received only two talents, was able to make two more talents from them. He could not make more than that but could only increase by the amount he was given. Therefore, the lord of that servant gave the exact, word-for-word commendation to him as to the servant who had made the additional five from his five talents. For again, the lord of that servant said:

> "Well done, good and faithful servant; thou hast been faithful over a few things, I will make thee ruler over many things: enter thou into the joy of thy lord" (Matthew 25:23).

Before going further, let's consider what these talents represent. As mentioned, the servants were able to produce more talents—but only up to the amounts they had each initially received. They could only reap from that which had been sown to them. This is why they both received precisely the same good report—because they were *faithful* with what had been imparted to them.

Now let's think of how this translates into spiritual matters, as this parable is surely not referring to financial gain. What exactly do we receive from the Lord? To what do we respond that came from His hands? With what are we to be faithful, after receiving it? Is it not His grace? For all that we are and all that we do come from God. And we cannot go beyond that which the Lord first gives us and works in us...

> "For of him, and through him, and to him, are all things" (Romans 11:36).

And as Jesus made clear:

> "Without me ye can do nothing" (John 15:5).

It may be helpful to look at these talents not so much as to the individual numbers given to each servant; rather, we should take note that each person was given a set measure—or amount—to use.

Let's look into this grace even further. Is there any other verse in the New Testament that sheds some light on the meaning of the talents in this parable?

A Measure of Faith

The answer is *yes,* for as mentioned in *Chapter 16: Faith— What If I Don't Have Enough?,* the Apostle Paul states:

> "God hath dealt to every man the measure of faith" (Romans 12:3).

In this verse we see that God has dealt, by grace, the measure of faith. And not only that, but He has dealt the measure to every person. This is a scriptural explanation for the talents mentioned in our parable of Matthew 25. But has every man received that which was offered?

The first two servants did receive and were faithful in that which was given to them. They both were able to multiply because they allowed this measure to become their own. And unlike the third servant who said of his lord, "I knew thee that thou art an hard man, reaping where thou hast not sown"—they knew this lord to be otherwise. They knew him *not* to be a hard man but one who first gave them the very thing they needed. Indeed, they received the grace given to them.

And this is why they were found faithful. It was not that they had earned some talents to gain some talents, nor was it that they were required to gain more than what they had at the beginning. No; for they only used what had been *given* to them. They simply received.

Looking at this spiritually, what do we first receive from the Lord? Salvation, is it not? For from the start of salvation, we begin our life and walk in the Lord. This is the beginning of using the measure of faith that is given to us. It is our saving faith.

Add To...and To...and To...

And as God works in us "to will and to do of His good pleasure" (Philippians 2:13), we find ourselves adding to our faith the many graces that are multiplied in us. For it's as if the Apostle Peter gave the interpretation of this parable when he wrote:

> "According as his divine power hath given unto us all things that pertain unto life and godliness...add to your faith virtue; and to virtue knowledge; And to knowledge temperance; and to temperance patience; and to patience godliness; And to godliness brotherly kindness; and to brotherly kindness charity [love]. For if these things be in you, and abound, they make you that ye shall neither be barren nor unfruitful in the knowledge of our Lord Jesus Christ" (2 Peter 1:3, 5-8).

Indeed, it is the Lord's divine power that "hath given unto us all things that pertain unto life and godliness." This is the grace and power that has changed our lives! And what did we do? We received it. That's all. We let this power rule in and through us, bearing the fruit of a life of abiding in Jesus. For as we grow in Christ, more and more of the Kingdom of God is multiplied in us. This is why Jesus could say:

"The kingdom of heaven is like unto leaven, which a woman took, and hid in three measures of meal, till the whole was leavened" (Matthew 13:33).

Yes, for as with this leaven that was hidden in three measures of meal, so is the Spirit of God transforming us from the inside out—spirit, soul and body.

And as Jesus also said:

"The kingdom of heaven suffereth violence, and the violent *take it by force*" (Matthew 11:12).

Surely the Kingdom of God has come in Spirit and we are taking it *by force.* This "force," translated into spiritual terms, is the result of fully receiving all that God has for us. For these words are a natural picture of the spiritual result of God's grace. It is His Kingdom that is being given to us, which we are taking, and it's His Kingdom that is working within us. This is what we see in the first two servants of the parable. They each had a reaction and a response to God's Spirit and the grace and calling which was given to them.

A Talent in the Ground

But with the third servant we see something very different, as he did not receive the grace that was given to him *at all.* For we see in Matthew 25:24-25 that he said:

"I knew thee that thou art an hard man, reaping where thou hast not sown, and gathering where thou hast not strawed: And I was afraid, and went and hid thy talent in the earth: lo, there thou hast that is thine."

You see, this servant did not know the lord of the parable. This is evident by the statement that he considered him "an hard man" and one "reaping where thou hast not sown." This is rather odd, since it's the exact opposite of what we just witnessed with the first two servants; they had demonstrated that only with what was first given to them could they bring forth anything.

We also see that the third servant never made the talent given to him his own. He never made it personal. For he said that he "hid *thy* talent" in the ground, thus revealing that he had never actually received ownership of it and therefore the talent did not become his. In the end it was still *"thy"* talent.

For it was the initial grace of salvation that this servant hid in the ground. He didn't respond to it. He didn't let it change him and multiply in him. He was offered a measure of faith but he let it just sit on the table, untouched. Again, consider the words of the Apostle Paul:

"God hath dealt to *every* man the measure of faith" (Romans 12:3).

And when unbelievers stand before God in judgment, they will realize what could have been theirs in Christ. They will know all that Jesus accomplished for them on that cruel cross, by His shed blood upon it. They will be reminded of all the times God reached out to them, in great or subtle ways, inviting them to turn toward Him in truth. These unbelievers will be aware of all that was sitting on their tables, and in this case, hidden in the ground—which God in His grace had offered them.

Truly, God's grace for salvation makes its way to each and every person. But as the Lord said in the time of Noah:

"My spirit shall not always strive with man" (Genesis 6:3).

This verse makes it evident that even in those dark times before the flood, God was striving with man to respond, calling men and woman to turn to Him. Clearly, He was "striving" for the souls of His creation to repent and allow Him to save them.

As for the Lord, it was a "striving" that ultimately led to His coming to the Earth and allowing Himself to be beaten and hung on a cross for the world's sin. As Jesus said of His mission:

"I have a baptism to be baptized with, and how am I pressed till it may be completed!" (Luke 12:50, *YLT*).

Indeed, this was the striving of a God who does in fact *only* reap where He sows, and who is not a hard man, but one who invites all to respond to Him, saying:

"Come unto me, all ye that labour and are heavy laden, and I will give you rest. Take my yoke upon you, and learn of me; for I am meek and lowly in heart: and ye shall find rest unto your souls. For my yoke is easy, and my burden is light" (Matthew 11:28-30).

Yet this third servant in the Parable of the Talents, like so many, would not accept the truth. He would not have God. For the grace that he hid in the ground was the very power for salvation. As it is written concerning the Gospel:

"It is the power of God unto salvation to every one that believeth" (Romans 1:16).

So you see, although he was a servant, he did not receive the talent the lord of the parable gave to him. He did not submit to his grace and lordship. There was a problem within the heart. And in this way, he was no different from the "wicked servant" found in Luke 19:22. For in this similar Parable of the Ten Minas, the servant was found to be as his lord's enemies, of whom it was said:

> "But those mine enemies, which *would not that I should reign over them*, bring hither, and slay them before me" (Luke 19:27).

The servants in these parables may have been around the things of their lord, but they didn't want his reign over their hearts. They didn't want to respond to Him.

They were like Judas, who was with Jesus and the other eleven disciples for over three years, yet chose his own way and his own plan over the way of grace before him.

Now when Scripture refers to a "servant," it does not necessarily pertain to one who is truly "born again" (John 3:3). This is made evident in Jesus' discussion with Nicodemus, who was a ruler of the Jews. Jesus made it clear to him that one must be born again to enter the Kingdom of God. Yet when Nicodemus said, "How can these things be?" (John 3:9), Jesus gave the reply:

> "Art thou a master of Israel, and knowest not these things?" (John 3:10).

So although Nicodemus was a ruler of the Jews, he did not know what it meant to be born of God's Spirit.

Indeed, the Kingdom of God is not like the kingdom of man. It is not seen in the external pomp of religion. It is found internally, in the humble hearts of those who need and want the living God. He will make Himself known to them. For that's why God's Spirit is in the world. As Jesus said:

"But the hour cometh, and now is, when the true worshippers shall worship the Father in spirit and in truth: *for the Father seeketh such to worship him.* God is a Spirit: and they that worship him must worship him in spirit and in truth" (John 4:23-24).

Truly, the Kingdom of God is found by those who respond to God's Spirit. There can be no games, no pretending, no imitation. God is real and He manifests Himself to those who receive Him in sincerity.

Beaten with Many Stripes?

The Bible has many warnings for those who play games with spiritual truths—being around them, misusing them and not actually receiving them. And it is better not to be around the things of God and Christianity than to be around them, know and experience them—and then reject them.

As Jesus said of another servant found in Luke 12:45-48:

"But and if that servant say in his heart, My lord delayeth his coming; and shall begin to beat the menservants and maidens, and to eat and drink, and to be drunken; The lord of that servant will come in a day when he looketh not for him, and at an hour when he is not aware, and will cut him in sunder, *and will appoint him his portion with the unbelievers.* And that servant, which knew his lord's will, and prepared not himself, neither did according to his will, shall be beaten with many stripes. But he that knew not, and did commit things worthy of stripes, shall be beaten with few stripes. For unto whomsoever much is given, of him shall be much required: and to whom men have committed much, of him they will ask the more."

In reading this Scripture, we find that he who knew more "and prepared not himself, neither did according to his will" was beaten with "many stripes." Why? Because he knew much and rejected much. For in this case, it would have been better to know less than to know more and then reject more. However, the outcome for rejecting God's will, whether knowing more or knowing less—is *never* good.

But what is God's will? As it is written:

"This is the work of God, that ye believe on him whom he hath sent" (John 6:29).

The will of God is in the simple act of true faith in Jesus, which brings about salvation. For it is Christ who bore our stripes on the cross, and "with his stripes we are healed" (Isaiah 53:5).

Indeed, Jesus was beaten with "many stripes," so that we could stand before God without any stripes of condemnation for sin (Romans 8:1). The Creator gave Himself for His creation, in love, by the atonement of the cross. To receive His gift of salvation is what it means to do "according to his will."

A Portion with the Unbelievers

Notice again what this verse in Luke says of the servant who did *not* do his lord's will:

"...appoint him his portion with the *unbelievers*" (Luke 12:46).

One might think it couldn't get much clearer, as to what kind of servant is being referred to here—but actually, it becomes crystal clear. For in Matthew 24:51, we find the parallel version of this Scripture saying:

"...and appoint him his portion with the *hypocrites*."

So obviously, the "servant" mentioned in this passage (as in our Parable of the Talents) is an unbeliever and not a true Christian. He is declared to be a hypocrite, which is pretending to be something *you are not*. As has been said, servants like this are *make-believers* who imitate true believers. They refuse to receive the measure of faith that is given to them, which begins with humility and the receiving of salvation itself. Indeed, they are like the servant spoken of here, who "knew his lord's will, and prepared not himself" (Luke 12:47).

Now let's get back to the Parable of the Talents and the servant who hid his talent in the ground. Simply put, this servant did not receive the single talent that was offered to him. In fact, *he didn't do that which was the least with it*. For as the lord of the parable spoke to him: "Thou oughtest therefore to have put my money to the exchangers [bankers], and then at my coming I should have received mine own with usury [interest]." This servant literally had *no response* toward the gift. Because of this, his lord spoke the words:

"For unto every one that hath shall be given, and he shall have abundance: *but from him that hath not shall be taken away even that which he hath*" (Matthew 25:29).

This verse may seem strange. Why should one who has, receive more, and one who has not, get even less? It seems unfair if you look at it naturally. But if you see it spiritually, it makes perfect sense.

For to him who has and receives of God and His grace, more will be given to him. Indeed, the Bible says of Jesus:

"For of his fullness we all received, and grace upon grace" (John 1:16, *NHEB*).

Yes, even into eternal life we shall receive. As the lord said to the first two servants who received their talents: "Enter thou into the joy of thy lord" (Matthew 25:21, 23).

But to those who reject God and His grace, all that they would seem to have will ultimately be taken away from them. For there is only eternal doom left for those who reject God and the gift of His Son, Jesus Christ. There is only loss. For the words to the third servant, who did not receive his talent but instead rejected his lord's will, are indeed chilling. His lord said:

"And cast ye the unprofitable servant into outer darkness: there shall be weeping and gnashing of teeth" (Matthew 25:30).

So this servant, like the servant mentioned in Luke 12:45-48, was found to deserve a portion with the unbelievers and hypocrites. Why? Because he was an unbeliever in heart and would not submit to the simple grace of salvation.

For God is always giving *first*. He reaches out to mankind with His love so that we might then respond to Him through the free will He has given us.

Oh saints, how good it is to know Him who *only* reaps where He sows. How wonderful it is to receive a salvation that is freely given by grace! I have often said that salvation is totally free, but you have to work hard to go to Hell. For it involves the work of one resisting the Spirit of God and His salvation through Christ—for an entire lifetime. And the day will come when it will be revealed to all who reject Christ— just how much divine grace had been offered and how much had been rejected.

May we not be found as these unbelieving servants, refusing to receive God's gift! For as it is written:

> "The word is nigh thee, even in thy mouth, and in thy heart: that is, the word of faith, which we preach; That if thou shalt confess with thy mouth the Lord Jesus, and shalt believe in thine heart that God hath raised him from the dead, thou shalt be saved" (Romans 10:8-9).

Those of us who have received this salvation in Christ can rejoice, for:

> "This hope we have as an anchor of the soul, a hope both sure and steadfast and entering into that which is within the veil" (Hebrews 6:19, *WEB*).

Thankfully, Jesus now looks at us beyond the eyes of servitude, for in our salvation He declares:

> "Henceforth I call you not servants; for the servant knoweth not what his lord doeth: but I have called you friends; for all things that I have heard of my Father I have made known unto you. Ye have not chosen me, but I have chosen you, and ordained you, that ye should go and bring forth fruit, and that your fruit should remain..." (John 15:15-16).

Chapter 20

Revelation 2-3 to the Churches?

The Definition of an Overcomer

The Book of Revelation has much to say about those who are in the church but are not of the church. I have used the term make-believer in this teaching, for the Bible clearly warns against "false brethren" (2 Corinthians 11:26) and hypocrites within the church body. It is because of this problem that Jesus gave warnings to the church, which are found in Revelation chapters 2 and 3.

Notice what Jesus said to each and every church when He addressed this issue. He gave the admonition:

> "...him that overcometh" or "...he that overcometh" (Revelation 2:7, 2:17, 2:26; 3:5, 3:12, 3:21).

Why would these words need to be spoken to the churches, except for the fact that many in the church had not overcome in their hearts and were not saved? Also, the Apostle John gave an explanation about an overcomer when He wrote:

> "For whatsoever *is born of God overcometh* the world: and this is the victory that overcometh the world, even *our faith*. Who is he that overcometh the world, but he that believeth that Jesus is the Son of God?" (1 John 5:4-5).

John stated emphatically that the victory that overcomes is brought about by faith and by being born of God, for "whatsoever is *born of God* overcometh the world." This is significant because John declared that the victory in overcoming and persevering as a Christian stems from the new birth itself. God gives the power through the Holy Spirit, as John also wrote:

> "But as many as received him, to them *gave he power* to become the sons of God, even to them that believe on his name: Which were born, not of blood, nor of the will of the flesh, nor of the will of man, but of God" (John 1:12-13).

It may not seem like it, but these words from John are similar to the words of Jesus in Luke 21:36, when He said:

> "Watch ye therefore, and pray always, that ye may *be accounted worthy* to escape all these things that shall come to pass, and to stand before the Son of man."

The King James Version uses the words "that ye may be accounted worthy to escape," but the oldest Greek manuscripts translate this as: "that you may *prevail* to escape" or "that you may *overpower* to escape." Indeed, it is similar to our word "overcome" spoken in these verses by John.

Jesus spoke these words in Luke concerning the receiving of the New Covenant that He was about to pour out—for only through Christ do we have the power to overcome and stand before Him. Only through Jesus are we made worthy.

For in Him we *are* overcomers. As it is written:

> "We are more than conquerors through him that loved us" (Romans 8:37).

And as the Apostle Paul also wrote, the Father has made us worthy to share in the Kingdom through Jesus:

> "...giving thanks to the Father, who has *qualified you* to share in the inheritance of the saints in the light" (Colossians 1:12, *NHEB*).

For Christ is He who has overcome *for us*, and in the New Covenant we are now *in Christ*. He has given us the victory and eternal life. Again, this is why John wrote so boldly:

> "For whatsoever is born of God overcometh the world" (1 John 5:4).

An Altar Call to the Lost

However, within the letters to the churches in Revelation, it is evident that not all had this relationship with Jesus, the Head of the church. Nothing makes this more obvious than the invitation that Jesus gave after addressing all the churches:

> "Behold, I stand at the door, and knock: if any man hear my voice, and open the door, *I will come in to*

him, and will sup with him, and he with me" (Revelation 3:20).

This Scripture definitely sounds more like an altar call to the lost than a message to the overcoming church. Notice how Jesus is saying that He is knocking on the door of their hearts, waiting to be invited in! He declares that "I will come in to him," indicating that He is *not yet* within many of them.

And this is no wonder because in the Lord's message to the churches, we see Him speaking to some that have known the "depths of Satan" (Revelation 2:24). They are described as being "wretched, and miserable, and poor, and blind, and naked" (Revelation 3:17). We also find those who need "white raiment, that thou mayest be clothed...that the shame of thy nakedness do not appear" and whose eyes need to be anointed with "eyesalve, that thou mayest see" (Revelation 3:18).

Without a doubt, the Lord is addressing some within the church who are blind to Him and to salvation itself.

In addition, there are many encouraging and reaffirming statements that the Lord gave to those who had received Him and were walking with Him. But his strong admonishment was aimed toward those without the life of Christ within them. For Jesus addressed one church with these words:

"Thou hast a name that thou livest, and art *dead*" (Revelation 3:1).

A dead church is a church *without* the life of Christ. This is the church in which the Lord also commends those Christians within it who "have not defiled their garments." For in the midst of this assembly they had remained in the truth, and Jesus said they will "walk with me in white: for they are worthy" (Revelation 3:4). This prophecy refers to true believers, who continued in their faith because they were indeed born of God's Spirit.

As Jesus said:

> "Either make the tree good and its fruit good, or make the tree corrupt and its fruit corrupt; for the tree is known by its fruit" (Matthew 12:33, *WEB*).

Make the Tree

Did you notice the verb, "make"? This word reveals the issue. How was the tree *made* in the first place? Was it born of God? Then it *will* last, for "that which is born of the Spirit is spirit" (John 3:6). If it's an imitation of the authentic, surely it will *not* last. This is why the Scripture encourages us:

> "Let that therefore abide in you, which ye have heard from the beginning. If that which ye have heard from the beginning shall remain in you, ye also shall continue in the Son, and in the Father. And this is the promise that he hath promised us, even eternal life" (1 John 2:24-25).

So why do we have this promise of eternal life—why such assurance? It's because this eternal life has *already* begun in the Christian believer! This is what Jesus promised when He said, "At that day ye shall know that I am in my Father, and ye in me, and I in you" (John 14:20).

Yes, it is "Christ *in* you, the hope of glory" (Colossians 1:27)! Indeed, this is a new heart that's *made good*, as Jesus stated, to bear good fruit. It is a new spirit, now connected to God's Spirit and eternal life itself, for Jesus asserted:

"But whosoever drinketh of the water that I shall give him shall never thirst; but the water that I shall give him shall be in him a well of water springing up into everlasting life" (John 4:14).

Did you grasp within this verse the promise of Jesus, assuring that one who drinks of Him will "never thirst"? That's because this well of water inside the heart will never be taken away! Truly, this water of Christ becomes in us "a well of water springing up *into everlasting life.*"

Since this fountain is a spring into everlasting life itself, how could Christians, having Christ *in* them, ever lose this "water"? For if believers could lose it, would they not become thirsty again? Yet Jesus declared that the one who drinks of Him shall "never thirst"!

Nevertheless, let us look at more of Jesus' words to the church found in these chapters of the Book of Revelation. In particular, let's examine one of the most misunderstood verses in the entire Bible.

Lukewarm & Spewed from the Lord's Mouth?

In Revelation 3:16 we read these words of Christ:

"Because thou are lukewarm...I will spue thee out of my mouth."

(The King James Version of the Bible uses the archaic spelling of "spue" for the current word, *spew.*)

This verse is found in the letter that was written to the church of the Laodiceans. Because it was written to the church, its meaning has often been misinterpreted to convey that a true believer could lose salvation. If we look at this verse more closely and *in context*, we will discover once again that this warning is actually pointing to those within the church who are merely pretenders. The entire verse of Revelation 3:16 reads as follows, with Jesus saying:

> "I know thy works, that thou art neither cold nor hot: I would thou were cold or hot. So then because thou art lukewarm, and neither cold nor hot, I will spue thee out of my mouth."

If Jesus is referring to a born-again believer with a new heart and spirit, why would He prefer one to be cold rather than being lukewarm? Wouldn't it seem better to be at least lukewarm instead of cold toward the things of God?

This verse doesn't make any sense unless we realize that Jesus is speaking to those in the church who are merely religious—and not in a personal relationship with Christ. In this context, the Scripture indeed becomes clear. In God's eyes, it is better to be cold toward Him and obvious in your sin than to be like the Pharisees of old, who were "lukewarm" in their religion. Why? Because these men were outwardly religious, but inwardly they were "a brood of vipers" (Matthew 3:7). And it is easier for those who are cold to come to the realization of their need for a Savior (as the prostitutes and tax collectors did in Jesus' day) than it is for those who think they are righteous in their own eyes (as did the Pharisees).

The religious and self-righteous person, who is in the church outwardly but not internally, has no true connection with Christ. To know Jesus is to receive Him in the heart, trusting Him as Savior. Those who are merely "playing church" are not actually in the true body of Christ, nor can they be assimilated into it without a surrender of the heart to Christ. Therefore, Jesus used the strong words: "Because thou art lukewarm, and neither cold nor hot, I will spue thee out of my mouth." He conveyed that they were not part of Him. And they never were part of Him in the first place. When we continue reading this letter to the Laodiceans, we discover even more evidence of this fact. Jesus said in verse 18:

> "I counsel thee to buy of me gold tried in the fire, that thou mayest be rich; and white raiment, that thou mayest be clothed, and that the shame of thy nakedness do not appear; and anoint thine eyes with eye-salve, that thou mayest see."

Here we see the Lord's counsel toward those who are spiritually poor. They do not have white raiment as clothing, they do not see, and they are in the shame of their sin, naked before God. This could hardly be true of a Christian who has trusted in Christ for salvation. For Jesus gives us His righteousness as a garment, He opens our eyes to the truth, and He takes away our shame with His mercy and forgiveness. Truly, Jesus has washed us and brought us back to the Father by His precious blood. As it is written:

> "And such were some of you: but ye are washed, but ye are sanctified, but ye are justified in the name of the Lord Jesus, and by the Spirit of our God" (1 Corinthians 6:11).

As we read further in this same letter, we come to that portion of Scripture mentioned a little earlier. It's always used when ministering to *unbelievers:*

"Behold, I stand at the door, and knock: if any man hear my voice, and open the door, I will come in to him, and will sup with him, and he with me" (Revelation 3:20).

This is clearly an invitation for someone *who does not have Christ in the heart already*. It's no surprise that we find this in the letter to the Laodiceans, which is full of correction for those *in* the church who are not *of* the church. It's for the lukewarm, who, just like the cold, need to receive Jesus as Savior.

Next, let's look at yet another verse in this same chapter. This Scripture is sometimes interpreted negatively to convey that Christians can be blotted out of the Book of Life and therefore lose their salvation (as it would *seem* that only believers would be written in the Book of Life in order to be blotted out of it).

Blotting Names from the Book of Life?

Jesus, in Revelation 3:5, promises:

"He that overcometh, the same shall be clothed in white raiment; and *I will not blot out his name out of the book of life*, but I will confess his name before my Father, and before his angels."

This is actually a word of comfort in Scripture. Isn't it good to know that God will not blot your name out of the Book of Life? For if you have accepted Jesus as your Savior and have been born again, you are an overcomer, as has been mentioned (1 John 5:4-5). Nevertheless, some have taken this verse to mean there is a possibility that God might blot you out of the Book of Life, because it appears to reveal that the Lord will do some blotting.

The Lord does actually do some blotting out of the Book of Life. However, we tend to think that the only names written in the Book of Life are of those who have made a confession of Jesus. But the Psalms present a different picture of this.

In his Messianic Psalm, David was speaking to God about the *unrighteous* when he said:

> "For they persecute him whom thou hast smitten, and they talk to the grief of those whom thou hast wounded. Add iniquity unto their iniquity, and let them not come into thy righteousness. *Let them be blotted out of the book of the living*, and not be written with the righteous" (Psalm 69:26-28).

In the context of this psalm, David had been referring to his enemies (verse 4) and to those who had "not come into thy righteousness."

Why were they even in the Book of Life in the first place?

One's name must first be written in the book in order to be blotted out of it. And these verses of Scripture reveal to us that initially *all* are written in the Book of Life.

David confirmed this when he wrote:

> "You have destroyed the wicked. You have *blotted out their name forever and ever*" (Psalm 9:5, *WEB*).

"Blotted out" in this text is the exact same Hebrew word that is used in Psalm 69:28, mentioned above, which means to "rub, blot out, put out, erase." For in these Scriptures we can clearly see that the book of life initially held the names of *all*.

David also said:

"Your eyes saw my body. *In your book* they were all written, the days that were ordained for me, when as yet there were none of them" (Psalm 139:16, *WEB*).

For God sees everyone and He never wanted separation from His creation. Scripture tells us that He wishes none to perish (1 Peter 3:9).

Jesus Himself said of infants:

"Their angels do always behold the face of my Father" (Matthew 18:10).

And the Apostle John wrote about Jesus:

"That was the true Light, which lighteth *every* man that cometh into the world" (John 1:9).

This is why babies, having not reached an age of accountability, go to Heaven when they die.

For David said concerning the death of his baby:

"I shall go to him, but he shall not return to me" (2 Samuel 12:23).

Therefore, the names that get blotted out of the Book of Life are those who come of age and *reject Jesus* and His salvation.

The blotting from the Book of Life does not refer to those who have received Christ as Savior—*but to the wicked who reject Him.*

But let us also consider this verse, in speaking of the wicked:

"They that dwell on the earth shall wonder, whose names *were not written* in the book of life from the foundation of the world..." (Revelation 17:8).

Doesn't this Scripture appear to contradict what David said previously about blotting out the names of the wicked from the Book of Life? And now the Word seems to say they were not written there in the first place?

Actually, it doesn't contradict what David said at all. Remember David's words about his enemies:

"Let them be blotted out of the book of the living, *and not be written with the righteous"* (Psalm 69:28).

So here we see that the wicked are blotted out of the Book of Life and thus, ultimately, they are *not written with the righteous.* Indeed, the meaning is that from the foundation of the world and in the foreknowledge of God, they were not found written in the Book of the Living. And that is how we find it worded in Revelation 20:15:

"And whosoever was not *found* written in the book of life was cast into the lake of fire."

Verses like these give a clearer understanding into the very last reference to the Book of Life in Scripture, which states:

"And if any man shall take away from the words of the book of this prophecy, *God shall take away his part out of the book of life*, and out of the holy city, and from the things which are written in this book" (Revelation 22:18-19).

This is merely a fulfillment of David's prayer in Psalm 69:26-28, as has been mentioned. For it is those who have "not come into thy righteousness" that Scripture declares to be blotted out of the Book of Life.

I should mention that this Scripture is from the King James Version of the Bible. And in this verse, the oldest and most reliable manuscripts do not say "book of life" but "tree of life." Either way, the truth of the verse is that those who do not bear the true fruit of salvation will not have part in the life of God.

Oh, what a blessing that as a believer in the Lord Jesus, a Christian has overcome through faith in Christ! For through Him we have received the new birth. And we have the promise:

> "He that overcometh...I will *not* blot out his name out of the book of life" (Revelation 3:5).

And thanks be to Jesus—you are chosen in Him! As Paul the Apostle said:

> "According as He has chosen us *in Him* before the foundation of the world...having predestinated us unto the adoption of children by Jesus Christ to Himself" (Ephesians 1:4-5).

And as Peter declared, you are:

> "Elect according to the foreknowledge of God, the Father, through sanctification of the Spirit, unto obedience and sprinkling of the blood of Jesus Christ" (1 Peter 1:2).

Chapter 21

The Prodigal Son in a Far Country

Publicans & Sinners

I have been asked the question, "What about The Prodigal Son? What if he had died in the wilderness?" The person with this inquiry wasn't literally asking the question to get an answer; he was saying it to deny eternal security, as a challenge to a Bible study I was sharing. He was trying to build an entire doctrine upon this parable, with the purpose of backing up the belief that Christians can lose their salvation. For that was the impression he came away with, after reading the story of The Prodigal Son. But this is not a legitimate argument for losing one's salvation. You will realize this by the manner in which the parable is presented. For at the beginning of the chapter in which Jesus shared this story, the Bible gives us a description of His audience...

"Then drew near unto him all the publicans and sinners for to hear him. And the Pharisees and scribes murmured, saying, This man receiveth sinners, and eateth with them" (Luke 15:1).

Now the Scripture could have said that Jesus gathered His disciples around Him before telling this story. Jesus had done this on many occasions, such as in Matthew 15:32, which reads: "Then Jesus called his disciples unto him." But the Lord didn't do that in this situation. Rather, we read that Jesus spoke these words specifically with the "publicans" (tax collectors) and "sinners" in mind. Again, He could have just gathered his disciples together to warn them, lest they fall away—but that is not the context of this Scripture. It is the *publicans* and *sinners* for whom He spoke this parable.

Also, one must keep in mind that this is a parable, which in the Bible is an allegorical picture or story that portrays a *real spiritual meaning*. The meaning itself may be open for interpretation and for this reason, the best practice is not to build a doctrine on an isolated parable alone.

Often there is more than one aspect when looking at a parable. This is why it is always a good idea to bring in other direct and relevant Scriptures to confirm its interpretation. In doing so, with the guidance of the Holy Spirit, we let Scripture interpret Scripture, and we are thus found "rightly dividing the word of truth" (2 Timothy 2:15).

Lastly, the Scripture does not say that the prodigal son died while away on his journey in a far country. An argument from the point of view that he died cannot be made with any soundness. How can one build a doctrine on what the Scripture *doesn't* say? But as for eternal security, the

Scripture is abundant in giving such a security for those in Christ Jesus.

Nevertheless, let's look into this beautiful story told by the Lord. It's one of my favorite parables.

The Parable

"And he [Jesus] said, A certain man had two sons: And the younger of them said to his father, Father, give me the portion of goods that falleth to me. And he divided unto them his living. And not many days after the younger son gathered all together, and took his journey into a far country, and there wasted his substance with riotous living. And when he had spent all, there arose a mighty famine in that land; and he began to be in want. And he went and joined himself to a citizen of that country; and he sent him into his fields to feed swine. And he would fain have filled his belly with the husks that the swine did eat: and no man gave unto him. And when he came to himself, he said, How many hired servants of my father's have bread enough and to spare, and I perish with hunger! I will arise and go to my father, and will say unto him, Father, I have sinned against heaven, and before thee, And am no more worthy to be called thy son: make me as one of thy hired servants. And he arose, and came to his father. But when he was yet a great way off, his father saw him, and had compassion, and ran, and fell on his neck, and kissed him. And the son said unto him, Father, I have sinned against heaven, and in thy sight, and am no more worthy to be called thy son. But the father said to his servants, Bring forth the best robe, and put it on him; and put a ring on his hand, and shoes on his feet: And bring hither the fatted calf, and kill it; and let us eat, and be merry: For this my son was dead, and is alive again; he was lost, and is found. And they began to be merry.

"Now his elder son was in the field: and as he came and drew nigh to the house, he heard musick and dancing. And he called one of the servants, and asked what these things meant. And he said unto him, Thy brother is come; and thy father hath killed the fatted calf, because he hath received him safe and sound. And he was angry, and would not go in: therefore came his father out, and intreated him. And he answering said to his father, Lo, these many years do I serve thee, neither transgressed I at any time thy commandment: and yet thou never gavest me a kid, that I might make merry with my friends: But as soon as this thy son was come, which hath devoured thy living with harlots, thou hast killed for him the fatted calf. And he said unto him, Son, thou art ever with me, and all that I have is thine. It was meet that we should make merry, and be glad: for this thy brother was dead, and is alive again; and was lost, and is found" (Luke 15:11-32).

Saved, Lost & Saved Again?

This is such a wonderful story, and I have often taught on it from the viewpoint of the father. It's interesting from this angle to see that the parable is more about what the father lost and got back again than even about the son himself. But the question is: Was the prodigal son saved, lost, then saved again? Can we apply this to *believers* in jeopardy of losing their salvation? *Is that what this parable is all about?* No...

When we read Scriptures containing the word *lost,* we find the reference is to those without God and without Christ. Regarding those who would say that the son represents a Christian who had not only gone wayward but had *lost* his salvation, they are missing the point to be made; in this story, the son actually left the father before salvation itself, in the same way the world goes its own way without God. For it is written that Jesus is:

> "...the true Light, *which lighteth every man that cometh into the world*" (John 1:9).

The Scriptures also declare:

> "For all have sinned, and come short of the glory of God" (Romans 3:23).

And all, by falling into sin, have become lost. As it is written:

> "Wherefore, as by one man sin entered into the world, and death by sin; and so death passed upon all men, for that all have sinned" (Romans 5:12).

The World Lost in Adam

Nowhere in this parable (before the son's departure) is it portrayed that the son was saved from sin within his heart. It indeed states quite the opposite, as it was *in his heart to leave the father.*

Yes, he was the father's son, but is not the world itself as the lost son? And was not the world lost in Adam?

> "*For as in Adam all die,* even so in Christ shall all be made alive" (1 Corinthians 15:22).

And Jesus was reaching out to the "publicans and sinners" around Him because this parable was directed *to them*. He was reaching out to a sinful world that had departed from the Father in original sin. This is the context of this parable.

Surely the lost of this world cannot be summed up as born-again Christians who have supposedly fallen from salvation—but as *unbelievers* who are in need of salvation.

This is an accurate representation of this parable. For what is one of the first things the father did when receiving his son? He called to:

"Bring hither the fatted calf, and kill it."

This is a picture of God receiving us on the basis of the sacrifice of Christ. A death had to happen for this acceptance; a price had to be paid for the sin, for:

"...apart from shedding of blood there is no forgiveness" (Hebrews 9:22, *NHEB*).

Jesus is the only "fatted calf" that was prepared for our salvation, as it is also written in Hebrews:

"Sacrifice and offering thou wouldest not, but a body hast thou prepared me" (Hebrews 10:5).

And Jesus is:

"...the Lamb slain from the foundation of the world. (Revelation 13:8).

Did you see how the father ran to the prodigal? This is a beautiful illustration of the verse:

"For God so loved the world, that he gave his only begotten Son" (John 3:16).

Has not God, in His grace, run to the world in giving us Christ? Does He not still run to the world in the sharing, teaching and preaching of the Gospel, through His Spirit? Have not all of us, who have come to Christ for salvation, been saved from "a far country"?

Two Covenants

This parable actually displays the comparison of two covenants. There is the New Covenant, in the grace shown toward the younger son and there's the Old Covenant, in the attitude of the elder son.

For the elder son came first, like the Old Covenant, reflecting the attitude of one under law. "Lo, these many years do I serve thee," was the first thing out of the elder son's mouth, who was upset with the father about the grace shown to the younger son. How often this is the case when living *under law*. Where there is blindness to the grace provided for us in Christ, there is reluctance to give grace and forgiveness to others. Yet the letter of the law, though righteous, only *kills*—because we are incapable of keeping it in our own power. This is why God has:

> "...made us sufficient as servants of a new covenant, not of the letter but of the Spirit. For the letter *kills*, but the Spirit gives life" (2 Corinthians 3:6, *WEB*).

For this older son was blinded in his self-righteousness and missing the point that he was, in fact, getting his brother back. And He was unable to recognize the love that his father already had toward him, a love revealed by the words:

> "Son, thou art ever with me, and all that I have is thine."

The prodigal, representing the New Covenant, was embraced, drawn near and given a ring, which would represent his acceptance and belonging within the family. It would be a symbol of the favor and authority granted him as the son of his father. He was also told to be given:

"...shoes on his feet."

How different this is when compared to Moses, who under law, was commanded:

"Do not come close. Take your sandals off of your feet, for the place you are standing on is holy ground" (Exodus 3:5).

The younger son was also given a robe, which is a picture of our righteousness in Christ. The Prophet Isaiah referred to this when he said:

"I will greatly rejoice in the LORD, my soul shall be joyful in my God; for he hath clothed me with the garments of salvation, he hath covered me with *the robe of righteousness*, as a bridegroom decketh himself with ornaments, and as a bride adorneth herself with her jewels" (Isaiah 61:10).

The message of this parable is an encouragement to us *all*, showing that salvation is God's wonderful grace for the lost world. That's why Jesus addressed this message of the prodigal to the "publicans and sinners"—but also to any "elder sons" who may think of themselves worthy of salvation in their own goodness. For Isaiah summed it up so poignantly in saying:

"But we are all as an unclean thing, and all our righteousnesses are as filthy rags; and we all do fade as a leaf; and our iniquities, like the wind, have taken us away" (Isaiah 64:6).

Yes, our own works are as "filthy rags" before the holiness of God. And the elder son, in self-righteousness, was at odds with the revelation of the coming New Covenant which states:

"For by grace are ye saved through faith; and that not of yourselves: it is the gift of God" (Ephesians 2:8).

Coins & Sheep: Found!

And to gain even more understanding of this, let's look at the backdrop to the telling of this parable. For Jesus had taught another story that *directly led* to the telling of The Parable of the Prodigal Son, which is:

"Either what woman having ten pieces of silver, if she lose one piece, doth not light a candle, and sweep the house, and seek diligently till she find it? *And when she hath found it*, she calleth her friends and her neighbours together, saying, Rejoice with me; for I have found the piece which I had lost" (Luke 15:8-9).

Did you notice the word "when" within these verses? You see, Jesus didn't say, "if she should find it, maybe" but "*when she hath found it.*" For there is no doubt with God about finding His own.

The Lord also shared yet another story, similar in meaning, which also led up to the telling of the Parable of the Prodigal Son. Jesus said:

"What man of you, having an hundred sheep, if he lose one of them, doth not leave the ninety and nine in the wilderness, and go after that which is lost, until he find it? And *when he hath found it,* he layeth it on his shoulders, rejoicing" (Luke 15:4-5).

You see, in the heart of God there is no "if" involved—only "*when*" for those who are ultimately His.

Now to be fair in dividing the Word correctly, we find in Matthew 18:13 the rendering of this verse as: "And if so be that he find it..." This is because the Scriptures in Matthew (which cover only this story of the sheep) are revealing that God indeed seeks out all so that they might be saved. Therefore, we see the "if" in Matthew's writing. For, as we know, some will not accept salvation.

Nevertheless, the writing in Luke reveals the *foreknowledge and predestination* of God. And like the woman who found her lost coin and the man who found his lost sheep, God *will* find His lost, called-out children.

For the sheep that are lost in the world, who are destined to be found by the Shepherd, will indeed come to Him. They will not perish in the wilderness because Jesus Himself gave His word:

"*All that the Father giveth me shall come to me*...And this is the Father's will which hath sent me, that of all which he hath given me *I should lose nothing...*" (John 6:37, 39).

Now saints, is that not a comfort?

Chapter 22

Forgive Us as We Forgive?

The Importance of Forgiveness

The Scriptures definitely state the importance of forgiveness. And the lack of forgiveness and bitterness in a person's life are sure signs of serious spiritual error. In fact, forgiveness is necessary for our close relationship with the Lord. If one does not forgive, how can the love of God flow through him? If one refuses to forgive, certainly one's initial salvation may be in question—but not the security of salvation itself. For to receive Christ is to receive forgiveness. And to know this forgiveness is to be enabled to then release it to others. It is a sure sign of the fruit of a converted life in Christ.

However, sometimes people have difficulty forgiving because they think if they forgive, they must also accept or allow the offenses to remain in their lives. But that is not the case. You can forgive without condoning the sin or the harmful situation. You can forgive and still commit the issue to the Lord Jesus. As the Apostle Paul said:

"Dearly beloved, avenge not yourselves, but rather give place unto wrath: for it is written, Vengeance is mine; I will repay, saith the Lord" (Romans 12:19).

The Lord asks us to forgive so we don't get preoccupied and ensnared with the pain of the situation. Indeed, He asks us to make place for the Lord's wrath *so that we won't carry the wrath ourselves.* And it is important to let go of all the bitterness and hatred that can devour us on the inside. Jesus has forgiven us and He asks us to do the same toward others. And sometimes we need to forgive ourselves as well. As Jesus stated:

"Thou shalt love thy neighbour as *thyself*" (Mark 12:31).

To forgive is to let the Holy Spirit have His way in your life, as forgiving allows you to experience God's love and healing. Offering forgiveness is to walk in the new life of Christ within you—and not in the old ways of the flesh.

Forgiveness in Sanctification

In the Lord's prayer we read,

"And forgive us our debts as we forgive our debtors" (Matthew 6:12, also Luke 11:4).

And Jesus conveyed the importance of forgiveness with these words:

"And when ye stand praying, forgive, if ye have ought against any: that your Father also which is in heaven may forgive you your trespasses. But if ye do not forgive, neither will your Father which is in heaven forgive your trespasses" (Mark 11:25-26, also Matthew 6:14-15).

These verses, like the parable of the unforgiving servant in Matthew 18:23-35 and other passages in the gospels, seem to present a somewhat conditional aspect of forgiveness. This "condition" seems to be that receiving my own forgiveness depends on my forgiving others.

It is important to understand that verses like these were spoken *before* the New Covenant, under the law and to unregenerate individuals. But you might ask, "Are not these words spoken in the gospels?" Yes, but as we will see, the New Covenant did not begin until the *end* of the gospels— when Jesus cried, "It is finished" (John 19:30) and sealed the payment for the New Covenant in His blood. He thus made the way for us to *stand* forgiven in the sight of God and become a new creation "in Christ" (2 Corinthians 5:17).

Yet our forgiveness to others plays a vital role in our spiritual health and growth. Forgiving is of utmost importance to our *sanctification*—as opposed to being a condition for keeping our *salvation.*

If Christians harden themselves and do not show forgiveness toward one another, they will find themselves tormented because they will be walking in the ways of the enemy. If we hold the Devil's hand, he will lead us into painful places. When we do not forgive, we block the flow of God's power in our lives. As Jesus said concerning our relationship with others:

> "Judge not, and ye shall not be judged: condemn not, and ye shall not be condemned: forgive, and ye shall be forgiven: Give, and it shall be given unto you; good measure, pressed down, and shaken together, and running over, shall men give into your bosom. For with the same measure that ye mete withal it

shall be measured to you again" (Luke 6:37-38, also Matthew 7:1-2).

For we are saved not just to go to Heaven but to be transformed and conformed to the likeness of Jesus. As it is written:

"Whom he did foreknow, he also did predestinate *to be conformed to the image of his Son...*" (Romans 8:29).

This is why we need to stay transparent with the Lord and receive His graces daily. For as the Scripture states:

"Can two walk together, except they be agreed?" (Amos 3:3).

And when we forgive others and admit our own failings, we receive His healing. As it is written:

"If we confess [agree with] our sins, he is faithful and just to forgive us our sins, and to cleanse us from all unrighteousness" (1 John 1:9).

All of this ties in with our sanctification. The word "confess" in the Greek literally means "to agree with." For when we are honest in our walk with the Lord, we draw close to Him and He cleanses us from all unrighteousness.

Forgiveness in Salvation

All these verses mentioned refer to forgiveness as it relates to a believer's daily walk with the Lord. But does Scripture indicate that forgiveness is a condition to keep our salvation? No. For although forgiving others is an important part of a believer's sanctification, we read about a complete forgiveness for those in Christ Jesus, granted once and for all, stated in the epistles. This forgiveness is granted upon our salvation and is based on the covenant that God set forth in Christ's blood.

We must remember that when Christ died on the cross, the veil of the temple was torn in two. For it is written:

> "And Jesus cried with a loud voice, and gave up the ghost. And the veil of the temple was rent in twain from the top to the bottom" (Mark 15:37-38).

A Torn Veil, A New Covenant

So for the first time in history, with this torn veil, the way was made for us to enter into the very presence of God. This is indeed when the New Covenant began. How horrified must the religious leaders have been, as they saw the veil of the temple—which separated the very holiness of God from man —ripped in half, from top to bottom...*torn by the very hand of God Himself!*

Yes, God accepted the sacrifice of His Son on the cross and made the way for all to be forgiven and restored to Himself.

And in the epistles, we now find the exhortation to forgive others *because we have been forgiven in this New Covenant.* As it is written:

> "Forbearing one another, and forgiving one another, if any man have a quarrel against any: *even as Christ forgave you*, so also do ye" (Colossians 3:13).

We also read:

> "And be ye kind one to another, tenderhearted, forgiving one another, even as *God for Christ's sake hath forgiven you*" (Ephesians 4:32).

This Scripture specifically states that "God *for Christ's sake* hath forgiven you." God has done the forgiving because it is based upon Christ. The condition for forgiveness rests solely upon the acceptance of Christ Himself. So for those who receive Jesus, there is forgiveness because of Christ and it is not based on their own actions. In fact, this forgiveness is expressed in the past tense, as completed. As it says, "even as God for Christ's sake *hath forgiven* you."

Consider again this verse in Hebrews, which states:

"For by one offering he has *perfected forever* those who are being sanctified" (Hebrews 10:14, *WEB*).

Truly, by this single offering of Christ, you are not only forgiven before God, but you have been *perfected* before Him —*forever*. This is God being true to the covenant that He brought forth in Christ! Your forgiveness was purchased with His atonement. This is the covenant that was ratified at the cross, where Christ bore your punishment upon Himself (Isaiah 53:5).

Let's look at yet another verse in the epistles:

"And you, being dead in your sins and the uncircumcision of your flesh, *hath he quickened together with him, having forgiven you all trespasses;* Blotting out the handwriting of ordinances that was against us, which was contrary to us, and took it out of the way, nailing it to his cross; And having spoiled principalities and powers, he made a shew of them openly, triumphing over them in it" (Colossians 2:13-15).

We know by this Scripture that believers in Christ are not only forgiven but "quickened together" with him. The word for this phrase in the Greek means—"to make alive together with." In other words, we received life upon salvation and are raised up in this new life with Jesus. This could only happen because our forgiveness is final in the eyes of God, who forgave us "all trespasses."

This speaks of the Christian's new birth. And this Scripture is declaring that our forgiveness is *so complete, so sure, so irreversible in salvation, that God has actually taken the next step and raised us up with Christ!*

A Covenant of Peace

And God has not only forgiven us in salvation but has given us a *covenant of peace.* This is reflected in the first four words Jesus spoke to His disciples when they were gathered together *after* His suffering and resurrection, when He told them:

"*Peace be unto you*" (John 20:19).

In fact, these words were so important to Jesus that He repeated them:

"*Peace be unto you*: as my Father hath sent me, even so send I you. And when he had said this, he breathed on them, and saith unto them, *Receive ye the Holy Ghost*" (John 20:21).

Notice in this verse, that for the first time in all His days spent with the disciples, Jesus "breathed on them," saying, "Receive ye the Holy Ghost." This is the beginning of the New Covenant indeed. For the disciples were just now receiving the Holy Spirit! And the forgiveness and peace that the Lord had purchased for them on the cross tied directly into the new birth He offered them. It is truly a covenant of peace, and the same offer is provided for us today!

It is this peace that the Lord foretold through the Prophet Isaiah, who wrote:

> "For this is as the waters of Noah unto me: for as I have sworn that the waters of Noah should no more go over the earth; so have I sworn that I would not be wroth with thee, nor rebuke thee. For the mountains shall depart, and the hills be removed; but my kindness shall not depart from thee, neither shall the *covenant of my peace* be removed, saith the LORD that hath mercy on thee" (Isaiah 54:9-10).

And Jesus shared this peace of His covenant with the disciples again, yet a third time. For it is also written:

> "And after eight days again his disciples were within, and Thomas with them: then came Jesus, the doors being shut, and stood in the midst, and said, *Peace be unto you*" (John 20:26).

Yes, peace. This is what Jesus has accomplished for you! And the New Covenant takes the forgiveness of God in salvation even further, by calling you "justified." That's like forgiveness on steroids. As it is written:

> "Therefore being *justified* by faith, we have *peace with God* through our Lord Jesus Christ" (Romans 5:1).

Chapter 23

Faith Without Works Is Dead?

Working for Salvation?

James 2:20 states:

"Faith without works is dead."

Many have interpreted this verse as meaning that one must work *for* salvation—that faith and grace are not enough and that salvation is dependent *upon* works. If this were the case, then indeed, salvation would *never* be secure for the Christian believer.

Yet James did not make works a foundation for faith. Works flow *from* faith—but saving faith will never flow from works. For Jesus made it clear that:

"No man can come to me, except the Father which hath sent me draw him" (John 6:44).

We cannot earn our salvation upon the foundation of self-effort. It costs too much. As it is written:

> "For the redemption of their life is costly, no payment is ever enough" (Psalm 49:8, *WEB*).

Surely man, being sinful, can never pay for the penalty of his sin. But Jesus, being the righteous sacrifice for our sin, has done what no man could do:

> "For Christ also hath once suffered for sins, the just for the unjust, that he might bring us to God..." (1 Peter 3:18).

Not Just a Nice Sentiment

Jesus has brought us to God. This is why salvation is not of works but by grace. This is not just a nice sentiment. The reality is that *we are helpless to save ourselves*. And Jesus made a way for us while we were still hopeless in sin. As the Scripture declares:

> "But God commendeth his love toward us, in that, while we were *yet sinners*, Christ died for us" (Romans 5:8).

James, in referring to works, is merely saying that there should be *evidence of true salvation*, by grace through faith, in a Christian's life.

He never put works *alone* or *before* faith. It is always *with* and *after* faith, as he says:

> "I will *shew thee my faith* by my works" (James 1:18).

In fact, James never separates works apart from faith but puts them both together, like the body and the spirit:

"For as the body without the spirit is dead, so faith without works is dead also" (James 2:26).

And the Apostle Paul has clearly—and abundantly—declared that our salvation is by grace through faith and *not* works. For he said:

"For by grace are ye saved through faith; and that *not of yourselves*: it is the gift of God" (Ephesians 2:8).

Paul also stated:

"Even so too at this present time also there is a remnant according to the election of grace. And if by grace, then *it is no longer of works*..." (Romans 11:5-6, *WEB*).

The apostle emphatically declares that salvation is *not of works* but of grace. In fact, he even went so far as to say:

"Therefore we conclude that a man is justified by faith without the deeds of the law" (Romans 3:28).

So why the seeming contradiction?

Again, the answer to this scriptural riddle is simple. If one is truly saved by grace, there will be works that *flow out from that faith,* proving it to be genuine. This is different from earning salvation *by* works. Therefore, the foundation of salvation is always by grace. Works flow *from* true faith but not *to* salvation. The works are only proof of salvation.

It is like my Dogwood tree. In the springtime it bears beautiful white flowers. Why does it do this? Because it's a Dogwood tree. Its flowers don't make it become a Dogwood tree; it already *is* a Dogwood tree. The flowers merely show proof of the type of tree that *already* exists. Likewise, the works that we bear as Christians are merely demonstrating the true faith that resides in our hearts.

Let's look at the analogy of a skydiver. If one was going skydiving and believed the parachute he was wearing to be secure, then jumping from an airplane would merely be the "work" of such faith. The faith came first in the acceptance that the parachute was sound, and from that faith came the "work" of jumping out. *Jumping did not make the parachute secure*—as it already *was secure.* Jumping was the result and proof of the skydiver's genuine faith, demonstrating his trust in the parachute.

For James was never saying that our salvation is *by* works. He was making the point that if we are truly saved by grace through faith, there should be genuine fruit or works of this new life, demonstrating *the reality of salvation.*

God of the Universe?

So we realize that James was merely separating the make-believer from the true believer. This is obvious in his context, as he stated:

> "Thou believest that there is one God; thou doest well: the devils also believe, and tremble" (James 2:19).

You see, James is getting to the heart of the matter. He's saying that to just believe in the reality of the God of the universe *is not enough.* Truly, one must go further; you need saving faith, resulting in a relationship with God. This happens when one is truly born again, receiving Christ as Savior. As has been stated over and over in this study, Jesus made it clear that:

"Ye must be born again" (John 3:7).

James actually compliments the words of Paul and is saying that genuine believers will have the works which *spring* from the well of God's saving grace within them. Indeed, those who receive the gift of salvation will be changed; and true works will be manifest from such amazing grace.

This is why Jesus also said:

"Verily I say unto you, Except ye be *converted*, and *become* as little children, ye shall not enter into the kingdom of heaven" (Matthew 18:3).

For in salvation you are *converted* and *become* a new creation in Christ. Again, as the Apostle Paul stated:

"Therefore if any man be in Christ, he is a new creature: old things are passed away; behold, all things are become new" (2 Corinthians 5:17).

And because we are new creations, the works that bear witness to this reality manifest through us.

As Christians—who are born again of God's Spirit—we have the parachute of Jesus strapped upon us. It is the parachute of salvation by grace through faith. Surely, it is a parachute that is most secure against our free-falling. For we have the promise:

"Now unto him that is able to keep you from falling, and to present you faultless before the presence of his glory with exceeding joy" (Jude 1:24).

Chapter 24

Ananias & Sapphira

Believers or Make-Believers?

In the New Testament Book of Acts, there is the account of Ananias and his wife Sapphira, who were both struck dead by the Lord during the formation of the early church. Were Ananias and Sapphira sincere believers joining the assembly of Christians? Let's look more closely into the hearts of Ananias and Sapphira, in order to understand their motives for joining the church. Starting at the end of chapter 4 and going into chapter 5, we read of the infant church:

> "And the multitude of them that believed were of one heart and of one soul: neither said any of them that ought of the things which he possessed was his own; but they had all things common. And with great power gave the apostles witness of the resurrection of the Lord Jesus: and great grace was upon them all. Neither was there any among them that lacked: for as many as were possessors of lands or houses sold

them, and brought the prices of the things that were sold, And laid them down at the apostles' feet: and distribution was made unto every man according as he had need. And Joses, who by the apostles was surnamed Barnabas, (which is, being interpreted, The son of consolation,) a Levite, and of the country of Cyprus, Having land, sold it, and brought the money, and laid it at the apostles' feet" (Acts 4:32-37).

Now the important point here is to notice the sincere love and harmony that was demonstrated within the early church. There were no power struggles or ulterior motives on display, but they simply cared for one another as each had need. None of them tried to pretend they were something they were not. No; they had one main thing in common—a love and desire to follow Jesus. But that honest devotion was about to be challenged...

"But a certain man named Ananias, with Sapphira his wife, sold a possession, And kept back part of the price, his wife also being privy to it, and brought a certain part, and laid it at the apostles' feet. But Peter said, Ananias, why hath Satan filled thine heart to lie to the Holy Ghost, and to keep back part of the price of the land? Whiles it remained, was it not thine own? and after it was sold, was it not in thine own power? why hast thou conceived this thing in thine heart? thou hast not lied unto men, but unto God. And Ananias hearing these words fell down, and gave up the ghost: and great fear came on all them that heard these things. And the young men arose, wound him up, and carried him out, and buried him. And it was about the space of three hours after, when his wife, not knowing what was done, came in. And Peter answered unto her, Tell me whether ye sold the land for so much? And she said, Yea, for so much. Then Peter said unto her, How is it that ye have agreed together to tempt the Spirit of the Lord? behold, the feet of them which have buried thy husband are at the door, and shall carry thee out. Then fell she down straightway at his feet, and yielded up the ghost: and the young men came in, and found her dead, and, carrying her forth, buried her by her husband. And great fear came upon all the church, and upon as many as heard these things. And by the hands of the apostles were many signs and wonders wrought among the people; (and they were all with one accord in Solomon's porch. *And of the rest durst no man join himself to them:* but the people magnified them. And believers were the more added to the Lord, multitudes both of men and women)" (Acts 5:1-14).

Ananias and Sapphira were two individuals who deliberately lied to the disciples and more significantly, to the Holy Spirit, during the time when the Lord was establishing His church. *It's important to note that their sin had nothing to do with the holding back of some of their money; it involved the deception they were portraying to the church.* For they were not joining the assembly as others had joined, with sincerity of heart. Rather, there was a different motive at play within them. For from the very beginning, they were trying to present an image of themselves as ones who had given and sacrificed more than they actually had given to the disciples. Theirs was a motivation of deception, pride, and falsehood, *not* of true faith in Christ.

There are a couple of very revealing words in this passage that give us insight into the hearts of Ananias and Sapphira, revealing that they were not true believers. For after both Ananias and Sapphira were struck dead by the Lord for their deception, we read:

> "And great fear came upon all the church, and upon as many as heard these things...and *of the rest* durst [did] no man join himself to them...And *believers* were the more added to the Lord, multitudes both of men and women" (Acts 5:11,13-14).

Of the Rest

We find two different groups of people in these Scriptures. First we read:

> "...*of the rest* durst [did] no man join himself to them."

Then we read:

> "...*believers* were the more added to the Lord."

Who were the "of the rest" ones? And with whom was this group (who no longer joined themselves to the disciples) associated? It becomes clear that they were *of the rest* of those mentioned previously, *Ananias and Sapphira.* These people, "of the rest," who no longer joined themselves to the disciples, were of the same as Ananias and Sapphira and in direct contrast to the *believers* who "were the more added to the Lord." Therefore, the "of the rest" group of whom Ananias and Sapphira were a part, were *unbelievers* or even more accurately—*false brethren*, joining the infant church.

Is it any wonder that the Lord would watch over and protect His flock? The result was clear that "of the rest did no man join himself to them." This is the rest of the kind of Ananias and Sapphira. The act of God upon Ananias and Sapphira dissuaded other individuals from joining the church for reasons other than true faith. These Scriptures are referring to the Lord's care for His own and His prevention of false brethren from entering the early church; they are not speaking of condemnation for true Christians *at all.*

Peter, in his rebuke to Ananias, went so far as to ask: "Why hath Satan filled thine heart to lie to the Holy Ghost...?" (Acts 5:3). A true converted believer has a new heart that is born from above. Satan may attack the mind through the old nature, but he can't fill the heart of a person who has the Holy Spirit dwelling there.

We are reminded that Jesus summed it up by His warning:

"Beware of false prophets, which come to you in sheep's clothing, but inwardly they are ravenous wolves. Ye shall know them by their fruits. Do men gather grapes of thorns, or figs of thistles? Even so every good tree bringeth forth good fruit; but a corrupt tree bringeth forth evil fruit. A good tree cannot bring forth evil fruit, neither can a corrupt tree bring forth good fruit" (Matthew 7:15-18).

Chapter 25

He Who Defiles
the Temple of God?

The Temple of the Church

The Apostle Paul wrote in 1 Corinthians 3:16-17:

> "Know ye not that ye are the temple of God, and that
> the Spirit of God dwelleth in you? If any man defile
> the temple of God, him shall God destroy; for the
> temple of God is holy, which temple ye are."

Are these verse speaking of the possible loss of salvation
even for God's own child, who was born again and bought by
Christ's blood? If this was the case, how could all the
Scriptures we have discussed so far hold true? But surely,
they are *all* true. For "Thy word is truth" (John 17:17).

It is important to understand that in the context of this
verse, Paul is speaking of the "the temple of God" as the

collective church and body of Christ. (This is not the same as the meaning of the phrase: "the temple of the Holy Spirit," as mentioned in 1 Corinthians 6:19, where Paul speaks of the physical body of each individual Christian.) Here in 1 Corinthians 3:16-17, Paul is referring to the church as being a temple, just as he wrote in Ephesians 2:19-21:

> "Ye are...built upon the foundation of the apostles and prophets, Jesus Christ himself being the chief corner stone; *In whom all the building fitly framed together groweth unto an holy temple in the Lord.*"

And the context of our verses of 1 Corinthians 3:16-17 shows that Paul is speaking of the church being a temple in this same way. For Paul is addressing the ministry to the church body when saying:

> "I have planted, Apollos watered; but God gave the increase. So then neither is he that planteth any thing, neither he that watereth; but God that giveth the increase. Now he that planteth and he that watereth are one: and every man shall receive his own reward according to his own labour. For we are labourers together with God: *ye are God's husbandry, ye are God's building*" (1 Corinthians 3:6-9).

Paul is speaking of the labor that he and Apollos brought to the Corinthian church. He says that "every man shall receive his own reward according to his own labour" and that *"ye are God's husbandry, ye are God's building."* The "ye" in this verse pertains to the Corinthian church or body of Christ. This is the context of the entire chapter. Their labor was not to themselves or to their own bodies but to *the body of Christ.*

And Paul goes on to discuss the work which one adds to that which he already laid, being the foundation of Jesus Christ Himself. He adds:

"Let every man take heed how he buildeth thereupon" (1 Corinthians 3:10).

The building materials or works that a believer manifests are that which Paul is referring to in this Scripture. He went on to say they are either "gold, silver, precious stones" or "wood, hay, stubble" (1 Corinthians 3:12). So he was basically asking: *With what materials are you building the church, which is the temple of God?*

And it's within this context that we find the verses we are examining, namely:

"Know ye not that ye are the temple of God, and that the Spirit of God dwelleth in you? If any man defile the temple of God, him shall God destroy; for the temple of God is holy, which temple ye are" (1 Corinthians 3:16-17).

The word "defile" in the Greek can also be translated as "corrupt." In fact, "defile" is just a different form of the same word as "destroy" in this verse. For the Scripture can also be translated:

"If any man *corrupt* the temple of God, him shall God *bring to corruption.*"

This verse is speaking of the Lord's protective care over the church, who are His people. They are the called-out ones who have received Christ. They are those who make up His temple.

If you who are reading this have a desire to realize your security in Christ *and* at the same time want to corrupt or destroy God's church—there is no comfort I can offer you. For how could your salvation be true with such bad fruit? How could it be genuine? How could you be *in Christ* and have such a desire in *opposition* toward *Him*?

Indeed, it's not a matter of losing salvation but of even possessing salvation in the first place.

Taken Away from the Book of Life?

These verses are somewhat similar to the Scriptures found at the end of the Book of Revelation:

> "For I testify unto every man that heareth the words of the prophecy of this book, If any man shall add unto these things, God shall add unto him the plagues that are written in this book: And if any man shall take away from the words of the book of this prophecy, God shall take away his part out of the book of life, and out of the holy city, and from the things which are written in this book" (Revelation 22:18-19).

For if a person wants to defile God's church in this way by taking away or adding to His Word, which is foundational to the church—then again, losing salvation is not the issue. Rather, the lack of salvation to begin with is the problem. Indeed, many harmful cults, against Christ, have arisen by adding to or removing Scriptures from the Bible. So verses like these are warnings to those who would prey upon God's church with the intent to corrupt it.

As has been stated in this study, Jesus declared:

"Either make the tree good and its fruit good, or make the tree corrupt and its fruit corrupt; for the tree is known by its fruit" (Matthew 12:33, *WEB*).

And we see that the Scripture regarding those who would defile the temple of God describes exactly what happened when the Lord dealt with Ananias and his wife Sapphira in the early days of the infant church.

As previously covered in *Chapter 24: Ananias & Sapphira*, these people were *not* of the fellowship of those who were true believers. In contrast, they were deceivers among the church, who were "of the rest" of those who did not believe. It was for this reason that the Lord dealt so swiftly with them. For He was protecting his emerging church from those who were joining the Christian assembly with improper motives (Acts 5:1-14). The warning of 1 Corinthians 3:16-17, concerning those who defile the temple, is likewise showing the Lord's protection for His genuine church body.

A Christian?
Let's Make the Argument...

Nevertheless, because Paul was speaking to the Corinthian church, it might be said that he was giving this warning of destruction to Christians. (Of course we know that the Scripture speaks not only to believers, but to unbelievers and make-believers as well.) But even if we make that argument, the full context of these verses would demonstrate that Paul wasn't speaking of *losing salvation*.

Having read 1 Corinthians 3:16-17 in regard to one defiling God's temple, let's now look at Paul's words which led directly up to that verse:

"For we are labourers together with God: ye are God's husbandry, ye are God's building. According to the grace of God which is given unto me, as a wise masterbuilder, I have laid the foundation, and another buildeth thereon. But let every man take heed how he buildeth thereupon. For other foundation can no man lay than that is laid, which is Jesus Christ. Now if any man build upon this foundation gold, silver, precious stones, wood, hay, stubble; Every man's work shall be made manifest: for the day shall declare it, because it shall be revealed by fire; and the fire shall try every man's work of what sort it is. If any man's work abide which he hath built thereupon, he shall receive a reward. If any man's work shall be burned, he shall suffer loss: but he himself shall be saved; yet so as by fire. *Know ye not that ye are the temple of God, and that the Spirit of God dwelleth in you? If any man defile the temple of God, him shall God destroy; for the temple of God is holy, which temple ye are*" (1 Corinthians 3:9-17).

Notice that according to Scripture, the works of a Christian will be openly manifest. These works are hopefully the fruit from a life of abiding in Christ, the true Vine. Without any doubt, this passage is saying that only the *works* of a believer will be judged and *not the believer himself.* Jesus has borne our condemnation, as it is written:

"But he was pierced for our transgressions. He was crushed for our iniquities. *The punishment that brought our peace was on him*; and by his wounds we are healed" (Isaiah 53:5, *WEB*).

And Jesus has declared emphatically that we will not be punitively judged:

> "Most certainly I tell you, he who hears my word and believes him who sent me has eternal life, *and doesn't come into judgment*, but has passed out of death into life" (John 5:24, *WEB*).

For this judgment of the Christian's works is not the same as the Great White Throne Judgment of unbelievers, found in Revelation 20:11-15, who are cast into the lake of fire.

Rather, this judgment of believers is to reveal and reward those who have yielded to Christ's Spirit in the godly works of gold, silver and precious stones. And for those who have built their Christian walk upon the works of the flesh, there will be loss of reward but not loss of salvation.

Quality vs. Quantity

It is interesting to note that it is not the *quantity* of work that is important but the *quality* (gold, silver, precious stones). For God is always looking to the humble heart that is yielded to Him. Jesus even declared in that day: "There are some who are last who will be first, and there are some who are first who will be last" (Luke 13:30, *WEB*). Indeed, even our sufferings in His name hold great reward. As Paul said, "For our light affliction, which is but for a moment, worketh for us a far more exceeding and eternal weight of glory" (2 Corinthians 4:17).

For no matter what your circumstances may be in the Lord, you can have no better quality of fruit than that which Jesus produces *through* you. Our walk with Christ never stops being through grace and by His Spirit. For bearing the fruit of God is not intended to be difficult for the Christian; it just requires surrender to His will. There may be suffering as He suffered, but this is because Christ is our life. And we can be assured that He knows our walk with Him, because "your labor *is not in vain in the Lord*" (1 Corinthians 15:58, *WEB*). For when we abide in Christ, the Vine (John 15:5), the "work" we bring forth is the very life of Jesus. And as we allow His grace to carry us in His will for our lives, He lives through us. As it is written:

> "God worketh in you both to will and to do of his good pleasure" (Philippians 2:13).

And as Jesus said:

> "My yoke is easy, and my burden is light" (Matthew 11:30).

What *is* difficult is to strive and continually perform the works of the flesh. These works of wood, hay and stubble of the flesh will not withstand the test of fire and will be burned away. But the believer, truly converted, who added such works of the flesh to the foundation of Jesus Christ and the church itself, *was still found to be saved.* For as Paul explained:

> "If any man's work shall be burned, he shall suffer loss: *but he himself shall be saved; yet so as by fire*" (1 Corinthians 3:15).

And strangely, it was directly after this statement that Paul added:

> "Know ye not that ye are the temple of God, and that the Spirit of God dwelleth in you? *If any man defile the temple of God, him shall God destroy*; for the

temple of God is holy, which temple ye are" (1 Corinthians 3:16-17).

These are the Scriptures we have been studying. Why did Paul suddenly put those words in there? If the argument is made that his statement could pertain to a true believer defiling the temple of God, the church—then surely he was referencing those whom he had just mentioned, who added "wood, hay, stubble" upon the foundation of Jesus Christ, whose works would be burned. If Paul was addressing them, he still said emphatically that such a one "shall suffer loss: *but he himself shall be saved; yet so as by fire.*" So how could Paul have been referring to his or her spiritual destruction? He could have been writing about physical destruction—of the flesh—but *not* of the spirit.

As has been mentioned in this study, the Apostle Paul spoke of such things in 1 Corinthians 5:5, where he wrote:

> "To deliver such an one unto Satan for the *destruction of the flesh*, that the *spirit may be saved* in the day of the Lord Jesus."

And it was also Paul who spoke of those believers who were mishandling the Lord's supper in disregard to the church:

> "For this cause many are weak and sickly among you, and many sleep. For if we would judge ourselves, we should not be judged. But when we are judged, we are chastened [disciplined] of the Lord, *that we should not be condemned with the world*" (1 Corinthians 11:30-32).

In both of these situations, a Christian's salvation was never in question. There may have been judgment but *not* condemnation. So either way you look at these verses of 1 Corinthians 3:16-17—as a warning for the unbeliever or even to a believer who is walking in an extreme situation of the wood, hay and stubble of the flesh—the loss of a *Christian's salvation* is not being referenced in the context of this chapter.

Indeed, the loss of salvation for a believer (one who is born again and in Christ) *is not spoken of anywhere in Scripture.*

The Terror of the Lord?

In 2 Corinthians, we find that the Apostle Paul had more to write concerning the judgment of the believer and unbeliever. He stated:

> "For we must all appear before the judgment seat of Christ; that every one may receive the things done in his body, according to that he hath done, whether it be good or bad" (2 Corinthians 5:10).

It is true that we will all give account, but believers and unbelievers *will not* be at the same judgment.

For the believer's judgment, as mentioned, will be a time of reward and not of damnation. There may be loss of reward for some, but there is no loss of salvation or the glories of Heaven.

In contrast, in the judgment for the unbeliever (who will be judged later), there will be damnation and not salvation. That is the lot for all who stand before the Great White Throne Judgment of Revelation 20:11-15. And when the Book of Life is opened at that time, no one who stands in that assembly will be found written within its pages.

Paul addressed this in his very next verse—and showed the difference between the believer and unbeliever—by saying:

"Knowing therefore the terror of the Lord, *we persuade men*; but we are made manifest unto God; and I trust also are made manifest in your consciences" (2 Corinthians 5:11).

Why was Paul persuading men? It's because he was speaking of the terror of the Lord as it applies to *unbelievers.* Paul was stating the reason for his preaching of the Gospel— to save the lost. For the terror of the Lord does not apply to believers who are already saved and "made manifest unto God." But it does apply to unbelievers, who will face Christ in the final Great White Throne Judgment (Revelation 20:11-15). Paul continued by saying:

"Now then we are ambassadors for Christ, as though God did beseech you by us: we pray you in Christ's stead, be ye reconciled to God. For he hath made him to be sin for us, who knew no sin; *that we might be made the righteousness of God in him*" (2 Corinthians 5:20-21).

Regarding the believer who has been made the righteousness of God, there is no longer the *terror* of the Lord. Indeed, he has already been persuaded and has come to Christ for salvation. Jesus is now *Savior.* And the Christian's works (whether gold, silver, precious stones or wood, hay and stubble) are all that will be judged; they will either remain or be burned away.

But according to God's Word, the believer in Christ will *never* be burned away!

303

Chapter 26

Converting an Erring Brother?

Anyone Among You

At the end of the Book of James we read the following:

> "Brethren, if any of you do *err from the truth*, and one convert him; Let him know, that he which *converteth the sinner* from the error of his way shall save a soul from death, and shall hide a multitude of sins" (James 5:19-20).

Some have taken these verses to mean that a Christian can lose salvation. After all, the Scriptures start with "Brethren..." and even say, "shall save a soul from death."

But as I have shared throughout this study, just because we are speaking of people outwardly as in the church, it does not necessarily mean we are dealing with those who are truly *converted inwardly* in Christ. James used the word "brethren" as a group term in this passage and said, "if any of you." He did not address the group with the more specific phrase, "if any brother." In fact, the wording of the Greek is much more descriptive, as it literally says: "if anyone *among* you." Being "among" a group of believers does not make you one of them. But Scripture always interprets itself, and John taught us that there are those among us who are not of us:

> "They went out from us, but they were not of us; for if they had been of us, they would have continued with us: but *they went out, that they might be made manifest that they were not all of us*" (1 John 2:19).

Erring from the Truth Himself

Notice that these individuals referenced in 1 John did "err from the truth" as James mentioned. For they "went out from us" but "were not of us." It was therefore manifested that they were not the same as those with a saving faith in Christ Jesus.

Paul wrote "unto *the church of God* which is at Corinth" (2 Corinthians 1:1), and yet he also said in the same epistle:

> "Examine your own selves, whether you are in the faith. Test your own selves. Or don't you know about your own selves, that Jesus Christ is in you?—unless indeed you are disqualified" (2 Corinthians 13:5, *WEB*).

Paul was confirming that there may be those who have *knowledge* of salvation without taking the step of *faith* to receive Christ unto salvation. Therefore, there may be those who "err from the truth" of salvation itself. They fail to receive Jesus, who is "the way, *the truth*, and the life" (John 14:6).

Notice also that our Scripture in James reads:

"...he which *converteth* the sinner from the error of his way" (James 5:20).

The word used for "converteth" is very interesting here, as it is the same Greek word that is found in Acts 3:19, which states:

"Repent ye therefore, and be *converted*, that your sins may be blotted out, when the times of refreshing shall come from the presence of the Lord."

This usage clearly demonstrates that James chose a word associated with salvation itself. For in salvation there is a rebirth when we turn to Christ for the forgiveness of sins, placing our trust in Him. There is a turning *to the truth* and with our conversion to Christ, there is a change of nature.

Converting the Sinner

Notice also that James does not say, "he who converteth *a brother* from the error of his way" but specifically says, "he which converteth *the sinner* from the error of his way." So James is not referring to a true brother; he speaks of "the sinner," who has *erred from the truth that can save him*. This is about a person coming to the brink of the things of true Christianity but still going astray.

James is writing in a similar fashion to the word found in Hebrews 12:15, which says *the church* should be:

"Looking diligently lest any man fail of the grace of God" (Hebrews 12:15).

The only way to fail of the grace of God is to not receive it, for it is a free gift to all who accept Christ as Savior.

An Impossible Contradiction

It's important to consider that those who believe these verses in James 5:19-20 pertain to a Christian who has lost salvation are also those who believe that the warning in Hebrews 6:4-6 (covered in *Chapter 12: The Warning of Hebrews 6*) is referring to Christians losing their salvation as well.

Yet in Hebrews 6, we have read that it "is impossible...to renew them again unto repentance" if they fall away. So how could James 5 be speaking of Christians coming back to their salvation, if Hebrews 6 was declaring it to be impossible?

Again, how can the writers of both James 5 and Hebrews 6 be speaking of Christians? If these verses are referring to believers, the Scriptures would completely contradict each other. For then James would be saying that you *can* bring such a one back (and encourages you to do so!), while Hebrews 6 would be stating you cannot.

But in truth, neither the warning in Hebrews 6 nor these words of James 5 apply to born-again Christians; rather, they are for those who have a knowledge (only) of Christian beliefs, falling short of faith in salvation. And because this is the case, these verses do not contradict each other *at all*.

Those who have been exposed to some truth may yet come to a saving faith in Christ, according to James.

However, the warning of Hebrews 6 goes further and applies to those who had tasted and experienced the presence and power of the Kingdom to come—yet still *did not receive Christ*. This is why it states: "For it is impossible...If they shall fall away, to renew them again unto repentance" (Hebrews 6:4-6). Why is it impossible? It's because they reject the personal known revelation of Christ's Spirit, and they choose to "crucify to themselves the Son of God afresh, and put him to an open shame" (Hebrews 6:6). There is no ignorance in this situation.

However, the Book of Hebrews offers words of comfort to all who have received Christ:

"But, beloved, we are persuaded better things of you, and *things that accompany salvation*" (Hebrews 6:9).

Chapter 27

Falling from Grace?

Returning to Legalism

The Apostle Paul, in admonishing the Galatians not to turn to Judaism and to the keeping of the law, wrote:

> "Christ is become of no effect unto you, whosoever of you are justified by the law; ye are fallen from grace" (Galatians 5:4).

In context, this verse is pertaining to specific individuals who looked for salvation in their works and not by the grace of God through the atoning work of Christ. Such individuals had turned from the grace of God to a system of law and effort, which does not provide *any salvation*. Indeed, as Paul admonished: "Christ is become of no effect unto you." This is not a verse addressing individuals who had gone back into the world; rather, it is a warning for those returning to *legalism*.

I was once in a church where believers were interceding for a brother who was stumbling in the ways of the world. During this prayer time a woman prayed aloud, saying that the brother had "fallen from grace." But wasn't it God's grace that embraced us while we were all in the world, lost and broken in sin? How could we then fall from it in this way? This grace picked us up so that we could join in singing with the saints of old: "Amazing Grace, how sweet the sound...that saved a wretch like me!" So why would we lose it and therefore be abandoned if we stumble? For the Lord's amazing grace is what met us in our initial need for salvation. Indeed, is not grace defined as God's *unmerited* favor?

Now of course, we prefer that a brother or sister *not* fall into the old ways of sin. It brings much grief and pain whenever we believe the lies of Satan and follow his ways. It hurts us and the people around us, as sin is not the path of healing but of destruction. However, I can tell you with certainty, that if such a brother or sister is truly saved, the condemnation of the Old Testament's law will not bring that believer back. For the Bible states clearly that:

"The law made nothing perfect" (Hebrews 7:19).

Amazing Grace—Betrothed Forever

And even within the pages of the Old Testament, we can see some of the most beautiful references to the New Covenant of grace that the Lord anticipated pouring out upon His people. One need go no further than this prophecy of Hosea:

"It will be in that day," says the LORD, "that you will call me 'my husband,' and no longer call me 'my master'...I will betroth you to me *forever*. Yes, I will betroth you to me in righteousness, in justice, in loving kindness, and in compassion. I will even betroth you to me in faithfulness; and you shall know the LORD" (Hosea 2:16, 19-20, *NHEB*).

For it is only God's grace that will bring the wanderers back, if they *do* have salvation. And as Hosea says in this Scripture, God has betrothed them to Him "forever." Who are we to say He cannot do so? The law may make you look good outwardly for a season, but it has no power to change who you are within, nor the way you think. No, this is done by His grace. Amazing grace.

Often Christians are afraid to believe there is this much grace for us! But since it's grace that saved you, why would the grace of God not keep you? How could we ever keep ourselves, since we were saved from the gutter in the first place? Consider these Scriptures in Romans 5:6, 8-10:

"For when we were yet without strength, in due time Christ died for the ungodly...But God commendeth his love toward us, in that, while we were yet sinners, Christ died for us. Much more then, being now justified by his blood, *we shall be saved from wrath through him.* For if, when we were enemies, we were reconciled to God by the death of his Son, much more, being reconciled, we shall be saved by his life."

Now if there are those who returned to the law and legalism—stopping short of faith in Christ and leaving the grace that was offered them in the Gospel—then truly they would have fallen from this high revelation of God's grace to a system of works. And this is surely the context in which the

Apostle Paul, in the Book of Galatians, was speaking when he referred to falling from grace. For Paul himself stated:

> "I do not make void the grace of God. For if righteousness is through the law, then Christ died for nothing" (Galatians 2:21, *NHEB*).

Following rules and righteous living will not save us. Only Christ can save us, through the grace He provided by dying for our sins on the cross. Any other way of self-effort will not and cannot do what the grace of God does for us. His grace reaches down from Heaven to lift us up. All we need to do is receive it by faith. This is the foundation of what it means to be born again and to become a Christian. For Christians are those who have acknowledged their sin and their need for the Savior. They are ones who have received what Jesus has done for them in the grace of salvation.

And it is *only* the grace of God that changes your heart and keeps you in salvation. This is why it can be said that if believers wander, being in Christ, the grace of God will bring them back. If others wander away *without* Christ, they are fulfilling the verse which has been quoted so often:

> "They went out from us, but they were not of us; for if they had been of us, they would have continued with us: but they went out, that they might be made manifest that they were not all of us" (1 John 2:19).

So when Paul was speaking of those who have "fallen from grace" in the Book of Galatians, he was not saying that they have sinned their way out of the grace of salvation. Rather, he was referring to those who instead returned to a system of legalism and works or of anything else apart from the saving grace of God.

Chapter 27: Falling from Grace?

Chapter 28

Peter & Some Falling

Calling & Election from God

The Apostle Peter stated in 2 Peter 1:10:

> "Wherefore the rather, brethren, give diligence to make your calling and election sure: for if ye do these things, *ye shall never fall.*"

Some may interpret this verse as meaning you can fall from grace (and thus salvation) because the wording implies the possibility of falling. But actually, this verse in context is merely stating that those who profess Christ should indeed see the fruit of Jesus in their lives—as *confirmation* of the salvation already within their hearts. This is what Peter means by the encouragement to "make your calling and election *sure.*"

We cannot make ourselves called nor elected; *only God can do that.* But those who *are* called and elected can demonstrate that their election is sure and genuine through their lifestyles.

The "falling" would only apply to one whose calling and election *was not sure* (and thus, to one not saved). For in context, Peter is merely saying to demonstrate the confirmation of this calling and election by bearing fruit.

Peter is speaking of salvation. Is it sure? Are you saved? Is there fruit? Then he declares: "Ye shall never fall."

This is good news! Indeed, this is a wonderful Scripture for the assurance of our eternal security. Peter is encouraging believers to know the genuineness of their salvation, which is revealed by the life of Christ working within them.

Again, this is Peter's way of saying exactly what had been written by Paul, who instructed the Corinthians:

> "Examine your own selves, whether you are in the faith. Test your own selves. Or don't you know about your own selves, that Jesus Christ is in you?—unless indeed you are disqualified" (2 Corinthians 13:5, *WEB*).

Falling from Steadfastness

Peter also shares a similar sentiment in 2 Peter 3:17-18:

> "Ye therefore, beloved, seeing ye know these things before, beware lest ye also, being led away with the error of the wicked, fall from your own steadfastness. But grow in grace, and in the knowledge of our Lord and Saviour Jesus Christ. To him be glory both now and for ever. Amen."

Peter used the phrase, "fall from your own steadfastness" in this case. In the original Greek, the word "steadfastness" translates as "stability, firmness or perseverance." Peter used it in direct contrast to his words in the previous verse, where he stated that the "unstable" twist (distort) the words of Paul (2 Peter 3:16). So Peter is clearly referring to one's stability.

To "fall from one's steadfastness" can be interpreted in two ways, with neither one describing a true believer falling from a position of *salvation* in Christ.

First, reading it in context, we can look at this from the point of view that Peter was warning a believer not to follow the error of the wicked and therefore fall from the stability of one's *walk* with the Lord. This would be a matter of sanctification and not an issue pertaining to salvation.

Jesus said:

"And ye shall know the truth, and the truth shall make you free" (John 8:32).

If we—as believers—follow error, we can be sure that our walk with Christ will suffer. Truth will set us free, but error will certainly bind us.

There are many verses in the Bible that encourage us in our life of sanctification with the Lord, and we need to always guard against allowing anything that does not line up with Scripture into our lives. In the Book of Proverbs we read:

"Keep thy heart with all diligence; for out of it are the issues of life" (Proverbs 4:23).

For as we walk with Jesus, we grow and experience more and more of His life and His peace in our lives. We are transformed and become more and more like Him. As it is written:

> "But we all, with open face beholding as in a glass the glory of the Lord, are changed into the same image from glory to glory, even as by the Spirit of the Lord" (2 Corinthians 3:18).

And Peter, in saying not to follow the error of the wicked, was warning fellow believers not to be influenced and get off-track by the erroneous behavior of the unstable who reject Christ. He encouraged Christians to stay on the right track and on sure footing in their walk of faith.

Secondly, we could look at the meaning of Peter's words as referring to one's perseverance in Christ—not to fall from it. This would be a deeper and more serious thought. For it is one's perseverance in Christ which manifests that the grace of his or her salvation was indeed real in the first place. Falling from that, however, would not be a loss of salvation. Rather, it would reveal that one *did not have salvation* to begin with. *For Christ Himself keeps us.*

Once again, our verse in 1 John makes it so clear:

> "They went out from us, but they were not of us; for if they had been of us, *they would have continued with us*: but they went out, that they might be made manifest that *they were not all of us*" (1 John 2:19).

And remember, as Paul wrote in Philippians 1:6:

> "Being confident of this very thing, that he which hath begun a good work in you will perform it until the day of Jesus Christ."

Either of these ways of interpreting "fall from your own steadfastness" would be true. But neither applies to a true believer falling from God's saving grace.

Of Incorruptible Seed

Notice that Peter ends our verses of 2 Peter 3:17-18, by saying:

> "But *grow in grace*, and in the knowledge of our Lord and Saviour Jesus Christ..."

And this is the mark of a true believer: growth. For growth is evidence of *life*, which is the eternal life inside of you. Peter referred to this life with these words:

> "Being born again, not of corruptible seed, but of *incorruptible*, by the word of God, which liveth and abideth for ever" (1 Peter 1:23).

Truly, this is a life "incorruptible," into which we have been born again!

For Peter was never implying that a true Christian could lose salvation. For Peter himself was the one who wrote:

> "Blessed be the God and Father of our Lord Jesus Christ, which according to his abundant mercy hath begotten us again unto a lively hope by the resurrection of Jesus Christ from the dead, *To an inheritance incorruptible, and undefiled, and that fadeth not away, reserved in heaven for you, Who are kept by the power of God through faith unto salvation* ready to be revealed in the last time" (1 Peter 1:3-5).

Chapter 29

Such Shall Not Inherit the Kingdom?

Speaking of Those Who Know Christ?

In Galatians 5:19-21, Paul wrote:

> "Now the works of the flesh are manifest, which are these: adultery, fornication, uncleanness, lasciviousness, idolatry, sorcery, hatred, strife, jealousy, wrath, factions, seditions, heresies, envyings, murders, drunkenness, revelings, and the like; of which I tell you before, as I have also told you in time past, that *they who do such things shall not inherit the kingdom of God.*"

In these verses of Scripture, we find the truth that those who live in and practice the works of the flesh will not inherit the Kingdom of God. That's good news because if this was not the case, Heaven would not be Heaven. There cannot be perfect love, peace and harmony where wickedness dwells. If only one person was able to curse in Heaven, it would become as fallen Earth and cease to be pure.

Paul emphatically declares that the Kingdom of God is not of such as these; therefore, we as believers should not live in the same manner as they do. This is the context of Paul's words.

But could it be that Paul is saying something else, as some imply? Is the apostle declaring that those who know Christ as Savior (those having new natures), who then fall into some sin—are now therefore lost and excluded from God's Kingdom and all the promises He made to them? Is that the meaning of these Scriptures? Do Christians become the same as those who will not inherit the Kingdom? Is there now condemnation for those in Christ? *Of course not!* If this was the case, what would happen to all the verses we have thus far mentioned (many of which were written by Paul himself!), proving a true believer's security in Christ? God's Word is *never* broken. Remember that Jesus said:

"The scripture cannot be broken" (John 10:35).

They That Are Christ's

When we look at these verses in Galatians in context, we discover that the apostle is simply making a distinction between the dead and the living. It is a distinction between those who live out their lives in the works of the flesh and those who bring forth the fruit of the Spirit in their lives. Paul is comparing two different types of people—those without Christ and those who are Christ's. And he is merely advising Christians not to live like the dead who will not see God. This comparison becomes evident as we read further in verse 24:

"And *they that are Christ's* have crucified the flesh with the affections and lusts."

Notice in this Scripture that Paul is stating, "they that are Christ's" are not the same as those practicing and living in the works of the flesh, who shall not inherit eternal life. And he further exhorts in verse 25:

"*If we live in the Spirit*, let us also walk in the Spirit."

You see, Paul is setting apart the true believer from the unbeliever. He is bringing out the fact that believers in Christ are not the same as unbelievers; and he is admonishing Christians that they should not be walking in the ways of the ungodly.

Paul is telling us in these verses to live out who we really are as Christians. And he warns that those who are alive only in the flesh—without any fruit or life in the Spirit—will not see the Kingdom of Heaven.

But notice the exhortation of Paul: "*If we live in the Spirit*, let us also walk in the Spirit." Did you notice the order there? We are alive in the Spirit *first* (being born again), then we walk in the Spirit. This indeed is salvation by grace and not by works.

The instruction could have been written: "*If we walk in the Spirit*, then we will live in the Spirit." But it wasn't expressed that way! Again, Paul encouraged: "If we *live* in the Spirit, let us also walk in the Spirit."

First we are alive in Jesus, then the fruit follows this new life. And because of this truth, Paul was exhorting believers not to walk in the old ways of the dead but to walk according to the new life that now abides in them.

325

And Such WERE Some of You

In addition, Paul more clearly brings out the comparison between those who are dead in the flesh and those who are alive by the Spirit, when he states almost the exact same thing in 1 Corinthians 6:9-10:

> "Know ye not that the unrighteous shall not inherit the kingdom of God? Be not deceived: neither fornicators, nor idolaters, nor adulterers, nor effeminate, nor abusers of themselves with mankind, nor thieves, nor covetous, nor drunkards, nor revilers, nor extortioners, shall inherit the kingdom of God."

Then Paul goes on to clarify his thoughts in verse 11:

> "And such *were* some of you; but ye are washed, but ye are sanctified, but ye are justified in the name of the Lord Jesus, and by the Spirit of our God."

Paul declared that those of whom he was speaking (those who shall not inherit the Kingdom), were not the same as those who were washed, sanctified and justified. For he clarified the difference by saying, "such *were* some of you." So in those previous verses, Paul was speaking specifically of "the unrighteous" and not of those who are righteous in Christ. As it is written:

> "He hath made him to be sin for us, who knew no sin; that we might be made the righteousness of God in him" (2 Corinthians 5:21).

And Paul definitively declared: "But ye are washed, but ye are sanctified, but ye are justified in the name of the Lord Jesus, and by the Spirit of our God." Our sanctification is not only in the Name of the Lord Jesus, who died for our sins, but it is also by the Spirit of God, who changes our hearts and keeps us from sin. And as previously mentioned, we are not only saved by grace; we are kept by it as well!

Keeping all this truth in mind, how could these verses by Paul ever be interpreted as addressing a Christian believer losing his or her salvation? Paul is merely giving the exhortation that as *the righteous,* we should not be walking in the manner of *the unrighteous*, who will not inherit the Kingdom of God. Why not? Because we have new life, being born again, and we are living in Christ now. Therefore, as we live, let us walk.

And the Bible confirms this in Colossians 2:6, where Paul also exhorts Christians:

> "As ye have therefore received Christ Jesus the Lord, so walk ye in him..."

by Richard O. Webb

Chapter 30

Sowing to the Flesh
& Reaping Corruption?

The Sowing & Reaping of Two Natures

The Apostle Paul, after making the argument in the Epistle of Galatians that Christians are *saved by grace* and *not by works*, winds down his thoughts in the last chapter by saying:

> "Be not deceived; God is not mocked: for whatsoever a man soweth, that shall he also reap. For he that soweth to his flesh shall of the flesh reap corruption; but he that soweth to the Spirit shall of the Spirit reap life everlasting" (Galatians 6:7-8).

Was Paul saying that a believer can lose salvation by reaping the corruption of the flesh? Not at all.

Paul wrote these verses about a Christian's *walk* after salvation. He was addressing the difference between the

Christian's old nature of the flesh and the new nature in the Spirit. As mentioned in *Chapter 3: The Security of Butterflies in Caterpillars*, we can refer to these natures as the old caterpillar and the new butterfly.

Paul is stating in these verses that God is not mocked; if you walk in the old ways of the caterpillar, you will incur the corruption inherent in that old nature. Indeed, if you sow to the caterpillar, you will reap from it. In the same way, if you sow to the butterfly (which is your true, born-again nature), you will reap the result of it, that being eternal life—which already abides in you. As Jesus said:

> "Verily, verily, I say unto you, He that heareth my word, and believeth on him that sent me, *hath everlasting life,* and shall not come into condemnation; *but is passed from death unto life*" (John 5:24).

Paul was not saying that every time you walk in the flesh you reap corruption and lose salvation, and every time you walk in the Spirit you gain eternal life back again. If so, we would probably die and be reborn daily—on and off in our salvation—as we endeavor to walk with the Lord. This thought, apart from being hopeless, has no biblical precedent in the Scriptures and was certainly not taught by the Apostle Paul.

Remember, it was Paul, when speaking of the carnal Christians at the Lord's supper (as covered in *Chapter 15: Damnation or Discipline?*), who said:

> "For this cause many are weak and sickly among you, and many sleep" (1 Corinthians 11:30).

This verse reveals that even in their rebellion, as Christians, they still were numbered with those who "sleep." This was Paul's term for believers *who died in the Lord, having salvation.* It was also Paul who wrote (when referring to a believer in a rebellious state, as covered in *Chapter 14: Branches, Fruit & Fire*):

> "To deliver such an one unto Satan for the destruction of the flesh, that the spirit *may be saved* in the day of the Lord Jesus" (1 Corinthians 5:5).

Surely, if Paul was referring to losing *salvation* by sowing to the flesh in a Christian's walk, he would not have made the statements that some "sleep" and "that the spirit may be saved." Paul would simply have called them *dead.* For they surely sowed to the flesh as believers.

But Paul was, after all, the one who spoke some of the greatest assurances of our eternal security found in God's Word. He stated emphatically that, as believers in Christ, we were sealed to the day of redemption (Ephesians 4:30), that nothing could separate us from the love of God (Romans 8:38-39), and that we have been predestined for glory (Romans 8:30)—to name just a few Scripture references that have already been stated in this study.

Sowing to the New Nature

These verses in Galatians 6:7-8, in regard to sowing to the flesh or the Spirit, pertain to the situation in which a Christian finds himself or herself after receiving Christ. For concerning the believer, Paul declared:

> "For the flesh doth desire contrary to the Spirit, and the Spirit contrary to the flesh, and these are

opposed one to another, that the things that ye may will—these ye may not do" (Galatians 5:17, *YLT*).

This verse undoubtedly shows that there is a passionate war between the two natures at work in the Christian, who is born again of God's Spirit. The flesh is contrary to the Spirit and the Spirit is contrary to the flesh. And as believers, though we are alive in our spirit (small "s") by our new birth, we are either *walking* in the Spirit of God or in the carnal nature of the flesh. We walk in either one or the other. Is it any wonder, therefore, that Paul the Apostle would encourage us to sow to the Spirit and our new nature?

But it is important to keep in mind that, as Christians, we don't sow to the Spirit *to attain* the Spirit and eternal life. No; for as a true believer in Christ, *we already have the Spirit and eternal life living in us.* We walk in the Spirit and sow to the Spirit so that we can live out this new life of Christ in us. And this is why Paul wrote:

> "For if ye live after the flesh, ye shall die: but if ye through the Spirit do mortify the deeds of the body, ye shall live. For as many as are led by the Spirit of God, they are the sons of God" (Romans 8:13-14).

Again, Paul is addressing one's choice, regarding which nature a Christian sows to *after* salvation.

Death Inherent of the Flesh

When Paul used the words that "ye shall die," he was referring to the loss of life and freedom that we experience when we walk in the flesh and allow it to dominate us in any circumstance. This is apparent in the verse's context. For although our spirit is alive in Christ, the flesh is dead in sin and *will* ultimately die. In fact, the Greek of this verse translates as:

"For if you live according to flesh, ye are *about* to die..."

This is a very interesting way of describing the experience of a believer walking in the ways of the old nature. *It's the experience of the presence of the flesh nature, as it tries to exert itself upon our new nature.* And this experience is a nearness to the death inherent in the old nature. For the nature of the flesh is full of all rebellion, strife and disharmony and indeed has the curse of death upon it. This is exactly what we, as believers, experience when we live in the old carnal ways of the flesh.

Paul's Interpretation

And we find in the previous chapter of Romans exactly how Paul interpreted the meaning of this death when he said:

"For I was alive without the law once: but when the commandment came, sin revived, *and I died.* And the commandment, which was ordained to life, I found to be *unto death.* For sin, taking occasion by the commandment, deceived me, and by it *slew me*" (Romans 7:9-11).

In these verses we can see, through Paul's own words, that the "death" he referred to was regarding the revival of the old nature—and not his actual physical or spiritual death.

Indeed, it is obvious that Paul did not die physically, nor did he die spiritually by losing salvation; if either happened, he could not have written this epistle. But Paul experienced the death inherent in the old nature. It was the sin of this fleshly nature that "slew" him.

This is not to say that continually walking in the ways of the flesh would not ultimately lead to physical death. It could lead to such, but this still would not be spiritual death for the true believer. As has been mentioned in this study, God may discipline a believer in a hardened state but will not condemn him, as Christ has borne the Christian's condemnation (Isaiah 53:5). And the believer's spirit, being born again, is "created in righteousness" (Ephesians 4:24) and is therefore "incorruptible" (1 Peter 1:23).

But in the context of this Scripture, Paul was describing what happened when sin revived in Him through the law and turned His eyes away from his walk with God in the Spirit and by grace. He experienced the walk of the flesh in all of its self-energies, waywardness and death. The caterpillar has no enduring life and cannot fly! Indeed, all its legs are earthbound.

However, the butterfly of the new life in the Spirit—which Paul has revealed can surely overcome and "mortify" (literally, "put to death") the deeds of the caterpillar—is eternal, and it flies in the power of God. We can only overcome the old nature through the power of God's Spirit in our new nature. As it is written:

"Greater is he that is in you, than he that is in the world" (1 John 4:4).

This is the walk made possible for us! It's available because God has re-created us in Christ and He has given us a new butterfly heart that's in harmony with His heart. For the butterfly of our new nature glides in the wind and power of

God's Spirit, overcoming the flesh of the caterpillar. And Paul, within these Scriptures, was encouraging believers in their lifestyles to walk in and live out the eternal life residing in them.

For unlike unbelievers who have only one nature (which is the flesh and of death), believers have *two* natures at war within themselves. There's the old and the new. And Paul was encouraging Christians to sow to the new nature inside them. It's that nature which is the *real you* in Christ, already possessing eternal life. This is why Paul could say to the Corinthian church:

> "Purge out the old yeast, that you may be a new lump, even as *you are unleavened.* For indeed Christ, our Passover, has been sacrificed in our place" (1 Corinthians 5:7, *WEB*).

You Really ARE Unleavened

The Apostle Paul is declaring that "you *are* unleavened." Many versions of the Bible translate this as "...you *really are* unleavened"—which shows the meaning of this verse more clearly. Leaven in this reference is symbolic of sin, and Paul is declaring that, as a new creation in Christ, you are without the leaven of sin. For even though sin still resides in the flesh —it does not reside in one's reborn spirit. This is who you really are in Christ!

This verse is a reference to the Old Testament Feast of Unleavened Bread, which was celebrated *after* the Feast of Passover. For it is only after our salvation through Christ's blood in the true Passover that we receive a new nature that is indeed "unleavened." This is why the Apostle Paul also said:

"Put on the new man, which after God is created in righteousness and true holiness" (Ephesians 4:24).

And it's why Jesus said:

"That which is born of the flesh is flesh; and that which is born of the Spirit is spirit" (John 3:6).

If you sow to this new man in the Spirit, you will indeed reap eternal life. It's not because you don't have this life but because you *do indeed have it;* and by sowing into it, you will be *experiencing* that eternal life that is *already* in you. As John declared:

"These things have I written unto you that believe on the name of the Son of God; that ye may know that ye have eternal life..." (1 John 5:13).

And as the Apostle Peter stated:

"Whom having not seen, ye love; in whom, though now ye see him not, yet believing, ye rejoice with joy unspeakable and full of glory: *Receiving the end of your faith, even the salvation of your souls*" (1 Peter 1:8-9).

So as believers, we are receiving the Kingdom of God within us—here and now—with a joy that is "unspeakable and full of glory."

If a believer sows to the carnal nature, he or she will receive the fruit of that nature—corruption. One cannot walk in the flesh and still demonstrate the fruit of the Spirit, which is:

"...love, joy, peace, patience, kindness, goodness, faith, gentleness, and self-control" (Galatians 5:22-23, *WEB*).

There is no benefit gained when not walking with God. One will only experience the death that's in the old nature. This is why God is not mocked. If one sows to the flesh, surely, he or she will of the flesh reap corruption. But it does not mean, nor was Paul implying, that the corruption involves loss of salvation for the born-again believer. Paul never even hinted at this, in his certainty that the new born-again nature is eternal.

Also, Jesus made it clear that the Holy Spirit given to us is a spring of *eternal life* within the soul, beginning on Earth and continuing into eternity. As He said:

> "Whosoever drinketh of this water shall thirst again: But whosoever drinketh of the water that I shall give him shall *never thirst*; but the water that I shall give him shall be in him *a well of water springing up into everlasting life*" (John 4:13-14).

Jesus never stated that this water would be turned on, then off again. *No; His promise to the one who receives it is that he "shall never thirst."* And Jesus gave the assurance that this water would continue to spring up "into everlasting life."

So it is no wonder that the Prophet Isaiah wrote:

> "Look, in the God of my salvation I will trust, and will not be afraid. For the LORD is my strength and my song, and he has become my salvation. *Therefore with joy you will draw water out of the wells of salvation*" (Isaiah 12:2-3, NHEB).

Chapter 31

Blasphemy Against the Holy Spirit?

Addressing the Unregenerate

Jesus stated in the Gospel of Matthew:

> "Wherefore I say unto you, All manner of sin and blasphemy shall be forgiven unto men: but the blasphemy against the Holy Ghost shall not be forgiven unto men" (Matthew 12:31, also Mark 3:28-30; Luke 12:10).

We must keep in mind that when Jesus spoke of the blasphemy of the Spirit, He was addressing unregenerate individuals, without the Spirit within them, who were attributing the works of the Spirit of God to the works of Satan. For the Pharisees had just finished saying:

"This fellow doth not cast out devils, but by Beelzebub the prince of the devils" (Matthew 12:23).

It is this very Holy Spirit (through whom Christ did cast out devils) who brings about conversion and the new birth. For the Spirit is the personal witness and power of God. This is why people, in their ignorance, can be forgiven for blasphemy toward Jesus. But to blaspheme *the Holy Spirit* involves a willful intent and knowledge of the true Spirit of God, whom the person is blaspheming. Ignorance is not an excuse in this case, for one would be blaspheming the very presence of God—the holy Presence that makes salvation known to man.

Individuals who knowingly and willingly blaspheme the Spirit of God from their hearts, thus prevent this very Spirit of repentance from granting them the forgiveness that leads to eternal life through Christ. Anyone fearful of having blasphemed the Spirit of God could not have done so—for this sin is a willful acknowledgment and rejection of God's revealed Spirit. In contrast, one who has blasphemed the Spirit of God would have no desire nor care for Jesus, nor repentance. Ultimately, however, this is the *willful sin* (Hebrews 10:26) of all who are found to have rejected Christ.

The Spirit & Conversion

The Spirit's role in conversion can be found in Zechariah 12:10, which prophetically speaks of Israel's turning to Christ in the Last Days:

> "And I will pour upon the house of David, and upon the inhabitants of Jerusalem, *the spirit of grace and of supplications*: and they shall look upon me whom they have pierced, and they shall mourn for him, as

one mourneth for his only son, and shall be in bitterness for him, as one that is in bitterness for his firstborn."

And this is the reason why Jesus said:

"No man can come to me, except the Father which hath sent me *draw him*: and I will raise him up at the last day. It is written in the prophets, And they shall be all taught of God. Every man therefore that hath heard, and hath learned of the Father, cometh unto me" (John 6:44-45).

Christians do not fall into the category of those who could blaspheme the Holy Spirit because believers have *already received* the Spirit of God, forgiveness and eternal life. Therefore, Christians have been born again of a new spirit "created in righteousness and true holiness" (Ephesians 4:24). And the reborn spirit *cannot* blaspheme the Holy Spirit because this renewed spirit is *one* with Him. As the Apostle Paul said:

"But he that is joined unto the Lord is one spirit" (1 Corinthians 6:17).

Remember that Paul also said of believers:

"Therefore if any man be in Christ, he is a new creature: old things are passed away; behold, all things are become new" (2 Corinthians 5:17).

Concerning our fallen nature, the Apostle John made it clear that:

"The blood of Jesus Christ...cleanseth us from *all* sin" (1 John 1:7).

341

Notice that to the one saved and in Christ, ALL sin is cleansed by the blood of Jesus. This verse proves that when Jesus was speaking of the blasphemy of the Spirit being unforgivable, *He could not have been referring to believers*. If this was the case, then how could it even be possible for ALL of a believer's sins to be forgiven by the blood, as John declared?

And you may recall that John stated concerning our *new nature in Christ:*

> "Whosoever is born of God doth not commit sin; for His *seed* remaineth in Him: and he *cannot* sin, because he is born of God" (1 John 3:9).

I suppose one could make the argument that if a law against blasphemy of the Holy Spirit did apply to the Christian, this very law in itself could provoke the flesh nature in its rebellion to blaspheme the Holy Spirit. In other words, you could be so afraid of doing it—that you do it. But that still would only be the flesh nature; it's not the real person of the new nature in Christ, whom God sees. The Lord always looks at the heart. And as a believer in Christ, you have a *new* heart!

For within every child of God, there is the fulfillment of the prophecy in Ezekiel 36:26, where God promises:

> "A new heart also will I give you, and a new spirit will I put within you."

And again, consider those words that Jesus spoke:

> "That which is born of the flesh is flesh; and that which is *born of the Spirit is spirit*" (John 3:6).

Christians, who are born of God, receive a new nature that is tuned to—and in harmony with—Christ. We literally become God's children in the spirit. This is why the Apostle Paul could write:

> "And because ye are sons, God hath sent forth the Spirit of his Son into your hearts, crying, Abba, Father" (Galatians 4:6).

And it's also the reason why Paul declared:

> "Wherefore I give you to understand, that no man speaking by the Spirit of God calleth Jesus accursed: and that no man can say that Jesus is the Lord, but by the Holy Spirit" (1 Corinthians 12:3).

"For it is God which worketh in you both to will and to do of his good pleasure."

Philippians 2:13

by Richard O. Webb

HEARTOFTHELORD.ORG

Chapter 32

Working Out Salvation with Fear & Trembling?

Working Out Salvation Within

Philippians 2:12 states:

> "Work out your own salvation with fear and trembling."

Some Christians have interpreted this verse to mean that one should always have fear and trembling regarding our salvation, and that we therefore have *no* eternal security. But that is not what this verse means *at all*. The Apostle Paul was writing to the Philippians, telling them to "work out" the salvation that was *already* in them. For he wrote in the very next verse:

> "For it is God which worketh in you both to will and to do of His good pleasure" (Philippians 2:13).

Sanctification—Shining as Lights

In this verse, Paul is actually speaking of personal growth in Christ and not of loss of salvation. When we look at the entire Scripture in context, we can clearly see that Paul, in his absence, was admonishing the Philippians to cautiously and wisely watch themselves—in the midst of a crooked world—as they continued to walk in their relationship with the Lord:

> "Wherefore, my beloved, as ye have always obeyed, not as in my presence only, but now much more in my absence, work out your own salvation with fear and trembling. For it is God which worketh in you both to will and to do of his good pleasure" (Philippians 2:12-13).

Why was Paul exhorting them in this way? Verse 15 explains:

> "That ye may be blameless and harmless, the sons of God, without rebuke, in the midst of a crooked and perverse nation, among whom ye shine as lights in the world" (Philippians 2:15).

This Scripture is not about *salvation* but about *sanctification* (becoming more Christ-like). For Paul never said to work *for* your salvation but to work *out* your salvation with fear and trembling. These verses refer to the watchful and contrite working out of that which had already begun in them, who—being "in the midst of a crooked and perverse nation"—shine as lights. Regarding their salvation, Paul had previously stated in the same epistle:

> "Being confident of this very thing, that he which hath begun a good work in you *will* perform it until the day of Jesus Christ" (Philippians 1:6).

The Harmony of Truth

Therefore, how could this verse *ever* be interpreted as referring to a lack of security in *salvation*?

The only reason for such an explanation in this case would be to misinterpret a Scripture, isolating it from its corresponding verses within the chapter and book. This is why it's important, with the help of the Holy Spirit, to prayerfully read all Scriptures in context. It takes more time to do this, but it's the only way to obtain accurate comprehension of the Bible—receiving the correct understanding of the messages that its writers intended to convey throughout the Word of God.

Think of any other study in life. If one opens a book from a particular study and reads only a few sentences, how can he or she possibly expect to understand its full meaning? If at school, would students pass a test with such a method? So why should we expect the Bible to be any different? Actually, the Scriptures are "harder" because we need the light of the Holy Spirit to understand them. Yet they are easier because we have the Holy Spirit to teach us and cause us to understand as little children!

With the Bible, readers should not drive by quickly, make a doctrine and simply move on. We need to see all Scripture within the context *and* in accordance with other statements the writers have shared in different locations of the Word of God. For the Lord has given us not only *verses* but *books* in the Bible! And His Word needs to be interpreted *in harmony*. For all of God's Word is truth. As Jesus prayed:

> "Sanctify them through thy truth: thy word is truth" (John 17:17).

Chapter 33

He Who Endures to the End Shall Be Saved?

Endure—in Order to be Saved?

It is written in the Gospel of Mark:

> "He that shall endure unto the end, the same shall be saved" (Mark 13:13, also Matthew 10:22-23, 24:13).

Some people have used this verse in saying that one cannot *ever* have an assurance of salvation. The argument is that you *cannot* know your salvation with any certainty *until* you make it to the very end of your days and enter into glory. Only then, they say, can you be assured.

Now it is true that if we endure, we reveal the salvation that we *already* have within us—and thus prove and demonstrate it. (This has been mentioned in this study and will be covered further in *Chapter 41: We Have Become*

Partakers of Christ!) But this is not the same as saying we endure—in order *to be saved.* That is something completely different and there are many verses in the Bible that contradict such a thought.

As a reminder of one of them, the Apostle John stated:

"These things I have written to you who believe in the name of the Son of God, *that you may know that you have everlasting life*" (1 John 5:13, *NHEB*).

John made it clear that we who believe *can know* and *should know* that we already "have everlasting life."

Nevertheless, to gain a better understanding of the meaning behind the Scripture to "endure unto the end," it it necessary to understand the other verses surrounding it. For this reason, I am going to deviate a little from our topic of eternal security in this chapter, in order to give a background of the coming biblical, end-time events. *(See page 457 for an accompanying end-time chart for this chapter.)*

I'm addressing this because this little verse about endurance in Mark 13:13 finds itself among the big end-time Scriptures. And without understanding those verses as well, one will not understand why this Scripture was spoken and how—if at all—it relates to our eternal security.

But though I detour a bit, I'm actually sharing more of the love of God which keeps us in salvation. And this chapter can be summed up by the words of David:

"For the LORD loves justice, and doesn't forsake his faithful ones. *They are preserved forever*, but the children of the wicked shall be cut off" (Psalm 37:28, *NHEB*).

Speaking of the End Times...

Now the first thing to realize about Mark 13:13 and those who "endure unto the end" is that this verse does not pertain to the end of one's life, but it is referring to the "time of the end" (Daniel 12:4). This is the period known as the Great Tribulation. It is a time of great trial upon the Earth, which occurs *before* the Second Coming of Christ—the actual physical return of Christ to Earth. Jesus referred to this time just a few verses later in Mark 13:19, by saying:

> "For in those days shall be affliction, such as was not from the beginning of the creation which God created unto this time, neither shall be."

During these days there will be believers on Earth. But they will only be those who were born again *after* the Rapture of the church.

A Meeting in the Air

The Rapture is a prophetic event spoken of by the Apostle Paul, in which believers on Earth will be:

> "...caught up...to meet the Lord in the air" (1 Thessalonians 4:17).

This is mentioned in the context of 1 Thessalonians 4:13-18, where Paul comforts the church regarding the physical resurrection and gathering together of the saints to be with Christ. Although the word "rapture" itself is not in the Bible, the word for "caught up" in the Greek is translated into Latin as "rapturo." This is the origin for the term, "the Rapture."

This word "rapturo" was translated from the original Greek word "harpazo," which means to "catch up, snatch or take away." Notice that the word not only has the meaning to be caught up, but to be *taken away*.

In this event, Christian believers will specifically meet the Lord *"in the air."* It is not to be confused with Christ's physical return to Earth (also known as the Second Advent), when His feet touch the Mount of Olives in Jerusalem to set up His Millennial Kingdom (Zechariah 14:4, Revelation 19:11-16). This meeting of the Lord is "in the air," with His believers being taken up *to Heaven*. This is what sets this event apart from the time of Christ's actual return upon the Earth. It is the fulfillment of Jesus' promise, when He said:

> "In my Father's house are many mansions: if it were not so, I would have told you. I go to prepare a place for you. And if I go and prepare a place for you, *I will come again, and receive you unto myself; that where I am, there ye may be also*" (John 14:2-3).

By these words, it is evident that Jesus was speaking of coming again, to take His own to His "Father's house." It is there that the Lord has prepared "a place," which is in Heaven itself, for those who have received Him. Jesus was not referring to His coming to reign on Earth at this time *at all*. For this *catching up* is to secretly take His bride, the church, away—*before* the great trials that will occur upon the Earth.

This is in fulfillment of the Parable of the Ten Virgins—of whom five were "taken away" when the bridegroom came for them. As it is written:

> "Then shall the kingdom of heaven be likened unto ten virgins, which took their lamps, and went forth to meet the bridegroom. And five of them were wise,

and five were foolish. They that were foolish took their lamps, and took no oil with them: But the wise took oil in their vessels with their lamps...the bridegroom came; and they that were ready *went in with him to the marriage*: and *the door was shut*" (Matthew 25:1-3, 10).

Notice that those who were ready did not remain where they were—but "went in with him to the marriage" and the "door was shut." They are in sharp contrast to the other five virgins, who were not true believers at all. As Jesus said:

"Afterward came also the other virgins, saying, Lord, Lord, open to us. But he answered and said, Verily I say unto you, *I know you not*. Watch therefore, for ye know neither the day nor the hour wherein the Son of man cometh" (Matthew 25:11-13).

First the Righteous

Again, this is *not* a picture of Jesus' physical return to Earth. For when Jesus returns to Earth in the Second Advent, He will send out His angels and they will separate and gather the *wicked first—then the righteous*. As Jesus said in the Parable of the Wheat and the Tares:

"Let both grow together until the harvest: and in the time of harvest I will say to the reapers, *Gather ye together first the tares* [the wicked], and bind them in bundles to burn them: but gather the wheat [the righteous] into my barn" (Matthew 13:30, see also 40-43).

But in the Parable of the Ten Virgins we see that the righteous are taken away *first,* separated from the wicked.

This is because the *catching up* or the Rapture of the church is the event that is being prophesied in that parable.

For in the Rapture, the righteous are taken away from the wicked in deliverance. In the Second Coming of Christ, the wicked are taken away from the righteous in judgment.

Also of significance regarding the five virgins left behind —who were imitations of the true—is the fact that they never saw the bridegroom. This is obvious because the "door was shut," and He was hidden from their eyes. That's why they said: "Lord, Lord, open to us." They could not see the bridegroom because when Christ comes in the Rapture for His bride, the church, *He is hidden to unbelievers*. But in the Second Coming of Christ, *He is visible to all*, because He is coming to set up His Kingdom upon Earth. As it is written:

> "...every eye shall see him, and they also which pierced him: and all kindreds of the earth shall wail because of him. Even so, Amen" (Revelation 1:7).

Door of Deliverance

Notice how the five wise virgins went through a "door." It's through this door that Jesus said he would deliver His believing church:

> "I know thy works: behold, I have set before thee *an open door*, and no man can shut it: for thou hast a little strength, and hast kept my word, and hast not denied my name...*I also will keep thee from the hour of temptation, which shall come upon all the world, to try them that dwell upon the earth*" (Revelation 3:8, 10).

In these verses, Jesus says that He has set "an open door" before His church and that He will deliver her from the trial that "shall come upon all the world." This is also the door of deliverance that the Apostle John saw, for after writing to the churches in Revelation 2-3, he stated in the next chapter:

> "After this I looked, and, behold, *a door* was opened in heaven: and the first voice which I heard was as it were of a trumpet talking with me; which said, *Come up hither*, and I will shew thee things which must be hereafter. *And immediately I was in the spirit...*" (Revelation 4:1-2).

It is important to notice the analogy here. John looks up, sees *a door in Heaven*, hears a voice *like a trumpet*, is *caught up to it* and is *instantly in the Spirit*. This is a strikingly clear picture of the Rapture itself.

Then John is told he will be shown the "things which must be hereafter." After what? It's after the catching up of the church, which John himself symbolized in these verses.

From this point on, the church is not mentioned on Earth in the Book of Revelation *at all* (throughout all the wrath and judgments), until her return *with Christ* in chapter nineteen:

> "Let us be glad and rejoice, and give honour to him: for the marriage of the Lamb is come, and his wife hath made herself ready. And to her was granted that she should be arrayed in fine linen, clean and white: for the fine linen is the righteousness of saints" (Revelation 19:7-8).

The reason why the church is not mentioned again on Earth until this point is because she had been taken away prior to the Tribulation period, as all these verses concur.

For throughout Revelation 2-3, we see the expression:

> "He that hath an ear, let him hear what the Spirit saith unto *the churches*" (Revelation 2:7, 11, 17, 29; 3:6, 13, 22).

Yet after John is taken up through a door to Heaven, we only read:

> "If any man have an ear, let him hear" (Revelation 13:9).

There is no longer any reference to the church, which has already been "caught up" (1 Thessalonians 4:17) to Christ. As Jesus said, "I will come again, *and receive you unto myself*" (John 14:3).

Once again, this is a picture of being *taken away* to Jesus, not returning to Earth with Him. The saints will indeed be returning to reign with Jesus, but not yet—for now is the time to receive their heavenly rewards (1 Corinthians 3:12-15).

Deliverance, Then Destruction

It is only *after* the church is "caught up" that the world enters the period of time known as the Tribulation (the last half of which is called the Great Tribulation). This was made evident when Jesus declared:

> "As it was in the days of Noah, even so it will also be in the days of the Son of Man. They ate, they drank, they married, and they were given in marriage *until the day that Noah entered into the ship*, and the flood came and destroyed them all. Likewise, even as it was in the days of Lot: they ate, they drank, they bought, they sold, they planted, they built; but in *the day that Lot went out from Sodom*, it rained fire and

sulfur from the sky and destroyed them all. *It will be the same way in the day that the Son of Man is revealed*" (Luke 17:26-30, *WEB*).

Notice the order of events here: It is *deliverance* (first), then *destruction*. This order demonstrates that those "caught up" *had* to be taken away *before* the Tribulation. Jesus could have used any pictures from the Old Testament, yet He chose to use the analogies of Noah and Lot.

Noah entered the ship, *then* came the flood. Lot went out from Sodom, *then* came the fire and sulfur. Both men were delivered from the coming judgment of God's wrath. This is why the angel who was sent to destroy Sodom, when speaking to Lot to escape to a nearby city, said:

"Hurry, escape...for *I can't do anything until you get there*" (Genesis 19:22, *WEB*).

We can see by these Scriptures that it is the catching up and taking away of God's saints that *triggers* many end-time events.

Those who will not turn to Christ now may very well be found remaining on Earth *after* the church has been "caught up" in these Last Days. They will still have the opportunity to repent and receive Christ during the Tribulation that follows. Yet, as it is written:

"Alas! for that day is great, so that none is like it: it is even the time of Jacob's trouble; but he shall be saved out of it" (Jeremiah 30:7).

Jacob's Trouble

The Scripture speaks of the Great Tribulation as "Jacob's trouble" because of the difficulty Israel (or Jacob) will face at this time. But it is during these troublesome days that Israel will turn to the Lord Jesus and receive the Messiah, whom they—as a nation—had rejected. For as mentioned in this study, it was prophesied in the Old Testament:

> "I will pour on David's house and on the inhabitants of Jerusalem the spirit of grace and of supplication. *They will look to me whom they have pierced*; and they shall mourn for him as one mourns for his only son, and will grieve bitterly for him as one grieves for his firstborn" (Zechariah 12:10, *WEB*).

And as the Apostle Paul wrote:

> "...and so all Israel will be saved. Even as it is written, 'There will come out of Zion the Deliverer, and he will turn away ungodliness from Jacob. This is my covenant with them, when I will take away their sins'" (Romans 11:26-27, *WEB*).

So the prophecy in Scripture is that God will restore the Kingdom to Israel and fulfill the many promises to her concerning the Messiah, Jesus. This is another reason why the church is "caught up" before this time. For in God's dispensation, He is turning His eyes back on Israel. For Jesus said of Israel in her rejection of Him:

> "Therefore say I unto you, The kingdom of God shall be taken from you, and given to a nation bringing forth the fruits thereof" (Matthew 21:43).

This was fulfilled by the birth of the church, where there is neither Jew nor Gentile (Galatians 3:28). In fact, of more importance than any national status is the Spiritual rebirth. For to be in Christ (2 Corinthians 5:17) is to become a son or daughter of the living God (Galatians 4:6).

But the Lord has an order and dispensation for His events. The Jews were initially meant to be the carriers of the Good News to all. However, in their rejection of Christ, the Gospel has been spread upon the Earth by the believing church.

Yet in these end-time days, God will revive Israel in preparation for His earthly Millennial reign from Jerusalem. For after the fullness of the Gentiles come into the Kingdom, Israel itself will also come in. As it is written:

> "For I would not, brethren, that ye should be ignorant of this mystery, lest ye should be wise in your own conceits; that blindness in part is happened to Israel, until the fulness of the Gentiles be come in. And so all Israel shall be saved..." (Romans 11:25-26).

This is why we read that the Lord is turning His attention back to the Jewish nation (and not to the church, which has been taken away) during the Tribulation. As it is written:

> "And I heard the number of them which were sealed: and there were sealed an hundred and forty and four thousand *of all the tribes of the children of Israel*...After this I beheld, and, lo, a great multitude, which no man could number, of all nations, and kindreds, and people, and tongues, stood before the throne, and before the Lamb, clothed with white robes...These are they which came out of great tribulation, and have washed their robes, and made them white in the blood of the Lamb" (Revelation 7:4, 9, 14).

It is thus revealed that the Lord is preserving a remnant of Israel and saving multitudes even during the Tribulation. For

God will be calling all to repent and receive Him. Indeed, part of the reason for the Tribulation itself is to cause the proud upon Earth to be humbled unto salvation.

Daniel's 70th Week: For the Jewish People

The Tribulation is actually the fulfillment of what is known as Daniel's Seventieth Week. The following verses are a little complicated but they are worth noting. Although I will be sharing of *times and years* here, I am in no way speculating on when Christ will return for the Rapture. For

> "...of that day and that hour knoweth no man, no, not the angels which are in heaven, neither the Son, but the Father" (Mark 13:32).

That is why Scripture calls it the "blessed hope" (Titus 2:13), as Christ could come for His church *at any time.*

But the following verses are not about the Rapture at all; they are about the Tribulation, before the Second Coming of Christ to Earth. I'm merely sharing that Christ's *first coming* (riding into Jerusalem) was prophesied to the very day in the Book of Daniel, which also speaks of the final Tribulation—its duration and with whom it finds its fulfillment.

Keep in mind when we look at the following prophecy that a *week of years* to the Jews is 7 years (just like a week of days). Thus *seventy weeks* of years would be 70 X 7 or 490 years. In these verses of Daniel, the angel Gabriel came to speak to him concerning his people (the Jews) and the End Times. As it is written:

> "Seventy weeks are decreed on your people and on your holy city, to finish disobedience, to make an

end of sins, to make reconciliation for iniquity, to bring in everlasting righteousness, to seal up vision and prophecy, and to anoint the most holy" (Daniel 9:24, *WEB*).

What these verses are stating is that 70 weeks or 490 years are decreed "on your people and on your holy city," referring to the *Jews* and *Jerusalem*. This prophecy is stating that by the end of this 490-year timeline, there will be "an end of sins." There will also be "everlasting righteousness" and "reconciliation for iniquity." This Scripture further declares that within the 70 weeks or 490 years, there will be the anointing of "the most holy" and "vision and prophecy" will be sealed up.

In other words, after 490 years, sin will be atoned for and the Messiah will set up His Millennial Kingdom! Thankfully, our sin has been atoned for in Jesus' *first* coming—by His death on the cross and resurrection. But as of yet, we have not seen all these words fulfilled. For the Messiah, the King, has not yet been received by the Jews, to "anoint the most holy." The sealing up of "vision and prophecy" has not come to pass either, as there are many prophecies yet to be fulfilled before Christ's return to reign on Earth. Certainly the bringing in of "everlasting righteousness" has not been fulfilled on Earth—yet. One needs only watch the news to know this fact. These are still pending for Christ's return (Second Advent) to Earth.

And although Jesus has died for our sins and thus made "an end of sins," His New Covenant has not been received by the Jewish nation as a whole.

The Scripture in Daniel continues:

"Know therefore and discern that *from the going out of the commandment to restore and build Jerusalem to the Anointed One, the prince,* will be *seven weeks* and *sixty-two weeks.* It will be built again, with street and moat, even in troubled times. After the sixty-two weeks the Anointed One will be cut off, and will have nothing" (Daniel 9:25-26, *WEB*).

So we read that after the "commandment to restore and build Jerusalem" (this was in the twentieth year of Artaxerxes the king, being 445 BC—see Nehemiah 2:1, 5-6), there will be 7 weeks and 62 weeks (or 69 weeks of years or 69 X 7 years, equaling 483 years). After this "the Anointed One will be cut off, and will have nothing." Note how it's written that after the "sixty-two weeks," "the Anointed One will be cut off." But it is not *just* "sixty-two weeks." For the prophecy is speaking of first the "seven weeks" and then the "sixty-two weeks"—in progression. The sum of these (7 + 62) are the 69 weeks or 483 years mentioned.

These 483 years from the "commandment to restore and build Jerusalem" led directly up to the "Anointed One," who is, of course, *Jesus.* What an amazing prophecy of the timing of Christ's first coming and suffering! What a verse showing Christ's love for us, in that "the Anointed One will be cut off, and will have *nothing.*" Jesus in His death had nothing so that He could give us *everything.* As it is written:

"For ye know the grace of our Lord Jesus Christ, that, though he was rich, yet for your sakes he became poor, that ye through his poverty might be rich" (2 Corinthians 8:9).

What a powerful summation of Christ's passion, written hundreds of years before its fulfillment!

For these Scriptures prophesy the Messiah being "cut off" after the fulfillment of the 69th week (7 weeks and 62 weeks equals 69 weeks or 483 years). The time period for the start of this prophecy "from the going out of the commandment to restore and build Jerusalem" to "the Anointed One, the prince" has been shown to be exactly 483 years—*to the day* —when Jesus rode into Jerusalem as King (Luke 19:28-40). (A biblical year is counted as 360 days. See Daniel 12:7; Revelation 11:2-3; 12:6, 12:14; 13:5.) It was then, for the first time in His ministry, that Christ presented Himself to the Jewish nation, among Messianic shouts of "Hosanna to the Son of David" (Matthew 21:9) and "Blessed be the King that cometh in the name of the Lord." As it is written:

> "And when he was come nigh, even now at the descent of the mount of Olives, the whole multitude of the disciples began to rejoice and praise God with a loud voice for all the mighty works that they had seen; Saying, Blessed be the King that cometh in the name of the Lord: peace in heaven, and glory in the highest. And some of the Pharisees from among the multitude said unto him, Master, rebuke thy disciples. And he answered and said unto them, *I tell you that, if these should hold their peace, the stones would immediately cry out*" (Luke 19:37-38).

The stones would cry out because this was the official day of Christ's presentation to Jerusalem and to Israel. This was the day to receive their Messiah! But as Daniel prophesied, He would be "cut off"—and this happened *only four days later!* For the elders of the Jews did not receive Him. And just as the sacrificial lamb was set apart for four days to be inspected before it was slaughtered, so it was the case with Christ in His sacrifice for us (Exodus 12:1, 6).

This prophecy of Daniel is one of the most amazing fulfilled prophecies in all the Bible. It is why Jesus wept and spoke to the Jews *on that very day*:

> "When he came near, he saw the city and wept over it, saying, 'If you, even you, had known *today* the things which belong to your peace! But now, they are hidden from your eyes. For the days will come on you when your enemies will throw up a barricade against you, surround you, hem you in on every side, and will dash you and your children within you to the ground. They will not leave in you one stone on another, *because you didn't know the time of your visitation*'" (Luke 19:41-44, *WEB*).

So at the rejection of the Messiah by the Jews, the 70 weeks of years (or 490 years) that are appointed for Israel STOPPED—having come to the prophesied 483 years. And because they refused to receive their King, the words Jesus spoke were fulfilled:

> "The kingdom of God shall be taken from you, and given to a nation bringing forth the fruits thereof" (Matthew 21:43).

This left the remaining 7 years on the table—still pending, for now—to reach the fulfillment of the 490 years appointed for the Jews. And this clock has been stopped at 483 years during the entire period of the church. This is because the Kingdom has come to the Gentiles through Israel's rejection of the Messiah. But once the church is "caught up," this clock of God will begin ticking again! For it is during this time that the Lord will turn His eyes back toward Israel and fulfill His end-time prophecies to that nation.

And since God is so faithful to Israel, will He not also be faithful to keep His children in salvation—those who have called upon Him and received Him by faith? Indeed, God is *always* faithful. As it is written:

"God is faithful, by whom ye were called unto the fellowship of his Son Jesus Christ our Lord" (1 Corinthians 1:9).

Our verses of Daniel continue, as we read the statement:

"...the people of the prince that shall come shall destroy the city and the sanctuary; and the end thereof shall be with a flood, and unto the end of the war desolations are determined" (Daniel 9:26).

This verse depicts how the city of Jerusalem has been destroyed many times over since Christ was "cut off." The "prince" in this case is not speaking of Jesus but of the coming Antichrist, as it refers to "the people of the prince that shall come." He is the one who will make a covenant or agreement with many for a week (7 years):

"He will make a firm covenant with many for one week. In the middle of the week he will cause the sacrifice and the offering to cease. On the wing of abominations will come one who makes desolate; and even to the decreed full end, wrath will be poured out on the desolate" (Daniel 9:27, *WEB*).

Again, the "he" in this verse is the Antichrist. He will make a "firm covenant with many for one week" that will bring about a temporary false peace (1 Thessalonians 5:3). In the middle of this week, he "will cause the sacrifice and the offering to cease" from the temple that the Jews will build at this time. This "one week" is our last 7 years which, when added to our stopped clock at 483 years, completes the 490 years or 70 weeks of Daniel's prophecy.

These last 7 years are the time of the Tribulation itself and they are still waiting to be fulfilled. "In the middle of the week" of those 7 years (or in three and a half years), the Antichrist will "cause the sacrifice and the offering to cease," as he "makes desolate." This begins *the Great Tribulation* and is why the Scripture repeatedly speaks of this time as three and a half years—or "a time, times, and an half," "42 months," or "1,260 days"—with a biblical year always being 360 days (see Daniel 12:7; Revelation 11:2-3; 12:6, 12:14; 13:5). Jesus referred to these verses in Daniel when He said:

> "When, therefore, you see *the abomination of desolation, which was spoken of through Daniel the prophet*, standing in the holy place (let the reader understand), then let those who are in Judea flee to the mountains...for then there will be great suffering, such as has not been from the beginning of the world until now, no, nor ever will be" (Matthew 24:15-16, 21, *WEB*).

These verses are unusual in that they contain the words:

"...(let the reader understand)..."

Why would the Scripture ever be worded this way? I know of no other place in the entire Bible were we find this little side note, speaking to *the reader.*

But it is addressed in this way because those who see these events at that time will be looking to the Scripture. And this verse is written specifically to those left behind upon an Earth *ready to go into its greatest trial of all time—the Great Tribulation.*

To sum it all up: Israel was promised 490 years until the Kingdom of the Messiah is fulfilled. The clock stopped at 483 years when the Jews rejected their Messiah. But at the end of days, the last amount of 7 years will be fulfilled in the Tribulation—the last half of which is called The Great Tribulation. It is a time of great trial upon the earth but at this time the Lord will cause Israel to turn to Him. The church, having been "caught up," is not mentioned in Daniel's prophecy at all, as this is the time of Israel's restoration. The dispensation of the church has reached its fulfillment with the fullness of the Gentiles being brought into the church, having been "caught up" before Daniel's Seventieth Week. *(See page 457 for the accompanying end-time chart to this chapter.)*

A False Peace—The Earth will Stagger

As mentioned, there will be people who receive salvation during the Tribulation. This takes place along with the setting apart and sealing of the 144,000 Jews at that time (Revelation 7:4). Those saved during the Tribulation will face great persecution and many unusual trials. The Scriptures declare it to be an unparalleled period of time when the Lord's righteous judgments and wrath will come upon the entire planet, due to the rebellion of its people toward God.

And believers who are saved during this time will be persecuted at a tremendous level. For although believers have been persecuted throughout the centuries, it will be a unique time about which Jesus said:

> "Then shall they deliver you up to be afflicted, and shall kill you: and ye shall be hated of all nations for my name's sake. And then shall many be offended,

367

and shall betray one another, and shall hate one another. And many false prophets shall rise, and shall deceive many. And because iniquity shall abound, the love of many shall wax cold. But he that shall endure unto the end, the same shall be saved" (Matthew 24:9-13).

These verses reveal the condition of the world *after* the church has been "caught up." For all nations remaining after the Rapture will be manifesting their hatred toward Christ. This is why Jesus said that "ye shall be hated of *all nations* for my name's sake."

Notice the context of our verse pertaining to "...he that shall endure unto the end, the same shall be saved" (Mark 13:13, also Matthew 10:22-23, 24:13). As mentioned earlier, its context is during these end-time events and is about being delivered out of them. But we will get to that topic in just a bit.

This "unity" of those who have rejected Christ is what will bring about a false peace at the beginning of the Tribulation. This is the time prophesied by the Apostle John:

"And I saw, and behold a white horse: and he that sat on him had a bow; and a crown was given unto him: and he went forth conquering, and to conquer" (Revelation 6:2).

This conqueror *is not* Jesus but the Antichrist, who shall conquer in a misguided "peace," which is an imitation of Christ's Millennial peace to come. It will end with the following three horsemen of: *war* (see Revelation 6:4), *famine* (see Revelation 6:5-6), and *death* (see Revelation 6:8) —during this Tribulation period.

For although the Tribulation will begin with a time of "peace," its latter half will end in utter destruction. As mentioned previously, this is the three and a half years known as the Great Tribulation. And as the Apostle Paul wrote:

> "But of the times and the seasons, brethren, ye have no need that I write unto you. For yourselves know perfectly that the day of the Lord so cometh as a thief in the night. *For when they shall say, Peace and safety; then sudden destruction cometh upon them*, as travail upon a woman with child; and *they shall not escape*. But ye, brethren, are not in darkness, that that day should overtake you as a thief...*For God hath not appointed us to wrath, but to obtain salvation by our Lord Jesus Christ*" (1 Thessalonians 5:1-4, 9).

Notice how Paul did not include believers in those times of destruction when he wrote: "when *they* shall say" and that "sudden destruction cometh upon *them*" and "*they* shall not escape." How could the church escape a global tribulation without being removed from it? Indeed, this is why Paul also said: "God hath not appointed us to wrath, but to obtain salvation by our Lord Jesus Christ."

So it is during this time that the Antichrist or *he who opposes Christ* will arise. But to be clear, the entire seven-year period of the Tribulation is considered a time of the Lord's judgments. For the Lord Himself will give those who have rejected Him over to a lie in receiving the false peace of the Antichrist. As it is written:

> "Because of this, God sends them a powerful delusion, that *they should believe a lie*, that they all might be judged who didn't believe the truth, but

had pleasure in unrighteousness" (2 Thessalonians 2:11-12, *WEB*).

The Scriptures clearly define this time to be a demonstration of God's judgment upon Earth. As we read in Revelation:

"For the great day of his wrath is come; and who shall be able to stand?" (Revelation 6:17).

And it is written:

"The earth will stagger like a drunken man, and will sway back and forth like a hammock..." (Isaiah 24:20, *WEB*).

As Jesus also said:

"The stars of heaven shall fall, and the powers that are in heaven shall be shaken" (Mark 13:25).

And as it is written in Hebrews:

"Whose voice then shook the earth: but now he hath promised, saying, Yet once more I shake not the earth only, but also heaven" (Hebrews 12:26).

These Scriptures reveal that the Earth and the heavens (stars, etc.) will be shaken from their balance! This is entirely in agreement with the words of Jesus, quoted previously:

"For in those days shall be affliction, such as was not *from the beginning of the creation which God created unto this time, neither shall be*" (Mark 13:19).

Worse Than the Flood of Noah!

Jesus said that the affliction of this time will be *worse* than anything yet to have occurred on the Earth from the beginning of creation! When I think of the worst event that has ever happened to the planet thus far, I think of the worldwide flood in the days of Noah (Genesis 6:16-7:24). What could *ever* be of greater destruction than the flood? How about the planet's complete removal from its orbit in the heavens?

Also consider this: Although the entire population will not be wiped out during the Tribulation as it was during the flood, except for eight people (Genesis 7:13)—the population of Earth in this modern day is *much greater* than that of the days of Noah. This means that *more will perish* in the Great Tribulation than ever did in the flood! Scripture confirms this fact by saying that the judgments in the Tribulation will make man more rare than fine gold! As Isaiah said:

> "Look, the day of the LORD comes, cruel, with wrath and fierce anger; to make the land a desolation, and to destroy its sinners out of it. For the stars of the sky and its constellations will not give their light. The sun will be darkened in its going forth, and the moon will not cause its light to shine. I will punish the world for their evil, and the wicked for their iniquity. I will cause the arrogance of the proud to cease, and will humble the haughtiness of the terrible. *I will make people more rare than fine gold, even a person than the pure gold of Ophir.* Therefore I will make the heavens tremble, and *the earth will be shaken out of its place* in the wrath of the LORD of hosts, and in the day of his fierce anger" (Isaiah 13:9-13, *NHEB*).

We learn from these Scriptures that man will be destroyed to such a great extent as to be rarer than "the pure gold of Ophir." This was a particularly fine and scarce gold in the ancient world. Again, we read that the Earth itself will be "shaken out of its place" by the "wrath of the LORD."

Deliverance in Christ

Therefore, is it any wonder that believers, saved before this time, are to be "caught up" (1 Thessalonians 4:17) and taken away—before the demonstration of God's wrath during the Tribulation? Why are they spared? It's because Jesus has *already* borne their judgment, wrath and punishment upon the cross. They have received Christ and are "in Christ" and won't be punished for what has already been forgiven by Jesus' atonement for them. For God keeps the covenant that He has made with us, who are *in Christ.* As it is written:

> "The punishment that brought our peace was on him" (Isaiah 53:5, *WEB*).

And as it is also stated:

> "There is therefore now no condemnation to them which are in Christ Jesus" (Romans 8:1).

And again, as the Apostle Paul declared in 1 Thessalonians:

> "God hath not appointed us to wrath, but to obtain salvation by our Lord Jesus Christ" (1 Thessalonians 5:9).

This is why it is so important to accept Christ and His gift of salvation *today,* before these events come to pass! For it is written:

> "Behold, now is the acceptable time. Behold, now is the day of salvation" (2 Corinthians 6:2).

Enduring to the End

Now let us get back to our verse:

"He that shall endure unto the end, the same shall be saved" (Mark 13:13).

This Scripture's context is referring to those believers who receive salvation *during* the Great Tribulation. They will be delivered from those trials by the Second Coming of Christ.

As mentioned, the Bible goes out of its way to say that the Great Tribulation is exactly three and a half years (Daniel 12:7; Revelation 11:2-3; 12:6, 12:14; 13:5). This is stated to comfort those believers on Earth at that time—that there will be an end to their suffering, manifested by the glorious Second Coming of Christ. This is in keeping with the words of Mark 13:20:

"And except that the Lord had shortened those days, *no flesh should be saved*: but for the elect's sake, whom he hath chosen, he hath shortened the days."

In this verse, we realize that the usage and context of the word "saved" is not speaking of salvation itself but of *survival*. It is stating that if the Lord did not shorten the days of the Great Tribulation, no one on Earth would be *saved from it* or *survive it!* But the days will get shortened for the sake of the elect—those believers who accepted Christ during the Tribulation.

In the same manner and context, survival through the Tribulation and to the Second Coming of Christ is the meaning behind our verse: "He that shall endure unto the end, the same shall be saved" (Mark 13:13).

This Scripture pertains to those believers who will be physically enduring to the end of the Tribulation, until the return of Christ.

For the Tribulation does not end in the compete and utter destruction of mankind and of the Earth; rather, it ends with the return of Christ and His saints and with the setting up of His Millennial Kingdom (Isaiah 65:25, Daniel 2:44, Revelation 20:1-6). Indeed, it is the planet's transformation and reclamation to the glory of God!

Jesus spoke to His disciples about His Millennial Kingdom:

"And Jesus said unto them, Verily I say unto you, That ye which have followed me, in the regeneration when the Son of man shall sit in the throne of his glory, ye also shall sit upon twelve thrones, judging the twelve tribes of Israel" (Matthew 19:28).

Sheep, Goats & Fruits of Faith

When Jesus returns to set up His Kingdom, He will separate the sheep from the goats—dividing those who accepted Him from those who rejected Him. These "sheep" are the people who survived the Tribulation, having received Jesus as their Lord and Savior. And the Millennial Kingdom will begin *only* with His sheep. As it is written:

"When the Son of man shall come in his glory, and all the holy angels with him, then shall he sit upon the throne of his glory: And before him shall be gathered all nations: and he shall separate them one from another, as a shepherd divideth his sheep from the goats: And he shall set the sheep on his right hand, but the goats on the left.

"Then shall the King say unto them on his right hand, Come, ye blessed of my Father, inherit the kingdom prepared for you from the foundation of the world: For I was an hungred, and ye gave me meat: I was thirsty, and ye gave me drink: I was a stranger, and ye took me in: Naked, and ye clothed me: I was sick, and ye visited me: I was in prison, and ye came unto me. Then shall the righteous answer him, saying, Lord, when saw we thee an hungred, and fed thee? or thirsty, and gave thee drink? When saw we thee a stranger, and took thee in? or naked, and clothed thee? Or when saw we thee sick, or in prison, and came unto thee? And the King shall answer and say unto them, Verily I say unto you, Inasmuch as ye have done it unto one of the least of these my brethren, ye have done it unto me.

"Then shall he say also unto them on the left hand, Depart from me, ye cursed, into everlasting fire, prepared for the devil and his angels: For I was an hungred, and ye gave me no meat: I was thirsty, and ye gave me no drink: I was a stranger, and ye took me not in: naked, and ye clothed me not: sick, and in prison, and ye visited me not. Then shall they also answer him, saying, Lord, when saw we thee an hungred, or athirst, or a stranger, or naked, or sick, or in prison, and did not minister unto thee? Then shall he answer them, saying, Verily I say unto you, Inasmuch as ye did it not to one of the least of these, ye did it not to me. And these shall go away into everlasting punishment: but the righteous into life eternal" (Matthew 25:31-46).

It has always been amazing to me to find in these verses that the righteous reply to the Lord by saying:

"Lord, when saw we thee an hungred, *and fed thee?*"

And the wicked reply:

"Lord, when saw we thee an hungred...*and did not minister unto thee?*"

Within these two dialogues we see the vast difference between the humility of the righteous and the arrogance of the wicked. This clearly reveals the contrast in their natures.

For by their fruits, it shall be exposed—those who indeed knew and received the Lord and those who rejected Him. And though these verses focus on the *fruit* of salvation, it is still *faith* in the heart that the Lord is seeking. This is made apparent by the words of Jesus:

"Nevertheless when the Son of man cometh, shall he find *faith* on the earth?" (Matthew 18:8).

And of those "goats," who did not receive Him, Jesus declared:

"...these shall go away into everlasting punishment: but the righteous into life eternal" (Matthew 25:46).

For although the Tribulation begins with the wicked remaining upon the Earth (after the Rapture), the Millennium begins with the righteous remaining upon the Earth (after the judgment of the wicked).

A Millennial Peace

And the Millennium, which is the one-thousand-year reign of Christ on Earth (Revelation 20:4-6), will be a time of blessed peace upon the planet. There will even be peace among the animal kingdom, as it is written:

> "The wolf will live with the lamb, and the leopard will lie down with the young goat; The calf and the young lion will graze together; and a little child will lead them. The cow and the bear will graze. Their young ones will lie down together. The lion will eat straw like the ox. The nursing child will play near a cobra's hole, and the weaned child will put his hand on the viper's den. They will not hurt nor destroy in all my holy mountain; for the earth will be full of the knowledge of the LORD, as the waters cover the sea. And in that day there will be a root of Jesse, one who stands up to rule over the peoples; to him will the nations seek, and his resting place will be glorious" (Isaiah 11:6-10, *NHEB*).

This "root of Jesse" is Jesus Himself. How wonderful! This is a time when: "They will not hurt nor destroy in all my holy mountain." For the Lord is demonstrating what His reign—and not man's—looks like.

I'm one who has always been saddened by the way animals hunt and eat one another. Yet by this Scripture, we know that this was never God's original intent for His creation. For it states: "The lion will eat straw like the ox." What a precious promise! The Lord will restore all creation itself from the fall of mankind's sin, as it is written:

> "For the creature was made subject to vanity, not willingly, but by reason of him who hath subjected the same in hope, Because the creature itself also shall be delivered from the bondage of corruption

into the glorious liberty of the children of God"
(Romans 8:20-21).

A Millennial Preview

Now we who are alive and remain to be "caught up" to meet the Lord in the air are among those who will be returning with Jesus when He comes to Earth to set up His Kingdom. Our home will still be Heaven itself (John 14:2), but we will join in the work of the Lord upon Earth. For Christ will reign in the Millennium with His resurrected saints! As it is written:

> "And I saw heaven opened, and behold a white horse; and he that sat upon him was called Faithful and True, and in righteousness he doth judge and make war. His eyes were as a flame of fire, and on his head were many crowns; and he had a name written, that no man knew, but he himself. And he was clothed with a vesture dipped in blood: and his name is called The Word of God. And the armies which were in heaven followed him upon white horses, clothed in fine linen, white and clean" (Revelation 19:11-14).

We will reign with Jesus, among those who had turned to Him during the Tribulation. They will still be in their natural state, having survived the trials of the Tribulation. This is similar to the snapshot we see in the gospels. For when Jesus was transfigured on the mountain, Moses and Elijah appeared and spoke with Him before the eyes of Peter, James and John:

> "After six days, Jesus took with him Peter, James, and John his brother, and brought them up into a high

mountain by themselves. He was changed before them. His face shone like the sun, and his garments became as white as the light. Behold, Moses and Elijah appeared to them talking with him..." (Matthew 17:1-3, *WEB*).

In this biblical account, we can see a preview of the Millennium itself—a sort of "coming attraction."

We have Jesus revealed in glory along with Moses and Elijah—with Peter, James and John admiring Him while in the earthly tents of their natural bodies. Oh, how wonderful:

"When he comes in that day to be *glorified in his saints* and to be *admired among all those who have believed*" (2 Thessalonians 1:10, *WEB*).

And the Millennium will ultimately culminate into the new heavens and the new Earth, re-created by the Lord, in which sin and death will be completely eradicated from the universe. As it is written:

"Nevertheless we, according to his promise, look for new heavens and a new earth, wherein dwelleth righteousness" (2 Peter 3:13).

Having said *all* this, let me share a little more about the verse with which we started this chapter, namely:

"He that shall endure unto the end, the same shall be saved" (Mark 13:13, also Matthew 10:22-23, 24:13).

It has already been stated that the context of this verse is in the period of the Tribulation and is about being saved from it. Those believers who are alive during that time, enduring through it, will see the end of those days and the trials of the Great Tribulation. Indeed, these believers will see the triumphant return of Christ to the Earth, upon the Mount of Olives! (Zechariah 14:4).

But let's cover every aspect of this verse...

Confirmed to the End

Who are they who *spiritually* endure to the end? Are they not the believers in Christ, who have been born of God and of His Spirit? For as previously mentioned in this study, the Apostle John wrote:

> "Whatsoever is born of God overcometh the world: and this is the victory that overcometh the world, even our faith. Who is he that overcometh the world, but he that believeth that Jesus is the Son of God" (1 John 5:4-5).

Why do they overcome? Because they have been "born of God." You see, endurance is a work of the Holy Spirit in the believer. As the Apostle Paul wrote:

> "So that ye come behind in no gift; waiting for the coming of our Lord Jesus Christ: Who shall also *confirm you unto the end*, that ye may be blameless in the day of our Lord Jesus Christ. *God is faithful*, by whom ye were called unto the fellowship of his Son Jesus Christ our Lord" (1 Corinthians 1:7-9).

Do you see how "God is faithful" in confirming you to the end? This is why God gave us the Holy Spirit to live within us. He knew we couldn't retain this salvation on our own. But unlike the Old Covenant that was external, the New Covenant is God saving us and keeping us *internally*!

Do you not see how much God has done to save you? The Father set the plan in motion, the Son died for your sins to save you, and the Spirit has come to change your heart and *keep* you! One God (in three persons) has given such a "great salvation" (Hebrews 2:3).

In these verses of 1 Corinthians 1:7-9, the word used for "confirm," in "Who shall also *confirm* you unto the end," also means to: "establish, guarantee, secure, make sure" according to the original Greek. It is sometimes translated as "strengthen" as well. But did you notice that word "secure" in the definition? It's part of the very title of this book: The Rose of God & The Eternal *Security* Found in Christ. For this verse in 1 Corinthians can also be translated:

> "...Who shall also *secure* you unto the end, that ye may be blameless in the day of our Lord Jesus Christ."

Saints, if that is not security in Christ, *then I don't know how it can ever be said more clearly!* Nevertheless, this verse can also be translated:

> "...Who shall also *guarantee* you unto the end."

Surely the promise of our security in Christ is declared for us in Scripture! Now this word "confirm" is also translated in some Bibles as "sustain."

Having played guitar for many years, I can relate to that translation. For I appreciate how good it is to have an instrument with nice sustain, one that can hold a note for a long time.

And how much better this is with God! He will lovingly hold you and "*sustain* you unto the end."

Chapter 34

If We Deny Him, He Will Deny Us?

The Division of Believer & Unbeliever

Paul the Apostle said in 2 Timothy 2:12:

> "If we deny Him, He will deny us."

But was he speaking about Christians in this verse? As mentioned in many of the previous Scriptures of this study, those who deny and reject the Lord *never* had salvation in their hearts in the first place. For:

> "Who is a liar but he that denieth that Jesus is the Christ? He is antichrist, that denieth the Father and the Son. Whosoever denieth the Son, the same hath not the Father" (1 John 2:22-23).

And again:

"They went out from us, *but they were not of us*; for if they had been of us, they would have continued with us: but they went out, that they might be made manifest *that they were not all of us*" (1 John 2:19).

Regarding this denial, Jesus said in Matthew 10:32-36:

"Whosoever therefore shall confess me before men, him will I confess also before my Father which is in heaven. But whosoever shall deny me before men, him will I also deny before my Father which is in heaven. Think not that I am come to send peace on earth: I came not to send peace, but a sword. For I am come to set a man at variance against his father, and the daughter against her mother, and the daughter in law against her mother in law. And a man's foes shall be they of his own household" (Similar words can be found in Luke 9:26, 12:9 and Mark 8:38).

These opposing fruits of the heart, between believer and unbeliever, cause such division that Jesus could say: "I came not to send peace, but a sword...and a man's foes shall be they of his own household."

These Scriptures clearly reveal the difference between those who believe and "confess" and those who do not believe and "deny."

That's why the verse: "If we deny Him, He will deny us" (2 Timothy 2:12) is not referring to saved Christians losing their salvation—but to unbelievers rejecting the salvation offered them in Christ (even if they *appear* as real Christians for a season).

Denial vs Faithlessness—Judas & Peter

You see, to deny the Lord is to reject Him. That is what Judas did. As it is written:

> "And while he yet spake, behold a multitude, and he that was called Judas, one of the twelve, went before them, and drew near unto Jesus to kiss him. But Jesus said unto him, Judas, betrayest thou the Son of man with a kiss?" (Luke 22:47-48).

But with Peter, it was a different situation. At the time of Jesus' crucifixion, Peter replied to those questioning him:

> "I know not this man of whom ye speak" (Mark 14:71).

However, he was not *rejecting* Jesus within the heart. Peter still believed in the Lord and still loved Him. He replied with those words because he was afraid. Although Peter denied Jesus outwardly out of fear, he never did it inwardly. That's why he wept over it later. As it is written:

> "And Peter remembered the word of Jesus, which said unto him, Before the cock crow, thou shalt deny me thrice. *And he went out, and wept bitterly*" (Matthew 26:75).

Peter may have been faithless in his denial at that moment, but he didn't deny Christ *Himself—not in his heart.*

If the verse: "If we deny Him, He will deny us" really applies to saved believers, why is it that the Lord did not deny Peter? In fact, after His resurrection, Jesus *went out of His way* to appear to Peter! And this verse tells us that Simon Peter was one of the first few who saw the risen Lord:

"And they rose up the same hour, and returned to Jerusalem, and found the eleven gathered together, and them that were with them, Saying, The Lord is risen indeed, *and hath appeared to Simon*" (Luke 24:33-34).

Peter never lost his salvation. Yet with Judas, who denied Jesus in the heart and was *never* a true believer (John 13:18, John 6:70), we find no such restoration.

For to truly deny the Lord means to reject *who He is—Himself.* A true believer cannot reject Christ in this way because he or she has been born again with a new heart that loves the Lord (John 3:6). Remember that Scripture found in Ezekiel? It is written:

"A new heart also will I give you, and a new spirit will I put within you: and I will take away the stony heart out of your flesh, and I will give you an heart of flesh" (Ezekiel 36:26).

And what about that prophecy of Jeremiah?

"And I will make an everlasting covenant with them, that I will not turn away from them, to do them good; but I will put my fear in their hearts, *that they shall not depart from me.* Yea, I will rejoice over them to do them good..." (Jeremiah 32:40-41).

This leads us to the precious promise that immediately follows the verse we have been discussing in 2 Timothy:

"If we are faithless, he remains faithful, for he cannot deny himself" (2 Timothy 2:13).

Did not Jesus remain faithful to Peter?

And since God has gone so far as to put *Christ in you* and *you in Christ*, will He not stay faithful to Himself—*inside of you*? For truly, "He cannot deny himself." So in remaining faithful to Himself, Jesus is faithful to us! Why? Because we are in Him and He is in us, by the new birth of salvation.

As Jesus declared with assurance:

"At that day ye shall know that I am in my Father, and ye in me, and I in you" (John 14:20).

And the Apostle Paul also affirmed that our very life is bundled up in Christ's life by saying:

"When Christ, *who is our life*, shall appear, then shall ye also appear with him in glory" (Colossians 3:4).

Certainly, this is why Scripture declares God's unerring faithfulness toward His children:

"The LORD's faithful love does not cease; his compassion does not fail. They are new every morning; great is your faithfulness" (Lamentations 3:22-23, *NHEB*).

Chapter 35

Not All Who Say, "Lord" Enter the Kingdom?

The Will of My Father

We read the words of Jesus in Matthew 7:21, declaring:

> "Not every one that saith unto me, Lord, Lord, shall enter into the kingdom of heaven; but he that doeth the will of my Father which is in heaven."

In this Scripture, was Jesus aiming His words at saved Christians? Was this statement spoken to imply that the security of salvation could be in question every time a believer finds himself or herself, unfortunately, stumbling in some way?

To answer this question we must ask: What is the will of the Father that Jesus was referring to in this verse? The Lord answered that very question when He was asked by the Jews:

> "Then said they unto him, What shall we do, that we might work the works of God? Jesus answered and said unto them, This is the work of God, that ye believe on him whom he hath sent" (John 6:28-29).

Now in our verse of Matthew 7:21, it becomes evident that Jesus wasn't addressing these words toward a true believer but to the *make-believer*. He was saying that just because someone calls Him "Lord," it doesn't necessarily mean this person knows Him and is saved.

When I was younger in the Lord, I always thought that if people said "Lord," "God," or "Jesus," they were saved. For I had assumed that only the redeemed would speak this way. But I have come to realize, as the Scriptures make clear, there are spiritual things that can be imitated by impostors. Just look at all the cults that have taken Christian words and Scriptures and twisted the real meanings! As the Apostle Paul warned of those:

> "Having a form of godliness, but denying the power thereof: from such turn away" (2 Timothy 3:5).

And Jesus never said you will know them by their words, but He did say:

> "Wherefore by their fruits ye shall know them" (Matthew 7:20).

For the fruit will ultimately reveal the real person. And thankfully, the *new birth* cannot be imitated. As Paul also stated:

"For our gospel came not unto you in word only, but also in power, and in the Holy Ghost, and in much assurance; as ye know what manner of men we were among you for your sake" (1 Thessalonians 1:5).

Jesus' words to those who called Him "Lord" in Matthew 7:21 are warnings to those who display an outward form of Christianity without the inward reality of *knowing* Him, as with genuine Christianity. For this Scripture has nothing to do with the possibility of losing one's salvation; it is actually the recognition of a *lack of salvation*. Jesus made this apparent when He continued His dialogue in the seventh chapter of Matthew...

I Never Knew You

"Many will say to me in that day, Lord, Lord, have we not prophesied in thy name? and in thy name have cast out devils? and in thy name done many wonderful works? And then will I profess unto them, *I never knew you*: depart from me, ye that work iniquity" (Matthew 7:22-23).

These verses were touched upon earlier, in *Chapter 12: The Warning of Hebrews 6*, and these strong words of Jesus demonstrate definitively that *He was speaking of those who did not have a relationship with Him.* For although they were supposedly performing Christian works, Jesus declared: "I never knew you."

Notice that Jesus' first response to them was not to say they weren't good enough. No; instead He declared that He *did not know them*, which revealed the lack of any relationship. And because of this lack of an actual connection with Him, Jesus made it known that they did not do His works but in fact, worked "iniquity."

Because of Relationship

It's strange that many in church have thought (and the world still *does* think) of entrance into Heaven in terms of outward good behavior. Consider this scenario:

Someone you don't know knocks on the front door of your home and asks to be allowed inside, saying, "I did something good today, so let me in!"

Would you let him or her in? This is someone with whom you have no relationship—a complete stranger—requesting entry, based entirely on performance. Would you trust this individual?

On the other hand, if the visitor was a friend or close member of your family, you would immediately allow this person inside. Why? Because of *relationship*.

And a trusting relationship is the requirement for entering Heaven. For to do the Father's will is to receive Christ. In so doing, you know the One who died for you— who gave His life to gain a *relationship* with you! Jesus spoke of this relationship when He said:

> "*My sheep hear my voice, and I know them, and they follow me*: And I give unto them eternal life; and they shall never perish, neither shall any man pluck them out of my hand. My Father, which gave them me, is greater than all; and no man is able to pluck them out of my Father's hand. I and my Father are one" (John 10:27-30).

For Heaven is a place that is populated with people who have one thing in common—a love and relationship with Jesus. This is what defines Heaven. Indeed, this is the entrance *into* Heaven. As Jesus also said:

> "Verily, verily, I say unto you, I am the door of the sheep. All that ever came before me are thieves and robbers: but the sheep did not hear them. *I am the door: by me if any man enter in, he shall be saved, and shall go in and out, and find pasture*" (John 10:7-9).

Chapter 36

Branches Not Spared?

Of Jews & Gentiles

In John 15:1-6, Jesus spoke of individuals being branches that are either *in Christ bearing fruit, in Christ not bearing fruit and taken up*—or *not in Christ and cast forth.* This was covered in *Chapter 14: Branches, Fruit & Fire.*

In the Book of Romans we find another branch allegory, which speaks of branches being "cut off." Could this be about born-again Christians losing their salvation or is there a different aspect to its meaning in these Scriptures?

In Romans 11:21-23, we read:

> "For if God spared not the natural branches, take heed lest he also spare not thee. Behold, therefore, the goodness and severity of God: on them who fell, severity; but toward thee, goodness, if thou continue in his goodness; otherwise *thou also shalt be cut off.*

And they also, if they abide not still in unbelief, shall be grafted in; for God is able to graft them in again."

In these verses of Romans, it is important to keep in mind that the Apostle Paul was referring specifically to the Jewish people and to the Gentiles (those not Israeli-born). The specific context of being grafted in or being cut off from Christ pertains to these two groups of people.

Paul was not speaking of individuals who were *saved* and being "cut off." He was referring to nations of people who were either in belief or cut off *due to unbelief and the rejection of the Gospel*. This is evident in the reading of the entire chapter of Romans 11.

The Apostle Paul started this chapter by stating that God has not cast away the Jewish people (though *as a nation* they *are* currently cut off from the Gospel). For God knows those whom He has foreknown and chosen to receive the Gospel—even among the Jews. As Paul stated:

"I say then, Hath God cast away his people? God forbid. For I also am an Israelite, of the seed of Abraham, of the tribe of Benjamin. *God hath not cast away his people* which he foreknew" (Romans 11:1-2).

And Paul added:

"I ask then, did they [the Jewish nation] stumble that they might fall? May it never be! But by their fall salvation has come to the Gentiles, to provoke them to jealousy. Now if their fall is the riches of the world, and their loss the riches of the Gentiles, how much more their fullness! For I speak to you who are

Gentiles. Since then as I am an apostle to Gentiles, I glorify my ministry..." (Romans 11:11-13, *WEB*).

In these verses, Paul is revealing that due to the rejection of Jesus as Messiah by the Jews, the Gentiles are now being grafted into Christ. As Jesus also stated:

> "And I say unto you, That many shall come from the east and west, and shall sit down with Abraham, and Isaac, and Jacob, in the kingdom of heaven. But the children of the kingdom shall be cast out into outer darkness: there shall be weeping and gnashing of teeth" (Matthew 8:11-12).

Yet Paul goes on to say that the Jews will eventually, as a nation, turn to Christ, the Messiah.

Carrying the Gospel

At the present time, the Jews are considered cut off from the Gospel because of unbelief. (Yet this is not the case for all of them, because some Jews have accepted Jesus as their Savior—Paul the Apostle being one of them.) But initially, it was the Jews who were meant to receive Jesus as their Messiah and spread the Gospel to the Gentiles.

However, the Jewish nation as a whole did not receive their Messiah, Jesus—and in the foreknowledge and plan of God, the Gospel went out to the highways and byways to whosoever would embrace it (Luke 14:16-24). As Jesus declared to the chief priest and elders of the Jews:

> "Therefore say I unto you, The kingdom of God shall be taken from you, and given to a nation bringing forth the fruits thereof" (Matthew 21:43).

So the believing church, made up mostly of Gentiles but of which there is "neither Jew nor Greek [Gentile], there is neither bond nor free, there is neither male nor female: for ye are all one in Christ Jesus" (Galatians 3:28), carries the message of the Gospel.

This is the age we are in now.

And though the Jewish nation is presently cut off, there is still a remnant of Jews being saved today; just as in Old Testament times, when the Gentiles as a nation were "cut off" from knowing God, the God of Israel was still saving Gentiles. A perfect example of this is king Nebuchadnezzar (Daniel 4:34-37). He came to know the God of Israel as His God. See also: Cyrus (Ezra 1:2-3), Rahab (Hebrews 11:31), Ruth (Ruth 1:16), the people of Nineveh (Jonah 3:5), etc.

As the Prophet Isaiah wrote:

"The God of the whole earth shall he be called" (Isaiah 54:5).

For the verses of Romans 11:21-23, which we are studying, reveal that mercy has been shown to the Gentiles as a nation. If they continue in this mercy, they will not be cut off (as a whole), and they will continue to show forth the light. In contrast, *if they do not continue to believe and receive the truth of the Gospel*, the Gentiles (as a whole) could be cut off as well. And the Jews, if they believe, can be grafted in again.

Indeed, biblical prophecy tells us that after the fullness of the Gentiles enters the Kingdom of God, all Israel shall be saved:

"For I don't desire you to be ignorant, brothers, of this mystery, so that you won't be wise in your own conceits, that a partial hardening has happened to Israel, until the fullness of the Gentiles has come in, *and so all Israel will be saved.* Even as it is written, 'There will come out of Zion the Deliverer, and he will turn away ungodliness from Jacob'" (Romans 11:25-26, *WEB*).

So the Scriptures of Romans 11 pertain specifically to nations or groups of people that are either in belief or unbelief. And Paul stated that the Gentile believers should not be conceited about the carrying of the Gospel which had come to them, because "you stand by your faith" (Romans 11:20, *WEB*) and God is able to graft the Jews back "into their own olive tree" (Romans 11:24).

Again, these verses refer to the Jews and the Gentiles being in belief or unbelief. *Those who are cut off are removed because of their rejection of the Gospel itself.* The meaning has nothing to do with a born-again believer's supposed loss of salvation *after* receiving Christ. For as it has been stated, the Lord Himself *keeps us* in belief. Remember that Jesus is He...

"Who shall also confirm you unto the end, that ye may be blameless in the day of our Lord Jesus Christ" (1 Corinthians 1:8).

But the message Paul is sharing in Romans 11 refers to God's dealings with the Jewish and Gentile nations and their acceptance or rejection of the Gospel of Christ.

Chapter 37

Losing Not Those Things We Have Wrought?

A Full Reward

In 2 John 1:8, the Apostle John wrote:

> "Look to yourselves, that we lose not those things which we have wrought, but that we receive a full reward."

In this verse, John encouraged believers to look to themselves in their Christian walk—that they should receive a "full reward." This is a theme that was also shared in many of the Apostle Paul's writings, as Paul often spoke of rewards for the believer in the coming Kingdom. For this Scripture in 2 John is not speaking about any loss of salvation but loss of *rewards.* John was admonishing believers not to turn aside in any way from the truth they had received. This is because John, as well as the other apostles, often warned Christians about false teachers and false doctrines. Notice the previous verse to this, as John had just written:

"For many deceivers are entered into the world, who confess not that Jesus Christ is come in the flesh..." (2 John 1:7).

Clearly John was warning believers not to follow such people and be led astray, thus losing the structure of truth that they had been taught. And as covered previously in this study (see *Chapter 28: Peter & Some Falling*), it was Peter who also admonished:

"Ye therefore, beloved, seeing ye know these things before, beware lest ye also, being led away with the error of the wicked, fall from your own stedfastness" (2 Peter 3:17).

Abiding Not in the Doctrine of Christ

And John continued by saying:

"*Whosoever transgresseth, and abideth not in the doctrine of Christ, hath not God.* He that abideth in the doctrine of Christ, he hath both the Father and the Son" (2 John 1:9).

Is John speaking of true Christians in this verse? Is he saying that born-again believers could, beyond the issue of loss of reward, face damnation because they "abide not in the doctrine of Christ"?

To show the obvious answer to this question, we will use John's very own words. (I imagine by now you have an idea of just what verse I'm about to quote!) For John summed it up quite nicely when he said:

"They went out from us, *but they were not of us*; for if they had been of us, they would have continued with us: but they went out, that they might be made manifest that *they were not all of us*" (1 John 2:19).

So the Apostle John made it evident that "*If they had been of us*, they would have *continued* with us." Therefore, those who left the faith were not "of us" and *never* had Christ to begin with. They may have been exposed to the "doctrine of Christ," but they did not have Christ Himself abiding in their hearts. If they had Him, they would have continued to "abideth in the doctrine of Christ." Situations like this one have been brought up many times in this study, reaffirming this truth.

And as John stated, he that "abideth not in the doctrine of Christ, *hath not God.*" Thus, those individuals who did not remain in the doctrine of Christ were exposed as not being truly saved in the first place.

Therefore, the answer is that John's words were *not* referring to true believers who had received Christ into their hearts but rather to make-believers who *could* walk away from Christ. For as he declared:

"They went out, that they might be made manifest that *they were not all of us.*"

Indeed, John's own writings explain his thoughts and clarify the meaning of his words. There is no loss of salvation referenced for true believers—only for the make-believers. As for Christians, the apostle was surely admonishing them to stay in the narrow but blessed walk of truth—whereby it could be revealed that each one indeed, "hath both the

Father and the Son" (2 John 1:9). This was John's delight. For he also said:

> "I have no greater joy than to hear that my children walk in truth" (3 John 1:4).

The fact that John the Apostle was assured of the security of the believer's life in Christ is apparent, as he wrote:

> "For the truth's sake, which dwelleth in us, and shall be with us *for ever*" (2 John 1:2).

How beautiful it is to think of the fact that as a believer in Jesus Christ, the truth shall abide in you *forever!* This truth abides in you by the Comforter Himself, the blessed Holy Spirit. As John wrote, quoting the uplifting words of Jesus:

> "And I will pray the Father, and he shall give you another Comforter, that he may abide with you *for ever*; Even the Spirit of truth; whom the world cannot receive, because it seeth him not, neither knoweth him: but ye know him; for he dwelleth with you, and shall be in you. I will not leave you comfortless: I will come to you" (John 14:16-18).

And as previously stated, it is certainly no wonder that John wrote:

> "These things have I written unto you that believe on the name of the Son of God; that ye may know that *ye have eternal life*" (1 John 5:13).

Notice that John did not say that "ye *will* have eternal life." No, he made it quite clear that "ye *have* eternal life." This is a promise held in the present tense and is not futuristic.

For it is while we are still in these earthen vessels that we enter into eternity by receiving Christ as Savior. Truly, eternal life begins *before* we get to Heaven, as the Apostle Paul wrote:

> "But we have this treasure in earthen vessels, that the excellency of the power may be of God, and not of us...While we look not at the things which are seen, but at the things which are not seen: for the things which are seen are temporal; but the things which are not seen are eternal" (2 Corinthians 4:7, 18).

Chapter 38

The Unhealthy Practice of Canceling Scriptures

That One Misunderstood Verse

Some years ago, I was sharing with a brother in Christ about this topic of the believer's security in Christ. Although I shared many Scriptures affirming this truth, there was one verse that made him believe he could lose his salvation. But before I continue to discuss that verse, I'd like to address how one can see such solid confirmations of our Christian security, yet throw all that truth aside for a single Scripture that may seem contrary. That's why in this study I have not only shared the affirming Scriptures of our security in Christ; I have also, with the help of the Holy Spirit, endeavored to explain those verses which may appear to speak otherwise.

To make a solid argument, it's fair to look at the entirety of Scripture and be "rightly dividing the word of truth" (2

Timothy 2:15). So why is it that situations often arise when someone will dispute the numerous biblical claims presented for our security in Christ, by merely quoting a single verse? To put it another way, if you want to dispute these truths (and you are, of course, entitled to your opinion), you should not only mention Scriptures that you think are contrary; you also need to explain why all the other Scriptures presented here (and others in the Bible) wouldn't actually mean what they say. For example, explain how "sealed unto the day of redemption" (Ephesians 4:30) doesn't really mean *sealed unto the day of redemption.* You would need to explain why "those whom He foreknew He also predestined" (Romans 8:29) doesn't in fact mean that *those whom He foreknew He also predestined.*

Also in need of explanation would be the words of Jesus when He said: "This is the Father's will which hath sent me, that of all which he hath given me I should lose nothing" (John 6:39). If this verse doesn't mean exactly what it says, how would one explain this affirmation of the Savior saying, *I should lose nothing,* as being interpreted to mean that the Lord would instead lose some?

Holding One & Canceling Others?

The point I want to make is that it's not enough, should one oppose this view, to think that a solid argument can be made by coming up with a single verse or two and saying, "There, that's it, and you're wrong." One can't just cancel out so many valid Scriptures, by clinging to a few that he or she claims to be contrary. You need to therefore explain the "difficult" Scriptures, those that seem to differ from your opinion, just as I have done in this study. Only then would you be giving a fair and balanced rebuttal.

And though it may appear that I've had much of the Word to expound upon, I can tell you: If I had to take the other stance and provide explanations in opposition to all the affirming Scriptures on eternal security, there would be just too many pages written in an attempt to clarify such an argument. The opposing book that would be written—if it *could* be written—would surely be too large to carry (or download!). For there are so many straightforward, solid Scriptures assuring our security in Christ, which would then have to be explained away to the contrary, and that cannot be done. With that being said...

Out of the many Bible verses that have been brought forth in this study, I could sum up the entire book by using only two Scripture references, which are:

"Jesus answered and said unto him, Verily, verily, I say unto thee, Except a man be born again, he cannot see the kingdom of God" (John 3:3).

And surely you know this one:

"They went out from us, but they were not of us; for if they had been of us, they would have continued with us: but they went out, that they might be made manifest that they were not all of us" (1 John 2:19).

If you understand only these two verses, you have the understanding of your eternal security in Christ. For although there are many more—those two verses give a complete summation of this truth.

However, if I were to go a step further and give a Christian merely one affirming Scripture, what would it be? It would be Jesus' promise to you about the Holy Spirit:

"And I will pray the Father, and he shall give you another Comforter, *that he may abide with* you *for ever*" (John 14:17).

For it is the Holy Spirit, who abides in us *forever*, who puts us "in Christ" (2 Corinthians 5:17). And nowhere in the Bible does it speak of Christians being removed from this high position, once we are "sealed" with Him (Ephesians 4:30) and seated with Him "in heavenly places in Christ Jesus" (Ephesians 2:6).

Why Difficult Scriptures?

Why do we have "difficult" Scriptures in the Bible, anyway? Why isn't it a little easier to understand without conflict? Well, there are two reasons. First of all, the Lord wants you to look to Him for understanding and not to yourself. Nothing gets this result for Him more easily than when you are in the humble position of being at the end of your own resources. This can bring you into a closer relationship with Christ, for *He is the goal* in reading and understanding the Bible. The goal isn't so much to simply have biblical knowledge; what's really important is to know the Lord Himself. For to draw close to Jesus is to experience the most wonderful grace of all! And when He teaches us, through His Spirit, we see His face and understand why David could say, "In thy presence is fulness of joy" (Psalm 16:11).

The second reason for encountering certain Scriptures is that all sorts of people read the Bible. There are some who have good hearts but also some without good hearts. And there is power in God's Word, both to comfort and to convict. That's why it's important to read the Bible *with the Lord*. You then receive His words *to you* as well as His understanding for you.

If you read the Scriptures without seeking Him, you might find yourself walking near the umpire and the first baseman. The umpire may be raising his voice to the first baseman, but he's not speaking to you; likewise, you don't want to mistake a biblical rebuke as aimed at you when that's not the case!

But most of the time, the issues with which Christians struggle arise because they do not read or understand the entirety of Scripture in context. We are never to "wrest" Scriptures out of the intended meaning for the purpose of creating a doctrine. As Peter wrote of those who twisted Paul's words:

> "As also in all his epistles, speaking in them of these things; in which are some things hard to be understood, which they that are unlearned and unstable *wrest*, as they do also the other scriptures, unto their own destruction" (2 Peter 3:16).

For we are to see each verse clearly and in context with the whole of Scripture. Only then, with the Holy Spirit's guidance, will we fully understand the truth clearly written in the text before our very eyes. It was always there, but we just didn't see it! And as Peter said:

> "We have also a more sure word of prophecy; whereunto ye do well that ye take heed, as unto a light that shineth in a dark place, until the day dawn, and the day star arise in your hearts" (2 Peter 1:19).

Now it's time to address that verse I mentioned earlier— the one my Christian brother allowed to prevent him from resting in the many promises of our security in Christ...

Chapter 39

Twice Dead?

Building a Puzzle—Piece upon Piece

In the Epistle of Jude, verse 12, it is written:

> "These are spots in your feasts of charity, when they feast with you, feeding themselves without fear: clouds they are without water, carried about of winds; trees whose fruit withereth, without fruit, *twice dead*, plucked up by the roots."

This is the Scripture that, in my Christian brother's mind, prevented him from accepting the security we have in Christ. Just one verse! For he had read "twice dead" and therefore concluded that a believer could lose his or her salvation. He figured that one must have first been spiritually dead, then alive (supposedly in Christ) and then dead again—in order to be "twice dead." That was it. That one verse seemed to overpower all the other Scriptures stating otherwise.

So it didn't appear to matter to him that Jesus said: "He that heareth my word, and believeth on him that sent me, hath everlasting life, and shall not come into condemnation; but is passed from death unto life" (John 5:24). Nor did it seem relevant that the Lord had promised: "I give unto them eternal life; and they shall never perish, neither shall any man pluck them out of my hand" (John 10:28). It also didn't seem important that the Scripture declares: "There is therefore now no condemnation to them which are in Christ Jesus" (Romans 8:1).

So many verses seemed to be pushed aside, no longer significant.

But as mentioned previously in this study: How can the Christian's reborn spirit, "created in righteousness" (Ephesians 4:24), *ever* die? The body incurs death but the spirit cannot die, since it is sinless. As the Apostle John declared, in speaking of the reborn spirit (and not the flesh) of a Christian:

"Whosoever is born of God doth not commit sin; for his seed remaineth in him: and he cannot sin, because he is born of God" (1 John 3:9).

Isn't it strange to deny all these Scriptures (and so many others), deeming them somehow less significant than the one verse that is not understood? Isn't it better to build a puzzle on what is clearly seen and understood, first putting those scriptural pieces together as a framework?

Isn't that a more logical posture for gaining understanding than pushing so much truth aside, picking up a single puzzle piece (one verse), placing it in the middle of the table and saying that it fits there?

False Teachers Without the Spirit

It's important to realize that in the context of verse 12 of his epistle, Jude was writing about false brethren and teachers who had worked their way into the church. He called them "clouds without water," meaning they were without the Spirit. They lacked the substance within them to provide true water and life, the way a rain cloud provides for the Earth. These individuals had no substance and could "water" nothing. This becomes more evident further in the chapter, where in verse 19 we read Jude's declaration:

> "These be they who separate themselves, sensual, having *not* the Spirit."

It is therefore obvious that the reference in this verse is not to brothers and sisters in Christ. These people were sensual; they were only of the natural flesh. *They have not the Spirit of God* and therefore there is no salvation within them. Once again, as Jesus asserted in John 3:3:

> "Verily, verily, I say unto thee, Except a man be born again, he cannot see the kingdom of God."

This letter by Jude is very similar to 2 Peter 2:1-22, which was also addressed earlier in this study (*Chapter 11: True Conversion?*). For Peter, in similar fashion to Jude, warned the church of false teachers. Both Jude and Peter were speaking of such individuals not as if they were out in the world—but within the church. These false brethren were therefore even more accountable for their deceit within the church body, and that's why there was such a strong rebuke toward them.

And Jude had described these individuals in verse 4 by stating:

"For there are certain men crept in unawares, who were before of old ordained to this condemnation, ungodly men, turning the grace of our God into lasciviousness, and denying the only Lord God, and our Lord Jesus Christ."

Again, Jude referred to "ungodly" men who were "denying the only Lord God"—and this is hardly speech that's applicable to true believers, who are alive through the Spirit of the living God and made one with His Spirit (1 Corinthians 6:17). Notice the wording used to describe these men, saying that they deny "*the* only Lord God." As mentioned in this study, they did not deny *their* Lord God (which would refer to a personal relationship) but "the" Lord God. Then Jude continued by saying, "...and *our* Lord Jesus Christ." For He was not *their* Lord Jesus Christ (as they were unbelievers) but He is *ours*—that is, belonging to the true Christian believers with salvation.

This verse also states that they were "before of old ordained to this condemnation." And we read in verse 13:

"...to whom is reserved the blackness of darkness for ever."

So their judgment was ordained and reserved ahead of time, due to God's foreknowledge. This definitely cannot be said of a true Christian's predestination. As it is written:

"For whom he did foreknow, he also did predestinate to be conformed to the image of his Son...Moreover whom he did predestinate, them he also called: and whom he called, them he also justified: and whom he justified, them he also glorified" (Romans 8:29-30).

Twice—in Rejection & Exploitation

Jude referred to these ungodly people as "spots in your feasts of charity" (Jude 1:12) in the King James Version. This would be more accurately translated in the original Greek as "hidden rocky reefs in your love feasts." The term "hidden rocky reefs" was used at that time to describe the dangers of a boat hitting an underwater object and running aground. So these were wicked people to avoid within the church, and the term "twice dead" is in no way inferring that they were ever alive in Christ. The context reveals this fact by exposing the hardness of their hearts and the utter extent of their lifelessness to the things of God. They were not only dead to God but having been inside the church and exposed to the truth, they were now doubly dead in their *rejection* and *exploitation* of that truth.

Notice how the Scripture is worded:

"...trees whose fruit withereth, without fruit, twice dead, plucked up by the roots" (Jude 1:12).

In this verse, the translation of "fruit withereth" (as in the King James Version) is misleading. It is accurately translated as "autumnal" and most versions of the Bible use a form of this very word. The picture is that they were late autumn trees that had *no* fruit in a time when they should be showing fruit. *For the verse is not stating that they had any fruit at all.* And the Greek for "plucked up by the roots" is literally "having been uprooted."

Therefore, an accurate understanding of this verse would be: "autumn trees without fruit, having been uprooted— twice dead." The past tense of "having been uprooted" is quite revealing, as it points to the very reason for the trees being dead the second time or "twice dead."

So the first death of the trees is evident because they were without fruit. After that, having been uprooted—they became twice dead. You can see how these two deaths of the trees went together, showing the double emphasis Jude placed on their condition. There is no life mentioned in the middle of these two "deaths." Jude is not even hinting that these individuals were ever saved. This is why he stated that they were "without fruit" in the first place.

Again, this Scripture exposes just how defiant these people were in their rejection and exploitation of the things of God. It does not pertain to true believers who were spiritually dead, then had life, then lost life. The context simply does not allow for this interpretation. Rather, this verse refers to false brethren within the church.

And Jesus warned of such people, when He said:

"Beware of false prophets, which come to you in sheep's clothing, but inwardly they are ravening wolves. Ye shall know them by their fruits. Do men gather grapes of thorns, or figs of thistles? Even so every good tree bringeth forth good fruit; but a corrupt tree bringeth forth evil fruit. A good tree cannot bring forth evil fruit, neither can a corrupt tree bring forth good fruit. Every tree that bringeth not forth good fruit is hewn down, and cast into the fire. Wherefore by their fruits ye shall know them" (Matthew 7:15-20).

With these words, Jesus teaches us that these false believers will be ravening wolves from the start, for a good tree cannot bring forth evil fruit; no, it is the *corrupt tree* that brings forth evil fruit. And these false brethren were found not only denying the Gospel but using it for their gain. The Apostle Peter also warned about them:

> "And through covetousness shall they with feigned words make merchandise of you" (2 Peter 2:3).

And this is why Jude emphasized their complete and utter depravity before God, using the term "twice dead" (Jude 1:12) when writing his epistle.

For Jude described the extent of their death—first having no fruit (which is indicative of the lack of salvation) and then being pulled up by their roots.

Our Twice-Dead Tangerine Tree

This picture within the Epistle of Jude is exactly what happened to our tangerine tree when my wife and I were living in Florida. First the tree died. It produced no fruit. Then a hurricane hit our area and although the strong wind didn't take down any of the living trees in our yard, it pulled that dead tree up by its roots. There it lay uprooted on the lawn. Why? Because it was already dead. It had no life nor water inside to anchor it down. It was totally, absolutely dead and now "twice dead, having been uprooted." The hurricane actually did me a favor. Since the tree was already dead, the storm saved me the trouble of having to cut it down.

So in these verses Jude isn't speaking of true believers *at all*. He's not referring to those who are reborn in God's Spirit, whom He has "raised...up together, and made...sit together in heavenly places in Christ Jesus" (Ephesians 2:6). Rather,

Jude's description applies to those who, as Jesus said, are wolves and "false prophets, which come to you in sheep's clothing."

The reason why they come to you in sheep's clothing is because they *never were sheep* from the beginning. That's why there is a need to cover the deception by wearing "sheep's clothing."

And as mentioned previously in this study, Peter referred to these same individuals when he wrote:

> "...whose sentence now from of old doesn't linger, and their destruction will not slumber" (2 Peter 2:3, *WEB*).

So how could these individuals have had eternal life if their "sentence now *from of old doesn't linger,* and their *destruction will not slumber*"?

This verse shows emphatically that those who are named "twice dead" (Jude 1:12) *never possessed salvation at all.* For if they had possessed it, their sentence would have indeed *lingered*—if even for a moment—and their destruction would have *slumbered.* But this verse reveals that they were *never* alive in Christ and thus never "lost" their salvation in becoming "twice dead."

Scripture has much to say regarding false brethren. And Paul summed it up in Romans 16:18, where he wrote:

> "For they that are such serve not our Lord Jesus Christ, but their own belly; and by good words and fair speeches deceive the hearts of the simple."

In verse 17 of that chapter, Paul also warned about their contrary doctrine and told believers to avoid them.

Jude's Words on Eternal Security

Jude does, however, have something significant to say concerning God's chosen people, who are His *true* sheep. It's very important to point out that Jude, who wrote this portion of Scripture we have been discussing, has great encouragement for the true believers in Christ Jesus. For in the beginning of his epistle, he gives us one of the most precious promises concerning our security in Christ in the entire Bible:

> "Jude, the servant of Jesus Christ, and brother of James, to them that are sanctified by God the Father, and *preserved in Jesus Christ...*" (Jude 1:1).

Wow, what a promise to believers in Christ! How emphatic are his comforting words, referring to "them that are sanctified" as being "preserved in Jesus Christ." Jude confidently states that our preservation in Christ is sure! This is indeed the wonderful truth that has been brought forth throughout this study.

But just in case that wasn't enough, and just in case someone didn't grasp it, Jude winds down his short epistle by giving us *even more* words of comfort:

> "Now unto him that is able to keep you from falling, and to present you faultless before the presence of his glory with exceeding joy" (Jude 1:24).

So Jude again reinforced our security in Christ by saying that God:

> "...is able *to keep you from falling,* and to present you *faultless...*"

421

Chapter 40

Some Tears, Some Glares

Why the Hostile Reaction?

Now if you have read everything thus far in this study, I do heartily applaud you! It demonstrates that you have taken the time to seriously look into this important subject. I encourage you, like the Bereans of old who "searched the scriptures daily, whether those things were so" (Acts 17:11), to seek the Lord and search these truths yourself. Bear in mind that God's Word will always set you free! For Jesus said: "The words that I speak unto you, they are spirit, and they are life" (John 6:63).

There have been times when I received very *hostile* reactions from the hearers of this foundational, life-changing truth of the Bible. I recall when I was asked to teach a men's Bible study in a church many years ago. I went into the meeting with much joy about sharing the wonderful truth of our security in Christ. I was holding a seven-page Bible study

I had written, which ultimately grew and became the basis for the book you are now reading.

While I was speaking, I could perceive two very distinct reactions. Some people were looking at me with eyes welling up with tears, as if the weight of the world was being lifted off their shoulders. Their faces revealed that they were grasping the assurance of God's saving grace in a way they had not previously understood. But there were others who were glaring at me, turning red in the face and becoming very angry; I could even say they were starting to gnash their teeth at me. (But I will let that go, as I'm sure you get the idea!) And I hope that as you're reading this, you don't fall into that latter camp.

For it has been my experience that those who disagree with the doctrine stated here are often (but not always) extremely hostile in their opposition toward those who believe in eternal security. When I shared my teaching so many years ago with that men's group, I was nearly tossed out of the church on the spot! And I had no idea that some of my brothers and sisters in the Lord would react so antagonistically to this truth.

The "Need" for Condemnation?

One reason that some may get so upset over the reality of our security in Christ is because *they fear that resting in grace may cause them to go back into sin.* In other words, they may think they "need" the condemnation to keep them sanctified. However, the Word of God tells us:

> "For the law made nothing perfect, but the bringing in of a better hope did; by the which we draw nigh unto God" (Hebrews 7:19).

Truly, it is grace that sanctifies us to become like Christ; this is not obtained through the law nor condemnation. Remember, the Apostle Paul specifically said:

"Wherefore the law was our schoolmaster to bring us unto Christ, that we might be justified by faith. *But after that faith is come, we are no longer under a schoolmaster*" (Galatians 3:24-25).

And Paul also said:

"For *sin shall not have dominion over you*: for ye are not under the law, but under grace" (Romans 6:14).

Sin's power is not broken by self-condemnation, but the victory *is* in our relationship with Christ. He alone is able to change us into His image. Our faith needs to be in Jesus and not ourselves, for in ourselves we have no lasting hope of transformation. As Jesus summed it up so simply:

"Without me ye can do nothing" (John 15:5).

For Christ is not only our Savior but *our salvation* as well. As it is written in the Psalms:

"The LORD is my strength and song, and is *become my salvation*" (Psalm 118:14).

And we know that Christ is:

"...made unto us wisdom, and righteousness, and sanctification, and redemption" (1 Corinthians 1:30).

Such a salvation provides grace to lay aside the sin which "doth so easily beset us" (Hebrews 12:1). Let us trust in Jesus for His work of sanctification in our lives. He will do what we cannot do for ourselves. Let us draw near in relationship to Christ so that the power of His grace indeed renews *every* aspect of our lives. Let us allow Him to *transform* us as well as save us!

There is an interesting verse in the Old Testament where King Josiah was speaking to the Levites who carried the Ark of the Covenant. The Bible states:

"And [Josiah] said unto the Levites that taught all Israel, which were holy unto the LORD, Put the holy ark in the house which Solomon the son of David king of Israel did build; *it shall not be a burden upon your shoulders*: serve now the LORD your God, and his people Israel..." (2 Chronicles 35:3).

What a wonderful picture of the New Covenant found in the Old Testament! Notice that it was only after they put the ark down that they could "serve now the LORD your God."

So it is with us; let us not carry the work of God in our own power, but let Christ carry us in His all-encompassing New Covenant of grace.

For it is Jesus Himself who still encourages:

"Come to me, all you who labor and are heavily burdened, and I will give you rest. Take my yoke upon you and learn from me, for I am gentle and humble in heart; and you will find rest for your souls. For my yoke is easy, and my burden is light" (Matthew 11:28-30, *WEB*).

And surely we do not carry salvation—but salvation carries us. So as believers, we have a security that is not of this world. It is a salvation that holds us as an anchor for the soul. As it is written:

"This hope we have as an anchor of the soul, a hope both sure and steadfast and entering into that which is within the veil" (Hebrews 6:19, *WEB*).

This is indeed why Jesus said:

"Peace I leave with you, my peace I give unto you: *not as the world giveth, give I unto you*. Let not your heart be troubled, neither let it be afraid" (John 14:27).

Salvation of Works?

But you see, when teaching salvation that is *fully* by grace, you risk hitting a nerve with anyone trying to live out salvation by his or her own works. For teaching salvation by grace strikes against human pride itself. This is another reason why some people react to this truth with such extreme anger. We all like to feel that we are accomplishing something, right? Yet our salvation is totally hands-off because it's fully by Christ.

It is a salvation that is by grace through faith *and not by works*. As Paul the Apostle said:

"For by grace are ye saved through faith; and that *not of yourselves*: it is the gift of God" (Ephesians 2:8).

The truth is: The work of salvation is not *to* God but *through* God. Do you see the difference in these two prepositions? Salvation *to* God involves your striving and presenting your own "righteousness" before God. In contrast, salvation *through* God is His work of grace and His righteousness *through* you. It is a surrender to the Lord's will, His grace and His power. So salvation is *received*—as a free gift...

> "For of him, and through him, and to him, are all things: to whom be glory for ever. Amen" (Romans 11:36).

And as Paul the Apostle also wrote:

> "Who hath saved us, and called us with an holy calling, not according to *our* works, but according to his own purpose and grace, which was given us in Christ Jesus before the world began" (2 Timothy 1:9).

Truly, it is far better for the soul to rest in God's grace than in its own pride. Pride will always deceive you, lead you astray and hurt those around you. In contrast, God's grace always brings healing to you and to those around you. And the Bible confirms that, before God, no one will be able to boast, as it is written:

> "But God chose the foolish things of the world that he might put to shame those who are wise. God chose the weak things of the world that he might put to shame the things that are strong. God chose the lowly things of the world, and the things that are despised, and the things that don't exist, that he might bring to nothing the things that exist, *that no flesh should boast before God.* Because of him, you are in Christ Jesus, who was made to us wisdom from God, and righteousness and sanctification, and redemption, that, as it is written, *'He who boasts, let him boast in the Lord'*" (1 Corinthians 1:27-31, WEB).

Do you see how much of this salvation is *His*? It is *all* in the Lord! That's why we love Jesus so much, as He is truly a wonderful Savior. For as it is written: "We love him, because he first loved us" (1 John 4:19). But if you are relying on your own efforts, you won't realize the beauty of Christ. And, as mentioned with the elder son toward the prodigal son, you'll find yourself getting angry because these "many years" (Luke 15:29) have you served Him in your own energies.

Some Pride, Some Prejudice?

This reminds me of yet another time when I was sharing eternal security with a fellow believer. This brother was striving in his relationship with the Lord in such a way that it was apparent his walk was based upon his own strength and power. The Scripture states, "Not by might, nor by power, but by my spirit, saith the LORD of hosts" (Zechariah 4:6). But this believer was of a different mindset. So he resisted what I shared about the grace of God being fully sufficient for us, balking at it because of his pride.

Then at a time when I was in prayer, the Lord told me exactly what to say to this brother. So the next time I met with him and we discussed this subject, I said, "Well, I guess I just have more faith in the blood of Jesus than you do." When I said that, his face changed, softening with humility. It was like a bomb went off. So for the first time in all of our conversations, his ears were open to hear what the Lord wanted him to understand. For God's truth struck where he was holding all his cards—his pride. And the Lord revealed to him that in all his striving, he was lacking what he really needed.

429

And that is exactly what God will do in our lives. He will find that spot of pride and take it down, as He did with the Rich Young Ruler who came to Him in all the energies of self. "What good thing shall I do that I may have eternal life?" (Matthew 19:16), he had asked the Savior. Unlike other sinners who threw themselves at Jesus' feet, this man had a plan of what *he* could do. He thought he was better than others and that he could do something good on his own.

But Jesus hit him with the five words that always come to those relying upon the law and themselves:

"Yet lackest thou one thing" (Luke 18:22).

Yes; for if we approach the things of God with our own self-righteousness and power—we, too, will find those words written upon the wall:

"Thou art weighed in the balances, and art found wanting" (Daniel 5:27).

Still, as in the case of the Rich Young Ruler, there is always hope. As Jesus said, regarding this salvation that He was bringing to the world:

"The things which are impossible with men are possible with God" (Luke 18:27).

For the pride of man is illogical. When I was giving my little teaching on eternal security in that church so many years ago, not one person who opposed it gave any sound scriptural rebuttal. They never even offered to do so, nor did they listen to the Scriptures I shared with them, because that wasn't the issue at hand. It had turned emotional with them instead of spiritual. Their pride was being threatened. And when that pride is stirred up, it refuses to listen to the truth, no matter how many Bible verses are given to support it. For only a heart that is humble before God will be taught by Him.

I remember another situation when someone said to me with disgust and marginalization, "Oh, you're one of those *once-saved, always-saved* people!" A prejudice was applied immediately, without any thought in regard to what my understanding of this doctrine might be. There was only the reaction that *you are one of those Christians, and I don't like this eternal security stuff—nor you.* Now saints, how is that the fruit of a close walk with Christ? How is it an attitude of openness to discussion, to learning and to the knowledge of God? How is that loving, even if you disagree? Is not love much better than knowledge? As Paul said:

> "Knowledge puffs up, but love builds up" (1 Corinthians 8:1, *WEB*).

Now knowledge of God is a wonderful thing when coupled with faith, and Scripture does exhort us to "grow in grace, and in the knowledge of our Lord and Saviour Jesus Christ" (2 Peter 3:18). But as Paul states, "If I have...knowledge...but don't have love, I am nothing" (1 Corinthians 13:2, *WEB*).

Now in reflecting on that statement toward me of being *once-saved, always-saved*, I must repeat that if one is *indeed truly saved, being born again,* then yes, he or she will stay saved. This *is* what the Bible makes clear. But the issue is whether or not one was actually saved from the start. That is what many people who oppose this view leave out of the equation altogether. They fail to see the make-believer or the "false brethren" (Galatians 2:4) in Scripture, and they misinterpret the warnings aimed at these people *as being for true believers.* In doing so, they leave no room for God's sanctification process for the child of God.

Why Bother with Sanctification?

If God was removing us from our salvation altogether, why would He bother to sanctify us? If this was true, a Christian's walk would then be easier, I suppose, because the years of being conformed into Christ's image would not be necessary. And Christianity would just be a matter of being lost and saved, over and over again. So how could you know exactly when you lost salvation? Under that doctrine, you would need to be sure to get "re-saved" continually— although Hebrews 6:4-6 would declare such a thing impossible (see *Chapter 12: The Warning of Hebrews 6*).

In fact, once my wife and I were counseling a woman who went to a church that offered no assurance of salvation in its teaching. She told us she was afraid of losing her salvation on a *daily* basis. She said that she was terrified she might get into a car accident and perhaps not be saved at that moment!

Dear saints, do you think this lack of peace is how God intended our salvation in Christ to be? Indeed, I wonder how many times in the church, altar calls have been made for the children of God to be "re-saved," again and again? But is it any wonder? For if we are taught that we have *no* assurance of our salvation in Christ, is this not the logical result? Sadly, this mindset leaves believers without any sense of the biblical comfort offered by our Lord. For with such unbelief in the keeping power of God, there is a lack of the sweet trusting intimacy that Jesus provides for His own. But without a doubt, God *does* sanctify us because He is with us, He is *for* us, and He is committed to us, as the Bible teaches and as has been mentioned:

> "For whom he did foreknow, he also did predestinate *to be conformed to the image of his Son,*

that he might be the firstborn among many brethren" (Romans 8:29).

It is also written:

"But we all, with open face beholding as in a glass the glory of the Lord, *are changed into the same image from glory to glory*, even as by the Spirit of the Lord" (2 Corinthians 3:18).

The Anointing Abides in You

And surely, as we allow ourselves to be taught by the Holy Spirit and to comprehend the totality of Scripture, we will begin to see how the Bible's seemingly contradicting verses *all* dovetail into one perfect truth. For God does not contradict Himself. Readers may often miss the truth of God's Word by not digging deeply into the context or by relying only upon what others around them are saying. Our walk with God always needs to be vertical *first*, for it cannot be found with true life if we only look horizontally. Jesus brought out this truth when He inquired of the Pharisees: "How can ye believe, which receive honour one of another, and seek not the honour that cometh from God only?" (John 5:44). Yes, these were the very Pharisees who, though quoting the written word, missed the living Word, the Messiah, standing right in front of them. But we have a perfect teacher in the Holy Spirit. As the Apostle John wrote:

"But the anointing which ye have received of him abideth in you, and ye need not that any man teach you: but as the same anointing teacheth you of all things, and is truth, and is no lie, and even as it hath taught you, ye shall abide in him" (1 John 2:27).

Chapter 41

We Have Become Partakers of Christ!

Saved to Endure

As we get close to the final chapter in this study, I thought I would share one of my favorite Scriptures concerning our security in Christ. I touched on this back in *Chapter 12: The Warning of Hebrews 6*, but it's worth another visit. This is one of my favorite passages because of the way it's worded, which makes it so interesting. The Word of God says in Hebrews 3:12-14:

> "Take heed, brethren, lest there be in any of you an evil heart of unbelief, in departing from the living God. But exhort one another daily, while it is called To day; lest any of you be hardened through the deceitfulness of sin. For we are made partakers of

Christ, if we hold the beginning of our confidence stedfast unto the end."

What is so amazing to me about this verse is the difference between what the Scripture *appears* to convey and what it actually *does* say.

Obviously, the beginning of the Scripture is speaking of those with *evil hearts*. How can a believer who has a new heart, with the Holy Spirit now dwelling within, be categorized as having an *evil* heart? For it is written in Ezekiel 11:19:

> "I will put a new spirit within you; and I will take the stony heart out..."

As has been covered in this study, our caterpillar flesh may still have the effects of sin, but our butterfly hearts have been "created in righteous" (Ephesians 4:24; Romans 7:22-23; 8:10).

Note also that the verse refers to an evil heart of *unbelief*. As has also been demonstrated throughout this study and as the Scriptures make abundantly clear, there may be those *in* the church assembly who are not really *of* the church. They still possess hearts of unbelief. Always remember our keynote Scripture of 1 John 2:19:

> "They went out from us, but they were not of us; for if they had been of us, they would have continued with us: but they went out, that they might be made manifest that they were not all of us."

That little verse in 1 John is like the hub of a wheel, tying all of its spokes together. It gives understanding into so many of the warnings found in the Bible. Those who do not remain are those who were never saved to begin with, and those who really are saved will endure—for God is the One who gives the power for salvation. Again, as John the Apostle wrote:

> "But as many as received him, to them gave he *power* to become the sons of God, even to them that believe on his name" (John 1:12).

If You Continue?

And this is the reason Paul the Apostle could write:

> "And you, that were sometime alienated and enemies in your mind by wicked works, yet now hath he reconciled...to present you holy and unblameable and unreproveable in his sight: *If ye continue in the faith grounded and settled, and be not moved away from the hope of the gospel...*" (Colossians 1:21-23).

Paul was not implying that your own self-enduring faith will keep you saved. Rather, the faith that endures is evidence of one who *is* saved. He is singling out those who will continue, having salvation, from those who will not continue. He is saying, as did John, that remaining in Christ is evidence of true salvation. Paul made this apparent when he said:

> "Moreover, brethren, I declare unto you the gospel which I preached unto you, which also ye have received, and wherein ye stand; By which also ye are saved, if ye keep in memory what I preached unto you, unless ye have believed in vain" (1 Corinthians 15:1-2).

Notice in this Scripture that the issue is not about a Christian's enduring strength; rather, Paul is actually questioning if some truly have salvation or have "believed in vain." *The issue is whether or not your salvation is genuine, having been received in the soil of a sincere heart.*

This is why Jesus said:

> "If ye continue in my word, *then are ye my disciples indeed*; And ye shall know the truth, and the truth shall make you free" (John 8:31-32).

For God's salvation in Christ, when truly received in the heart, will take root and keep you. This is why we have that blessed promise in the Word of God:

> "Being confident of this very thing, *that he which hath begun a good work in you will perform it until the day of Jesus Christ*" (Philippians 1:6).

Already Partakers

This brings me back to our verse in Hebrews 3:12-14, which is the one I find so interesting. This verse in Hebrews gives us the same promise as the verse just stated in Philippians, about our perseverance in Christ. Look specifically at Hebrews 3:14, where it says:

> "For we are made partakers of Christ, if we hold fast the beginning of our confidence steadfast unto the end."

When reading such a verse, some may think it means *we WILL BE partakers of Christ if we hold fast our confidence to the end*—as if we are self-reliant *for* salvation, in order to keep it. But that is not what this Scripture is saying *at all*. Rather, we are enduring *by* salvation, because we possess it.

Notice again the verb tense: "We ARE MADE [present tense] partakers of Christ, if we hold fast..." The actual Greek tense of the verb demonstrates this even more clearly, for it reads:

"We *have become partakers* of Christ, if we hold fast..."

Do you see? We *already have Christ* to begin with, as we "have become partakers of Christ." This verse is stating that by reason of holding our confidence to the end, we are manifesting that we indeed *already* have Christ! This is why we hold our confidence to the end! Let's read John 1:12 again, this time with verse 13:

> "But as many as received him, to them gave he power to become the sons of God, even to them that believe on his name: *Which were born, not of blood, nor of the will of the flesh, nor of the will of man, but of God*" (John 1:12-13).

Yes, we who are Christians hold fast our confidence to the end because we received power to become the sons of God, having been *born of God!* And as John went on to say:

> "For whatsoever is born of God overcometh the world" (1 John 5:4).

Should this be any surprise? Has not God covered our *entire* salvation in Christ? For it is written:

> "I will give thanks to you, for you have answered me, and *have become my salvation*" (Psalm 118:21, *WEB*).

Surely, to God be the glory!

Chapter 42

Jesus, the Rose of Our Salvation

God's Word is Perfect

As we have looked deeply into these Scriptures on eternal security, it's good to remember some important truths.

First of all, God's Word is perfect and does not contradict itself. It's strange how we can read a hundred Bible verses affirming our security in Christ, but if we read one that seems to imply otherwise, it's the tendency of human nature to give more weight and precedence to that verse. I believe this is because we live in a world where it's hard to simply be comforted. What I mean by this is that it's easier to have fear than faith. But God's Word is true and He is good and completely loving. He is not like the natural world around us that takes and takes again. The Lord gives and gives and gives even more, which is foreign to this world. This is why it involves seeking Him to understand Him. Truly, such goodness is of another Kingdom, based on love. And this is no wonder, for "God *is* love" (1 John 4:16).

The Sum of Thy Word is Truth

Secondly, we must keep in mind that Scripture interprets Scripture. For this reason, we must look at "all the counsel of God" (Acts 20:27) in determining any doctrine. As the Apostle Paul also instructs us:

> "Study to shew thyself approved unto God, a workman that needeth not to be ashamed, *rightly dividing the word of truth*" (2 Timothy 2:15).

Sometimes a Scripture can only be understood in light of other Scriptures. For as has been mentioned, God's truth is like putting together a puzzle. As the pieces come together here and there, a picture starts to form. And that picture is Jesus!

When interpreting God's Word, it is always best to view the verse or verses we are reading in full context. If we take a verse aside and isolate it, we may miss its application entirely.

Psalm 119:160 declares, "Thy word is true from the beginning." Young's Literal Translation of the Bible defines this verse as: "The sum of Thy word is truth," which I think is beautiful. For the Word of God builds upon itself, adding layer upon layer of truth, with all the layers being brought together to reveal one sum truth. This is why it's so important to allow Scripture to interpret Scripture, through the help of the Holy Spirit. As Jesus said:

"Howbeit when he, the Spirit of truth, is come, he will guide you into all truth: for he shall not speak of himself; but whatsoever he shall hear, that shall he speak: and he will shew you things to come" (John 16:13).

The Tree of Life

And this leads to my third important point...

The Bible was never meant to be studied like a biology book, using our own power and mental energy. No; in fact, the reason why it appears to not make sense at times is because the natural mind can't comprehend its spiritual meaning. But God reveals His truth to little children! He gives eyes to see what His Word is truly conveying when we humble our hearts before Him. As Jesus prayed:

"I thank thee, O Father, Lord of heaven and earth, because thou hast hidden these things from the wise and prudent, and hast revealed them unto babes" (Matthew 11:25).

That's just it. God wants us to humble ourselves so that He may reveal truth to us. As has been mentioned, He didn't plan for us to understand it on our own, without Him. You know why this is so? It's because God is much more interested in relationship than in merely imparting knowledge. Adam and Eve ate from the Tree of the Knowledge of Good and Evil and it never brought them closer to God, nor will knowledge *alone* ever bring anyone closer to Him. This is the reason why the Bible tells us to seek the Lord:

"When thou saidst, Seek ye my face; my heart said unto thee, Thy face, LORD, will I seek" (Psalm 27:8).

We also read:

"I will cause him to draw near, and he shall approach unto me: for who is this that engaged his heart to approach unto me? saith the LORD" (Jeremiah 30:21).

And praise His wonderful Name! When we receive Jesus, we partake of *The Tree of Life!* We learn and grow by His Spirit. We grow in the knowledge of Him—and by Him. This is indeed true knowledge...and true life. As Jesus prayed:

"And this is life eternal, that they might know thee, the only true God, and Jesus Christ, whom thou hast sent" (John 17:3).

In Christ Jesus

Finally and most importantly, if there is one thought to take away from this study, it's the reality of what it means to be "in Christ" (2 Corinthians 5:17). Such a little preposition carries so much weight when it places you *in* Jesus! And the heart of the message of eternal security is revealed by being *in Christ.* He is our life, our salvation, our redemption, our righteousness, our strength, our wisdom and yes—our security.

Truly, the most important message in this entire book is that which expresses the significant words Jesus spoke to Nicodemus and with which I started this study.

Indeed, these are words that Jesus still speaks to all who have not turned to Him:

"Marvel not that I said unto thee, *Ye must be born again*" (John 3:7).

This is the beginning and end of the subject. Turning to Jesus in sincere faith and admitting your sin and need for salvation is the only requirement to receive the new birth, by which you are placed *in Christ*. You see, God just wants your heart. He won't force His way there. You have to allow Him to save you and impart His eternal life to you.

I'm thankful I did this over forty years ago. Many hobbies have come and gone and personal ambitions have changed as well, but Jesus has remained sure and faithful since the day that I asked Him into my heart. For His salvation will take root in you and grow like a tree "so that the birds of the sky can lodge under its shadow" (Mark 4:32, *WEB*).

Christ, the Rose of God

I hope this teaching has been helpful to you. What's so important about knowing your security in Christ, anyway? One word...grace. And perhaps another one...love. How can we know love when we are striving in some way to earn what has been freely given to us?

Many years ago, I was in Boston with a friend around Valentine's Day, and I purchased three long-stemmed red roses to give out for free. My friend just put up with me, but I was thinking of God's free gift of grace in salvation and wanted to give some flowers to people I thought seemed lonely. As I proceeded to give the flowers away, I realized what a difficult task I had undertaken. Nobody wanted to take them because they couldn't believe they were really for free—with no strings attached. In fact, it took me all day to give away those three roses.

On one occasion, after the sun had already set, I was pleading with a woman to receive the free rose. I said, "Please, I've been trying all day to give three flowers away. Please take it."

She finally did accept the rose, much to her disbelief and my joy. And as I walked away, I turned back to see her looking at me—dumbfoundedly—with an ever-so-slight smile.

How hard it can be to let go and just receive! And how pleasing it is to our God as He gives and we freely receive the gift of His Son and inherit everlasting life!

May we all remember the words of Jesus, which He spoke of the Pharisees:

> "To whom little is forgiven, the same loveth little" (Luke 7:47).

May we therefore be found receiving *much* forgiveness, that we may, in return, love much.

For Christ is indeed the Rose of God, who was manifested into this world to bear the thorns of our sin. Jesus, the Rose without thorns, was separated from the face of God in the darkness of the cross so that we may never be separated from the light of God's love. And all this took place so that we could be reconciled to God and truly *know* Him.

For truly, in Christ Jesus, *much is forgiven.*

Secure in Christ

I can rest assured, from law I am free
For God, in grace, is taking care of me.
The faith I have is all in Thee,
I but yield to Thee, in me.

For I've struggled hard to climb the tower,
To get the strength, perfection and power.
But in frustration, I cried, "no more,"
And then I found what I was looking for.

Not I to Thee, but Thee to me,
The life I live is rest in Thee.
Not I to Thee, but Thee to me,
This life I live – secure in Thee.

For I am weak, but You are strong,
And You have become redemption's song.
So at moments like this and day by day,
I yield my pride and humbly say:

The Lord is my Shepherd, my Vine and my Life;
I am His pearl, His pearl of great price.
And I need not strive in life to attain
A love that was mine, before time began.

Not I to Thee, but Thee to me,
The life I live, You live through me.
Not I to Thee, but Thee to me,
This life I live – is Christ in me.

R.O. Webb

An Invitation to Receive Christ...

The first words Jesus spoke in His ministry were:

"Repent: for the kingdom of heaven is at hand" (Matthew 4:17).

Jesus came to bring salvation to a world that had turned away from God. He paid the price for the sin debt of the world, by taking its punishment upon Himself on the cross. When we admit our need for help and receive Christ's salvation, we then enter into the plan He has purposed for our life—to be restored to God.

How do you receive salvation? It's a simple act of yielding and inviting Christ, by faith, into your heart. Jesus said:

"Behold, I stand at the door, and knock: if any man hear my voice, and open the door, I will come in to him, and will sup with him, and he with me" (Revelation 3:20).

When you sincerely accept Christ, He will keep His promise and come into your heart. You will be born anew by His Spirit, within your innermost being.

Have you asked Jesus into your heart? Do you know Him personally? Do you know you *have* salvation and that you are positively going to Heaven? If not, it is simply a heart-felt prayer away. The Bible says:

> "...if you acknowledge with your mouth that Jesus is Lord and believe *in your heart* that God raised him from the dead, you will be saved" (Romans 10:9, *NHEB*).

Why has God orchestrated salvation in this way? Why must you allow Him into your heart? *Because Jesus will not go where He's not invited.* Those who are redeemed have this vital act in common: We have said "Yes" to Jesus Christ, allowing Him to enter our hearts for eternity. If you have not done this simple but important act, I encourage you to *sincerely* do so now. *God needs your permission to save you!* It's as simple as praying:

"Jesus, I admit that I am a sinner and ask you for forgiveness. I believe you died for my sins on the cross and that you rose from the dead to give me everlasting life. I accept you as my personal Savior and invite you into my heart. Amen."

If you have now asked Jesus into your heart, I suggest that you write it down. It's a way to confess what God has done in you! God doesn't need to see it, as He knows all things. But so that *you* can see it and be assured of the fact that you received Christ, I encourage you to sincerely declare:

I, _____, *received Jesus on this date:* _____.

I pray that you will indeed say such a prayer from your heart. For in so doing, you will have made the most important decision of your life—receiving Jesus, the Rose of God.

Special thanks to Lois M. Webb
for her help and support in this project.
This work would not be complete
without her.

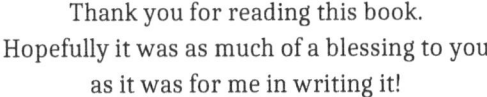

Thank you for reading this book.
Hopefully it was as much of a blessing to you
as it was for me in writing it!

Please consider sharing a review of this book
in the place where you purchased it.
Your review helps others when deciding
to read this study.

**Visit us at HeartoftheLord.org
to hear our worshipful music
and discover more of this ministry!**

*"The LORD bless you, and keep you. The LORD make his face
to shine on you, and be gracious to you. The LORD lift up his face
toward you, and give you peace."*

(Numbers 6:24-26, NHEB)

End-Time Chart

(For Chapter 33)

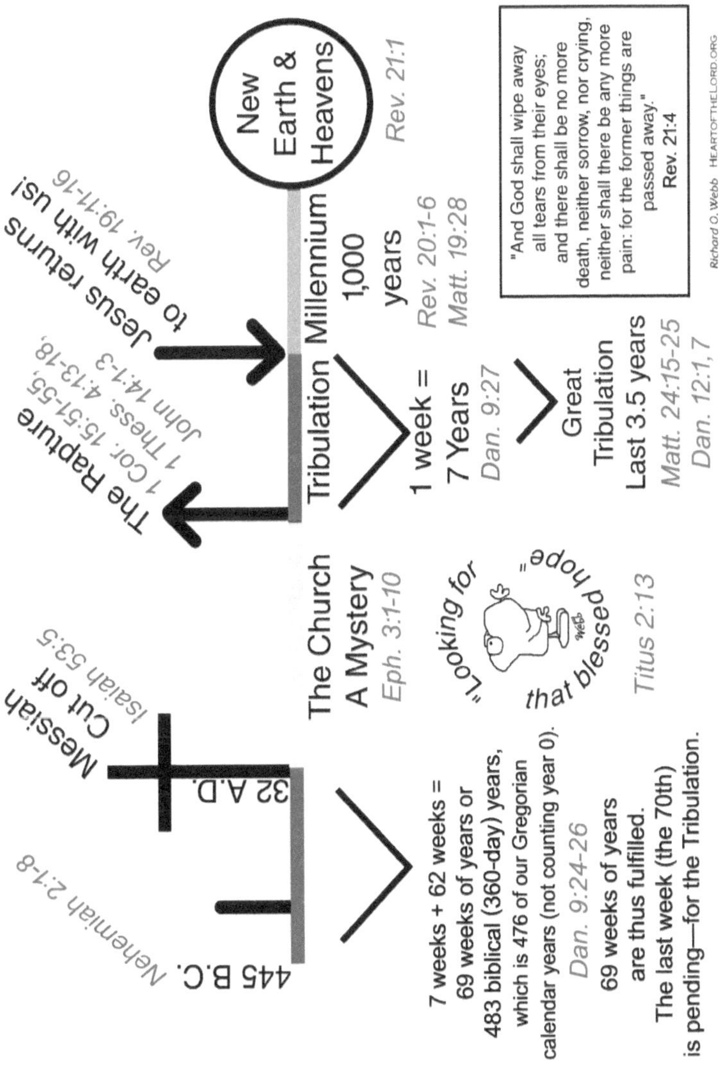

New Earth & Heavens — Rev. 21:1

"And God shall wipe away all tears from their eyes; and there shall be no more death, neither sorrow, nor crying, neither shall there be any more pain: for the former things are passed away." Rev. 21:4

Richard O. Webb   HEARTOFTHELORD.ORG

Jesus returns to earth with us! Rev. 19:11-16

The Rapture — 1 Cor. 15:51-55; 1 Thess. 4:13-18; John 14:1-3

Millennium — 1,000 years — Rev. 20:1-6, Matt. 19:28

Tribulation

1 week = 7 Years — Dan. 9:27

Great Tribulation — Last 3.5 years — Matt. 24:15-25, Dan. 12:1, 7

The Church — A Mystery — Eph. 3:1-10

"Looking for that blessed hope" — Titus 2:13

Messiah Cut off — Isaiah 53:5

32 A.D.

445 B.C. — Nehemiah 2:1-8

7 weeks + 62 weeks = 69 weeks of years or 483 biblical (360-day) years, which is 476 of our Gregorian calendar years (not counting year 0). Dan. 9:24-26

69 weeks of years are thus fulfilled. The last week (the 70th) is pending—for the Tribulation.

INDEX of BibleHearts™ (Alphabetical)

INDEX of Scriptures (Alphabetical)

- *M* -

- *N* -

- *P* -

Notes: